Northern Italy in the Roman World

Northern Italy in the Roman World

From the Bronze Age to Late Antiquity

Carolynn E. Roncaglia

Johns Hopkins University Press
Baltimore

Printed in the United States of America on acid-free paper
9 8 7 6 5 4 3 2 1

Johns Hopkins University Press
2715 North Charles Street
Baltimore, Maryland 21218-4363
www.press.jhu.edu

Library of Congress Cataloging-in-Publication data is available.

ISBN-13: 978-1-4214-2519-1 (hc)
ISBN-10: 1-4214-2519-X (hc)
ISBN-13: 978-1-4214-2520-7 (electronic)
ISBN-10: 1-4214-2520-3 (electronic)

A catalog record for this book is available from the British Library.

Johns Hopkins University Press uses environmentally friendly book materials, including recycled text paper that is composed of at least 30 percent post-consumer waste, whenever possible.

For Mom

Contents

Figures and Tables

FIGURES

TABLES

Preface

This book is a history of a region created by the Roman Empire. Geographically, the region that the Romans called Cisalpine Gaul is a combination of varied features: Alps, plains, delta, piedmont, karst, glacial lakes, and solitary volcanic hills. While this region, broadly considered, served as a nodal point in trade between peninsular Italy, Europe, and the Mediterranean throughout its history, it was not a region unified in any political, cultural, or economic sense until the Roman conquest of the second century BCE. It was an artificial creation, an agglomeration of Po and Venetic plains with the Ligurian coast and of isolated Alpine valleys with the marshy Po Delta. Yet its creation provides insight into Roman fears and imperial aspirations, just as its development over time elucidates the ways in which being part of a larger, interconnected Roman world shaped the lives of individuals and communities.

METHODS

Through the analysis of northern Italy as a region, this book aims both to understand how the Roman Empire created its own geography and also to examine the consequences of that creation. This work thus falls into a much-debated and long-established area of study, that of the nature of change in the territories of the Roman Empire. The changes undergone by the Roman provinces has been alternatively termed *bricolage*, *creolization*, *hybridization*, or—more frequently—*Romanization*.[1] This work does not attempt to offer a new term for *Romanization* but rather outlines some of the mechanisms by which individuals and systems changed the human and natural landscape in one particular region. Change in Roman northern Italy happened at varying rates, and this book argues that the often fast-moving political history of the Roman state not only intersected with long-term trends in northern Italian societies, economies, and networks but repeatedly directed those trends. Northern Italy, as the following chapters attempt to show, presents a case for the interconnection of political, social, economic, and cultural history in the Roman world. So while northern Italy is in many ways peculiar and distinct from other provinces, I hope that it can serve as a model for changes in other regions.

Since the conceptualization of the area between the Apennines and the Alps as being part of "Italy" was not static over time, the region also presents an opportunity to look more critically at the concept of Roman Italy, which was a creation born of a political and cultural moment and not a static, monolithic being. To do so, this book also examines the evolution of both northern Italian and Italian identity. I do not address the political elephant in the room—the prominent place of "northern Italian" identity in the politics of the Lega Nord, a federalist party that dabbles in Padanian nationalism—since that complicated issue requires lengthier discussions of Celtic revivals, European separatist movements, anti-immigration policies, and modern Italian politics than this book is able to give.

As a history of a region, albeit an artificial one, the book owes a significant debt to the study of the Mediterranean by Fernand Braudel and later by Peregrine Horden and Nicholas Purcell, and while the task of gathering and analyzing evidence for ancient northern Italy is not as daunting as for the Mediterranean as a whole, the scale of the inquiry does require some selectivity.[2] This book cannot and does not claim to be exhaustive, and while the following pages use a combination of archaeological, epigraphic, and literary evidence, the reader will note a preponderance of epigraphic material in the middle chapters, sometimes at the expense of other types of evidence. This reliance on Roman inscriptions allows a partial reconstruction of social networks and local ideologies but unfortunately does not give the fullest consideration to contributions from archaeology and literature. The reader may also find that the use of case studies excludes or minimizes important areas, sites, and persons, and where possible I point the reader to fuller treatments of those topics.

ORGANIZATION

The three parts of this book trace the creation, development, and eventual destruction of Roman northern Italy. The creation of this region is largely a story of the Roman Republic, but in order to provide context and to argue for the unique nature of the Roman conquest, the first part looks back first to the Bronze and Iron Ages and the worlds of the Terramare and Golasecca before examining the Roman conquest and the subsequent political and cultural incorporation of northern Italy into the Roman world.

The second and largest section of the book follows the evolution of the region under the Roman Empire in the first and second centuries CE, and since the corpus of material from this period is so extensive, case studies of particular areas and cities—the Aemilia, Tanaro Valley, Novum Comum, and Aquileia—are used selectively to illustrate particular points.

The invasions and subsequent Roman restructuring of northern Italy in the third century mark a turning point in the region's history, and the book's third and final section details how towns and networks in the region responded to the changing Roman world of Late Antiquity. Here again the large amount of evidence requires a more selective approach, and this section's sole chapter functions as a miniature of the imperial section, with smaller case studies tracing Late Antique developments as well as the final dissolution of northern Italy, both as a unified region and as part of a larger Roman world.

Acknowledgments

Many people have encouraged and improved this book, which has its origins in a dissertation overseen by Erich Gruen and Carlos Noreña. Their guidance, patience, and wisdom have enriched the project through all its stages, and they have been role models and mentors. Most of all, their encouragement in the darkest periods of the job market is a debt that I can never fully repay.

I owe thanks as well to Santa Clara University for its support throughout multiple phases of the writing of this book. Lissa Crofton-Sleigh, Bill Greenwalt, John Heath, Angela Holzmeister, Helen Moritz, Michael Taylor, and Daniel Turkeltaub answered queries, read chapters, and provided many insights. Marie Bertola's instruction, both in Italian and in driving a standard transmission car, made possible much of the research in Italy. Writing companions Amy Leuck, Roberto Mata, Danielle Morgan, and Michael Schermann shepherded the project to its various deadlines. Sierra Cirimelli-Low and Keegan Pincombe cheerfully labored for hours on the thankless tasks of scanning chapters and running books back and forth from the library.

Beyond the mission walls of Santa Clara, Elizabeth Meyer kindly offered comments and guidance on the entire manuscript. Shane Bjornlie corrected many errors in the discussion of Late Antique Italy. I also thank Nandini Pandey, Paul Scotton, Jason Schlude, Amy Russell, Kris Seaman, Jeffrey Pearson, and Tim Doran for their time and comments on sections of the manuscript.

I inflicted immeasurable suffering on members of the Soprintendenza with my poor Italian, and their patience and knowledge has been invaluable. I owe particular thanks to Maria Cristina Ronc and Giovanna Gambacurta.

For creating the index I thank Kate Mertes, and for the maps I thank the staff at the Ancient World Mapping Center. Barbara Lamb fixed countless errors and inconsistencies. I am grateful to the staff and readers at Johns Hopkins University Press and especially to Matt McAdam.

Abbreviations

For ancient authors, the abbreviations from *The Oxford Classical Dictionary* (edited by S. Hornblower and A. Spawforth, 3d ed., Oxford: Oxford University Press, 2005) are used. Commonly used abbreviations for epigraphic collections are listed below.

AE — *L'année épigraphique*. Paris, 1888–.

CIL — *Corpus Inscriptionum Latinarum*. Berlin, 1863–.

CLE — *Carmina Latina epigraphica*, edited by Buecheler and E. Lommatzsch. Leipzig, 1895–1926.

IAquil — *Inscriptiones Aquileiae*. 3 vols., edited by J. B. Brusin. Udine, 1991–93.

IG — *Inscriptiones Graecae*. Berlin, 1873–.

ILLRP — *Inscriptiones Latinae Liberae Rei Publicae*. 2 vols., edited by A. Degrassi. Florence, 1963–65.

ILS — *Inscriptiones Latinae Selectae*. 3 vols., edited by H. Dessau. Berlin, 1892–1916.

LegioXVApo — *Die Steindenkmäler der legio XV Apollinaris*, edited by M. Mosser. Vienna, 2003.

Lupa — Ubi Erat Lupa, http://lupa.at/.

Smallwood — *Documents Illustrating the Principates of Nerva, Trajan, and Hadrian*, edited by M. Smallwood. Cambridge, 1966.

A Note on Geography and Names

DEFINING NORTHERN ITALY

This book traces the evolution of an area whose conceptualization as a distinct geographic concept was a new creation of the Roman period and whose borders themselves evolved over time. What the Romans called Cisalpine Gaul was not static even during the Republic, and for consistency the book defines northern Italy throughout as those areas composing the Augustan *regiones* VIII (*Aemilia*), IX (*Liguria*), X (*Venetia et Histria*), and XI (*Transpadana*). This large area is slightly bigger than the borders of modern Italy and is roughly analogous to the Italian administrative regions of the Aosta Valley, Piedmont, Lombardy, South Tyrol, Trentino, Veneto, Emilia-Romagna, and Friuli-Venezia-Giulia, plus the parts of Slovenia and Croatia on the Istrian peninsula. Since these Augustan borders were the longest lasting of the Roman period, they were chosen as the parameters of the study.

The following chapters will rely on case studies of individual regions and towns to highlight larger general changes in northern Italy over time. By necessity of this design, discussion of certain areas within the northern Italy defined above has been truncated or omitted. Coastal Liguria, Istria, and the upper Adige valley have largely been omitted, although these areas are important and have their own special dynamics. More attention is paid to the large plains of the Po River, Emilia, and Veneto than to the valleys of the Alps and the Apennines, and discussion of the Friuli-Venezia-Giulia is limited largely to Aquileia at the expense of Iulium Carnicum (Cividale), Forum Iulii (Zuglio), and Tergeste (Trieste), all three of which have a substantial history of excavation and rich collections of finds.

THE GEOGRAPHY

The essential feature of northern Italy's geography is a broad river plain, bounded by the Alps in the north and west, the Adriatic in the east, and the Apennines in the south. The major drainage basin is that of the Po River, which runs Italy's longest river, from the western Alps to the Adriatic, but in the east a series of mostly north-south-running rivers—the Adige, Brenta, Livenza, Piave, Tagliamento, and Natisone—cut through the Venetic plain. The Po and Venetic plains together create a large expanse of flat land, encircled alternatively by mountains and sea. In the east is the Adriatic coastline, whose important features are the Po Delta and a series of lagoons. In the Roman Empire, Italy went as far east as the agriculturally rich Istrian peninsula, much contested in the twentieth century and now shared by Croatia, Slovenia, and the Italian village of Muggia. Along the northern edge of the central Po Plain, long glacial lakes cut through the Alpine foothills. To their north are the narrow valleys and high passes of the Alps. In the west, the Po Plain gives way to the hills of the Piedmont and after them the Cottian and Maritime Alps. In the south, the less formidable Apennines run at an angle from the southeast to the northwest, making the Ligurian coast mountainous.

Since the geography of northern Italy may be unfamiliar to many readers, brief descriptions of some potentially confusing geographic terms are given below.

Aemilia (the modern Emilia). The Augustan region, including the southern Po Plain and its adjacent Apennine foothills. The important Roman towns here were Ariminum (Rimini), Bononia (Bologna), Ravenna, Mutina (Modena), Parma, and Placentia (Piacenza).

Cisalpine Gaul. Before the triumviral era at the end of the first century BCE, the Roman province between the Apennines and the Alps. Under the Empire this was sometimes used generically to refer to northern Italy.

Istria. The Istrian peninsula, located in the northern Adriatic.

Liguria. The Augustan region in northwestern Italy south of the Po, north of the Ligurian Sea, and east of the Maritime Alps. The most important towns here were Genua (Genova), Libarna, Dertona (Tortona), Alba Pompeia (Alba), and Albintimilium (Ventimiglia). Throughout the text this definition is meant unless otherwise specified.

Po Plain. The large plain created by the Po River and its tributary rivers. In this work the "Po Plain," unless otherwise specified, is also taken to include the Venetic plain and the plains of the Emilia Romagna, even though these areas are separate drainage basins, since the three plains are not separated by other features and form an unbroken expanse of plain.

Transpadana. (a) Before the Augustan era, the area of Cisalpine Gaul north of the Po River.(b) From Augustus through the third century CE, the

Augustan region north of the Po River and stretching from Lake Iseo and the central Po Plain to the western Alps. The most important towns here were Mediolanum (Milan), Augusta Taurinorum (Torino), Ticinum (Pavia), Augusta Praetoria (Aosta), Vercellae (Vercelli), and Eporedia (Ivrea).

Venetic Plain. The plain in the Veneto between the Adige River and the Carnic Alps.

Venetia et Istria. The Augustan region including the Veneto, Friuli-Venezia-Giulia, and the Istrian peninsula. The most important Roman towns here were Aquileia, Patavium (Padova), Verona, Brixia (Brescia), Cremona, Tergeste (Trieste), and Altinum (Altino).

Veneto. The region of northeastern Italy bordered on the south by the Po River and stretching east to Lake Iseo and the central Po Plain.

PLACE NAMES

Throughout the book the modern names of rivers, mountain ranges, lakes, and seas are used. Hence the reader will find the Po River and not the *Padus* or *Eridanus*.

For towns, cities, and other human settlements, ancient place names—when known—are used in place of modern ones. For sites whose ancient names remain lost, the modern place name is given. For most places, the name used during the Roman Empire is used. For the select few for whom an earlier name is known, that is provided when appropriate. To mitigate confusion, in the index both ancient and modern names are given. The decision to use ancient settlement names was dictated by the incorporation of multiple Latin inscriptions and office titles into the main text.

PERSONAL NAMES

For personal names, the original spelling is kept as often as possible, and Latinization of Greek names is avoided. Exceptions are made for those individuals much better known by an Anglicized name, such as Pompey, Livy, and Pliny.

PART I / The Creation of Northern Italy

Chapter One

Northern Italy before the Romans

Writing in the Augustan age, the Roman writer Livy opened his history of the Roman Empire with an account of two city-founders:

> It is generally accepted that after the fall of Troy the Greeks kept up hostilities against all the Trojans except Aeneas and Antenor. These men had worked consistently for peace and the restoration of Helen and for that reason, added to certain personal connections of long-standing, they were allowed to go unmolested. Each had various adventures: Antenor joined forces with the Eneti, who had been driven out of Paphlagonia, and, having lost their king, Palaemenes, at Troy, wanted someone to lead them as well as somewhere to settle. He penetrated to the head of the Adriatic and expelled the Euganei, a tribe living between the Alps and the sea, and occupied that territory with a mixed population of Trojans and Eneti. The spot where they landed is called Troy and the neighboring country the Trojan district. The combined peoples came to be known as Veneti.[1]

Then, going on to describe the wanderings of Aeneas and the subsequent establishment of Rome by a Latino-Trojan dynasty, Livy situates the origins of his fellow townsmen of Patavium (Padova) in the mythic timeline of the Trojan War, which by Livy's time was already shared cultural property across the ancient Mediterranean.

Yet the origin story that Livy gives the Veneti places them within another common narrative, that of continual migration, displacement, and adaptation within pre-Roman northern Italy. Hence in Livy (and Cato the Elder's) Italy, Etruscans displace Euganeans, Gauls displace Etruscans, and Romans displace Gauls. The narrative provides a convenient justification for Roman colonization, but it also reflects a historical reality in which northern Italy, situated between central Europe, peninsular Italy, and the Adriatic (in turn the gateway to the Aegean and Eastern Mediterranean), adapted to changing circumstances. Communities moved, peoples changed, and networks evolved. The Roman state was not the only external force to change the area and to understand its impact requires context.

There were no empires in northern Italy before the Romans, but there were a series of organized political and economic systems that had shaped and reshaped the physical and human landscape before the Romans. De Marinis aptly notes: "La storia della campagna padana aveva avuto inizio circa 4000 anni fa con l'età del bronzo ed è stata, almeno fino a Rinascimento, una successione di alterne vicende di colonizzazioni e abbandoni, sistemazioni idrauliche e degrado di canalizzazioni e bonifice, crescite demografiche e spopolamenti, di opposizione tra foreste e paesaggio incolto da una parte, campi coltivati e pascoli dall'altra."

The history of the Po countryside had its beginning around four thousand years ago, with the Bronze Age (fig. 1), and was, almost until the Renaissance, a succession of alternating events of colonization and abandonment, hydraulic systemization and the decay of canals and works, demographic growth and depopulation, and the opposition between forests and uncultivated landscape, on the one part, and cultivated fields and pastures, on the other.[2]

This chapter examines changes—real and imagined—made to that landscape between the Bronze Age and the fourth century BCE.

The People on the Lakes

The Bronze Age saw the first substantial reworking of the landscape, particularly along the lakes and in the central Po Plain.[3] In the Early Bronze Age (approximately 2200–1600 BCE), the inhabitants of Lombardy, Piedmont, the western Veneto, and Trentino began building their communities on piles jutting out over lakes, marshes, and rivers.[4] These people were united by a uniform phase or complex of material culture called the Polada, generally divided into two phases: an early phase in BA I (2200–1900 BCE), marked by settlements built on platforms over existing bodies of water or marshy ground, and a second phase in BA II (1900–1700/1600 BCE), in which the settlements became more standardized

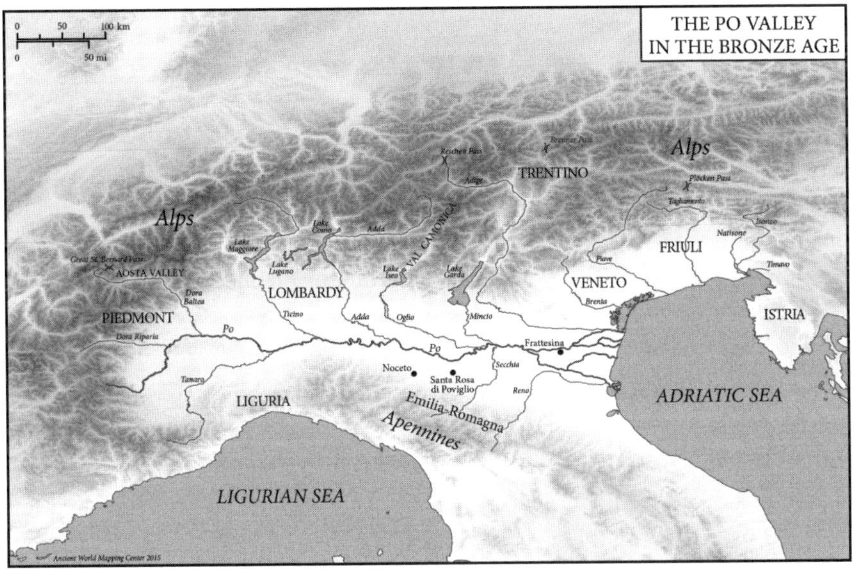

Figure 1. Northern Italy during the Bronze Age. Map by Ancient World Mapping Center.

and rectangular and were built more frequently over reclaimed land.[5] In both phases these communities were densely packed along the shores of northern Italy's glacial lakes, particularly Lake Garda.

The lake villages around Lake Garda were not unique but were part of larger developments across the Alpine sphere. Similar lake villages could be found in Switzerland, southeastern France, Austria, Slovenia, and Germany. This Alpine "lake-dwelling phenomenon" can be traced back to the fifth millennium BCE and continued, with important and sometimes lengthy interruptions, up to the end of the Bronze Age (around 1200–900 BCE), although it spread the fastest in the Early and Middle Bronze Ages.[6]

The prosperity of these communities was based not only on agriculture and pastoralism but also on the trade in metals with central Europe. Copper deposits opened up in the Bronze Age Tyrol, and the Salzkammergut encouraged trade through the Brenner Pass and benefitted lake-dwelling communities at the southern end of that pass.[7] The exploitation of that Alpine trade enriched Polada settlements. The second major phase of development in the Early Bronze Age (BA II) saw established communities increase in size and also saw the creation of new settlements in an expanded orbit, stretching from the Trentino in the north to the Po River in the south and from Lombardy in the west to the Veneto in the east.[8]

In the Middle Bronze Age these newer pile-dwelling settlements, also known as *Palafitte*, prospered. Made of densely packed houses supported on piles and surrounded by palisades, these settlements were centers of production, exchange, and exploitation of local lake resources.[9] Partly built on the shore and partly jutting out onto the lake, the communities in later phases built rectangular wooden grids on the lake bed to give order and support to the planned settlement above.[10]

The Terramare

As Palafitte communities proliferated along the lakes in the Middle Bronze Age, so too did the Terramara villages of the Po Plain.[11] The Terramare were so named after the dark, heavily organic, multilayered mounds of earth—the *terre marne* in the local Emilian dialect—left by their settlements and exploited for fertilizer by farmers in the seventeenth and eighteenth centuries CE.[12] The Terramare occupied homogenous, rectangular settlements surrounded by ditches and canals, and the material culture of these settlements had much in common with that of their Palafitte neighbors to their north. Their emergence in the Po Plain was dramatic, and by the height of the Middle Bronze Age, as Europe was recovering from a period of lower economic activity at the end of the Early Bronze Age, more than two hundred Terramara settlements dotted the southern Po Plain.[13] Population growth had been steady but gradual since the start of the Bronze Age, but by BM IIA, the increase in population so outpaced demographic expectations that colonization and migration must have been at work.[14] Indeed, both the spread of the Terramare and the Palafitte represent the result of striking economic and demographic expansion in Middle Bronze Age northern Italy.[15]

Equally dramatic was the way these Middle Bronze Age inhabitants altered the landscape. The Terramara settlements were small, typically around 1–2 hectares in size, but were densely concentrated, in some areas as much as one settlement per 10 km^2.[16] These settlements required forests of timber; one estimate places the forest land needed to furnish the wood for one settlement's base of pilings at 48 ha.[17] The Terramare then used the cleared land for cereal production (around 30%–40%) and livestock raising (60%–70%).[18] The Terramare deforested their territory at a rate unequaled elsewhere in Italy or Switzerland and not to be seen again until the Roman era.[19]

As did the Palafitte, the Terramare relied heavily on control of water and waterways. The reliance was not just practical but also ideological. The most striking example of the importance of bodies of water in Terramare culture and religion comes from Noceto, just a few kilometers west of Parma. In the late Middle Bronze Age, this Terramara community built a large wooden basin, 4m deep and 22m by 13m around, into which were thrown a variety of votive offerings both utilitarian and ritual: loom weights, wooden utensils, and antlers, as well as figurines of humans, animals, and miniature wheels.[20] Also found were the remains of small turtles and frogs, which indicate that for a significant amount of time the basin was filled with water, creating an aquatic sacred space.[21]

The Late Bronze Age can be divided into two distinct phases, BR1 (c. 1350/1300–1200 BCE) and BR2 (1200–1150 BCE), the latter of which saw the collapse of the *Terramare* on the central Po Plain and resettlement and reorganization in much of the rest of northern Italy.

During the first phase, many of the *Terramare* settlements in the central Po plain—namely, the Emilia and the Valli Grandi Veronesi—were abandoned, while a few settlements grew larger.[22] The area of the *Terramara* settlement at Santa Rosa di Poviglio, for example, grew from 1 to 7 hectares, and others grew to as large as 20 hectares.[23] The cultivated areas around sites increased accordingly; at Santa Rosa di Poviglio the area of extramural cultivation expanded from 1km to 4km wide.[24] As settlements grew both fewer and larger, a greater percentage of them added artificial fortifications.[25]

By the first half of the twelfth century (BR2), the abandonment of Terramara settlements accelerated, and by the end of the Late Bronze Age, the system had collapsed. Of the last few Terramara settlements surviving in BR2, all had some form of artificial fortification, and even these were eventually abandoned. These last settlements show significant signs of stress. At Santa Rosa di Poviglio, within a short period of time, wells along the settlement's fringe were dug and then redug in attempts to bring water up from decreasing water tables, while canals were allowed to go dry.[26] The settlement's inhabitants also began to build their houses in the block-house technique instead of on the previously ubiquitous piles.[27] This new technique used far less wood and suggests that wood was becoming scarcer after four centuries of intensive deforestation.

Explanations for the collapse of the Terramare have generally been multicausal. Favorite culprits have been the well-documented overexploitation of the Po Plain's resources coupled with dramatic population increases.[28] The desperate search for water at Santa Rosa di Poviglio has been linked with a larger Dry Event attested by lower lake levels around Garda, the Swiss plateau, and the Jura Mountains.[29] That the Terramare's problems coincided with the collapse of Bronze Age communities and empires across the Aegean and Eastern Mediterranean at the beginning of the twelfth century suggests not only that these environmental stresses were widespread but also that the collapse of trade routes compounded economic distress.[30] Simultaneously, the system of metals production and trade, which had been crucial to the economy of northern Italy, was shifting. Starting in the thirteenth century BCE, copper and tin oxide ore mining in the Colline Metallifere in southern Tuscany increased, competing with alpine copper sources in the Trentino, which show declining production in the eleventh century.[31] Complicating matters further was the development and spread of Urnfield culture in central Europe and the appearance of a new type of weapon, the Naue Type II sword, in the eastern Alps at the end of the thirteenth century.

The collapse of the Terramare was locally catastrophic; the Emilian part of the Po Plain remained largely depopulated until the eighth and seventh centuries.[32] In the area of the plain north of the Po, however, many of the sites inhabited in the Late Bronze Age were abandoned, but the area did not become depopulated. Rather, the inhabitants moved and created new settlements, densely concentrated along the rivers.[33] Around Lake Garda and in the Trentino there was greater continuity, and whatever caused the devastation in the south had few effects in the old areas of the Polada.[34] In Istria, too, there were signs of stress, with many of the *castellieri*—the typically Istrian fortified settlements common on that peninsula since the beginning of the second millennium—disappearing in the twelfth century BCE.[35]

The differing reactions to the problems of the twelfth century signal what would become a prominent feature of northern Italy in the ancient world and arguably up to the present: a strong and persistent regionalism. The topography of the land is partly to blame. In impoverished and isolated Liguria, for example, where Bronze Age settlement density was low and where long-distance connections were slow to develop, the Ligurian Apennines divided the land from the Po Plain and connected it to an area of the Mediterranean not fully incorporated into long-distance trade routes.[36] Nevertheless, geography was not destiny, and the borders of regions in ancient northern Italy were as fluid as their Renaissance counterparts. The areas encompassed by the Palafitte (around northern Italy's lakes) and the Terramare (the central Po Plain) for the most part do not align with either cultural or political divisions in the Iron Age or the Roman era. The origins of the evolving configurations of northern Italian regions ought to be sought not just in geography but also in other areas.

The Final Bronze Age

By the start of the Final Bronze Age (1150–975 BCE), new settlement patterns were emerging in areas affected by the Terramare collapse. In the central Po Plain, communities had moved to more mountainous areas or to the banks of major tributaries, although population levels were much lower than before. In the Po Delta, whose inhabitants had previously favored building their settlements in marshy areas along minor waterways, communities were now situated along the Po's major branches, especially the Po di Adria.[37] This move to the Po's major waterways took greater advantage of the transport possibilities that the Po provided.

The reorganization of settlement patterns was accompanied by cultural changes. Inhabitants in Istria—which shared cultural and economic connections with central Europe, the Balkans, and northeastern Italy—suddenly shifted in the twelfth and eleventh centuries from inhumation to cremation.[38] This shift to cremation was characteristic of the end of the Bronze Age and early Iron Age throughout central Europe and Italy and was particularly characteristic of the former's "Urnfield culture," named after the commonly found fields of cinerary urns, and the latter's "protovillanovan" and "villanovan" cultures, named after a mid-nineteenth-century archaeological site of Villanova near Bologna.[39] In Italy, the relatively homogenous Villanovan koine stretched from the southern Veneto and eastern Lombardy south to Latium and parts of Campania and encompassed nearly a third of Italy.[40]

Frattesina

One of these new urn-using communities was the Final Bronze Age / Early Iron Age settlement at Frattesina in the Po Delta.[41] The settlement developed during the late twelfth and eleventh centuries BCE along a main channel of the Po alongside two other nearby settlements, Gognano and Villamarzana, and exemplifies the settlement shift following the collapse of the Terramare.[42] Capitalizing on the decline of the Terramara communities in the nearby Valli Grandi Veronesi, the settlement at Frattesina took advantage of its location along the Po di Adria, then the main channel of the Po Delta.[43] Frattesina prospered as a center of production and exchange until the hydrology of the Po Delta changed and the Po di Adria lost its preeminence to the Po di Spina; the settlement itself disappeared in the ninth century BCE.[44]

Before its disappearance, the three-hectare community was the hub of economic activity in the Po Delta.[45] The inhabitants of Frattesina produced ceramics, worked antler, and textiles, and it is the rare Bronze Age site in Europe to show signs of glass production.[46] Frattesina dominated regional trade in those objects, and its Italian trade connections into Etruria across the Apennine passes appear to have been strong. A few pieces of Mycenaean-type pottery found at Frattesina indicate connections with southern Italy, where the Aegean-inspired pottery was produced.[47] Similarly, ivory pieces and an ostrich shell point to even more distant connections with the eastern Mediterranean.[48]

The amber finds from Frattesina and its surrounding area are particularly instructive. Frattesina, its necropolis, and nearby settlements have produced numerous amber pieces, both finished and unfinished, which have been identified as succinite and thus most likely Baltic in provenance.[49] The unfinished pieces indicate that amber was worked on site, and the concentration of pieces around Frattesina suggests that the site was a point of hub for the manufacture and distribution of finished amber. Amber had been imported into Italy since the Early Bronze Age, when it appeared in southern Italian sites such as Laterza.[50] In the Middle and Late Bronze Age, it appeared in Terramara and Palafitte sites and increased in quantity, which underlines the economic power and extensive trade connections of those communities.[51] In the Final Bronze Age, the geographical distribution of amber grew, in the west to Sardinia and in the east to the Aegean and Ionian islands, and even though there are small sources of amber in Italy, supply from the Baltic seems to have been sufficient, and these Italian sources were not explored in the Bronze Age.[52] The settlement at Campestrin di Grignagno Polesine, across the river from Frattesina, even seems to have specialized in amber finishing.[53] In amber, Frattesina acted as a key part in trade between central Europe, peninsular Italy, and the Mediterranean, a position similar to that held by the earlier Palafitte and Terramare communities.

Frattesina's position as the commercial and production center of the upper Adriatic in the Late Bronze Age and early Iron Age was similar to that occupied in later centuries by Etruscan Spina and Atria, Roman Aquileia, and medieval Venice. That certain communities in northeastern Italy acted as intermediaries in trade between central Europe and the Mediterranean is not in itself extraordinary. Significant is how the shape of that trade changed over time and how those changes affected northern Italy. The lake-dwelling settlements around Lake Garda were made possible by the demands for metals in the Early Bronze Age, while climate change and the stresses put on long-distance trade by the Bronze Age collapse in the eastern Mediterranean helped ruin the Terramare. Frattesina

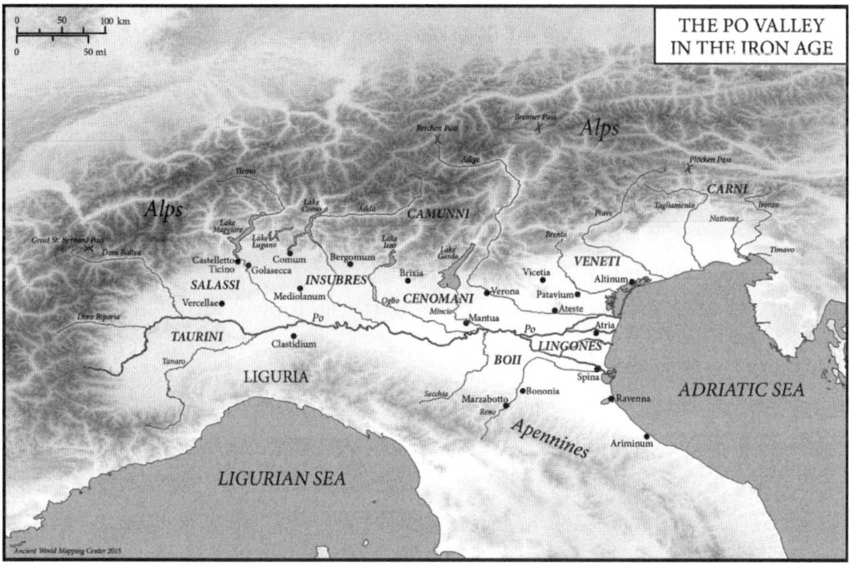

Figure 2. Northern Italy during the Iron Age. Map by Ancient World Mapping Center.

benefitted both from the vacuum left by the decline of the Terramare and from a demand for items of personal adornment in early Villanovan communities across Italy.

The Iron Age and Urbanization

The importance of northern Italy both as a source of resources, particularly agricultural, and a place of exchange between Europe and the Mediterranean meant that as long-distance trade networks recovered in the Iron Age, so too did northern Italy. The Iron Age (fig. 2) created the northern Italy that the Romans encountered when they themselves invaded and colonized the area in the third to first centuries BCE.

The Iron Age in Italy was not an absolute horizon, and distinct regional cultures emerged at different times in different places.[54] In general, the tenth and ninth centuries BCE were marked by shifts in settlement patterns and material culture, although these were not uniform across the region.

Nevertheless, in the following centuries one trend was clear: the development of proto-urban and urban centers across most of northern Italy, excepting parts of the Alps. By the ninth century, significant although still small settlements were developing at Bologna, Este, and the area near the exit of the Ticino River from

Lake Maggiore, where the communities of Golasecca, Sesto Calende, and Castelletto Ticino seem to have synoecized.[55] During the eighth and early seventh centuries, Etruscan colonization in the Po Plain and the development of the Venetic centers at Ateste and Patavium created large proto-urban settlements, in the cases of Este and Felsina (Bologna) up to 100 and 300 ha, respectively.[56] In late eighth-century Liguria, densely populated areas along the coasts began to reorganize into proto-urban centers, which had trade links with the Golasecca area in Lombardy and with northern Etruria.[57] Imports from both Etruria and central Europe increased substantially in northern Italy in the eighth century.[58]

The late ninth- to eighth-century revival of trade and urbanism in northern Italy was part of a larger trend across Italy and the Aegean, as populations increased and as long-distance trade routes across the eastern Mediterranean came back to life. The new wealth and power accrued by clans and communities across the Mediterranean found expression in the tomb paintings of Tarquinia and the earliest Doric temples of the Peloponnese. Out of the Villanovan culture in Etruria and northern Italy, communities consolidated, expanded, and formed defined group identities.[59]

The sixth century saw further urbanization, with the entrance of the Umbrians into the Romagna and the development of important urban centers at Comum (at the expense of Golasecca, Sesto Calende, and Castelletto Ticino), Genua, and Altinum.[60] At the same time Venetic settlements at Ateste and Patavium began to show increased complexity, with groups of houses along an organized street layout ringed by sanctuaries and cemeteries.[61]

Along the Adriatic coast, the success of the emporia Atria and Spina underscored the economic revival. Like Frattesina before them, these centers took advantage of increased trade between Italy, the eastern Mediterranean, and central Europe. They were also quite cosmopolitan. Etruscan predominates in inscriptions from Spina, but Greek graffiti are common, and other languages of the Adriatic coastline—including Venetic, Illyrian, and Picentene—are also represented.[62] Here Greek traditions such as the Anthesteria were practiced and even adapted to their new, culturally multilingual environment. Here women participated in symposia, a Greek social ritual adapted to Etruscan sensibilities.[63] Hence defining either Atria or Spina as either definitively Greek or Etruscan communities has proved elusive, and this cultural middle ground induced confusion even in ancient authors.[64]

By the fifth century BCE there was an advanced urban network in the Po and Venetic Plains, with both primary (Concordia, Opitergium, Bononia/Felsina,

Ateste) and secondary (Marzabotto, Spina, Vicenza, Oppeano, Montebelluna) urban centers, complete in some cases with fortifications, internal networks of canals (Mantova), external canals linking to other centers (Atria and Spina), and orthogonal street plans, with sidewalks and sewers (Marzabotto, Como, Castelletto Ticino).[65]

In Livy and other historians, this urban development is compressed into a story of Etruscan dominance, one in which the Etruscans colonized and controlled nearly the whole of the Po Plain apart from the northeast corner, kept by the Veneti. They had twelve northern colonies, to match a federation of twelve cites in Etruria proper. But this seems to have been an exaggeration, possibly a projection back to the later Roman conquest. Moreover, defining what is and what is not Etruscan in northern Italy is more difficult than in Etruria, with its different city states celebrating collective religious celebrations at Fanum Fortunae, near Orvieto, with a pantheon of relative uniformity and with at least a collective group name, *Rasenna*.

There are a few communities, such as Felsina (Bologna), with its distinctive horseshoe-shaped *cippi*, and Marzabotto, a planned settlement in the Apennines southwest of Bologna, that are almost certainly Etruscan.[66] Outside this southeastern corner of the Po Plain, the evidence for defining a community as Etruscan is nearly always inconclusive. In the Piedmont, there is the occasional imported Etruscan helmet or razor through the early seventh century, but even in the seventh and sixth centuries there were sustained trade and significant cultural exchange but no clear signs of colonization or political control.[67]

Contrary to Livy's presentation of twelve northern Etruscan colonies, Etruscan dominance of the Po Plain was largely limited to the southeast, clinging to the line of the Apennines around the major centers at Felsina and Verucchio.[68] Yet the reality was less important to the later history of the region than the myth, whether that myth was promulgated by Etruscans in Etruria reacting to their loss of influence in the region after the fourth century, or by the Romans in the Middle Republic explaining and justifying their own conquest, or by later historians Polybius and Livy.

Livy, Polybius, and the Veneti

For the historian Livy the fantasy of a widespread Etruscan dominion in the north did have its uses. It emphasized the antiquity and strength of the Veneti, whom he describes in book 5 of *Ab Urbe Condita Libri* as inhabiting the only area of Cisalpine Gaul not ruled by the Etruscans.[69] Venetic maintenance of independence while living next to a large and wealthy Etruscan federation parallels Livy's depiction of early Rome in the first four books of the history, in which Rome was often at war with threatening Etruscan neighbors. That the Veneti were never ruled by any immigrant Etruscan kings made the comparison all the more favorable to the Veneti and to Livy's Venetic hometown of Patavium.

Livy's description of *Etruria Padana* and Venetic independence immediately precedes his descriptions of Celtic invasions into Italy and their eventual capture of Rome itself at the end of book 5. Successful Venetic resistance to Celtic invasion also contrasts favorably with Rome's inability to protect itself against the Gauls. Livy had set up a comparison of Rome and the Veneti as early as the first sentence after the preface, in which Aeneas and Antenor are paired as Trojan refugees fleeing with their people to Italy.[70] That early comparison highlights the connection between Livy and Rome's origins, and it is the only time before book 5 that the Veneti are mentioned.[71] When they reappear, between the discussion of the Etruscans and the Celts, the Veneti are established as Rome's worthy cousins—more successful in resisting foreign invaders if perhaps less successful in establishing an empire. In short, Livy's description of the entire political situation in sixth to fourth century BCE northern Italy paints a conveniently rosy portrait of the Veneti through comparisons not just with the rest of Cisalpine Gaul but with early Rome itself.

Livy's defense of the Veneti may have been a reaction to historians claiming that Antenor was a traitor. The Roman senator and historian Sisenna, writing in the early first century BCE, says that Antenor betrayed Troy to the Greeks, and in Greek historians the story of Antenor as traitor goes back to at least the fifth century BCE.[72] Livy's positive portrayals of the Veneti and their founder were thus part of a larger historiographical dialogue and should also be seen in the larger cultural and political context of the mid and late first century BCE, when upper-class northern Italians were making inroads into Roman political, social, and literary circles. Valorization of Antenor and the Veneti created a suitably honorable history for Livy and other elites from Venetia and thus justified their new places in Roman hierarchies.

In contrast, the Greek historian Polybius, writing in the second century BCE, places his brief description of the Veneti in a narrative of Celtic invasions:

> Those [Celts] who first settled in the district near the source of the Po were the Laevi and Lebecii; after them came the Insubres, the largest tribe of all, and finally the Cenomani, who lived along the banks of the river. The part of the

> plain which borders the Adriatic had always belonged to another very ancient tribe, that is the Veneti; in their customs and their dress they scarcely differed from the Celts, but they spoke a different language and the tragic poets have many fabulous tales to tell about them. On the southern bank of the Po, that is the side nearer the Apennines, the first settlers beginning from the west were the Anares and later the Boii. Eastwards of them in the direction of the Adriatic lived the Lingones, and beyond these and near the sea the Senones.[73]

Polybius ascribes to the Veneti the same antiquity and independence that Livy did but groups them physically and culturally with the Celts, whom he describes as ignorant of art, science, and civilization.[74] Since there was significant and sustained cultural borrowing and hybridization among the Veneti, Cenomani, Golasecca, and Insubres throughout the Iron Age, Polybius's description of the Veneti is an oversimplification, but not entirely inaccurate.[75] Missing entirely from Polybius's histories is Antenor. A short and dismissive reference to the tales of the tragic poets is the only allusion to any mythical origin story about the Veneti. For Livy, the Veneti were part of his history and identity. For Polybius, the Veneti were a footnote in the larger drama of what ancient authors characterized as the Celtic invasions.

The Celts

Polybius's interest in the Celts lay in their importance to both Roman and Greek history in the third and second centuries BCE. In the third century Celts had invaded Greece, and Hellenistic monarchs in the eastern Mediterranean used military defeats of the Celts as political capital for generations, even as they eagerly employed Celtic mercenaries in their own forces.[76] Polybius came from a world in which Celts were seen as a barbaric, brave, and erratic enemy, and as a hostage in Rome he entered a world in which the Roman defeat at the hands of the Celts was commemorated in the calendar and in which fear of a Celtic invasion was real enough to be written into town charters.[77]

Yet the "Celts" were largely a Greek and Roman construction. Throughout Iron Age Europe, people spoke Celtic languages, and in the Iron Age a diffused Hallstatt (eighth to sixth centuries BCE) and La Tène (fifth to first centuries BCE) culture meant that most of central and western Europe shared a broadly similar material culture.[78] Yet there were significant local and regional differences and even more political divisions. These divisions, at least in their third- to first-century forms, are sometimes recorded in Greek and Roman writers, but little effort was made to distinguish beyond those. To the Romans, the inhabitants of Europe were *Galli*, Gauls, and to the Greeks they were *Keltoi*, Celts.

Polybius and Livy both present a narrative in which waves of Celts cross the Alps and settle in northern Italy, displacing the Etruscans.[79] The reality was more complicated and has been much debated.

In northwestern Italy there was a relative continuity in settlements and population in the early Iron Age. In Lombardy the Protogolasecca evolved almost seamlessly into the Golasecca culture of the early Iron Age.[80] Inscriptions there show an early presence for Celtic languages. A late seventh-century inscription from Sesto Callende indicates that the Golasecca peoples spoke a Celtic language, while similar inscriptions in the area occupied by the Cenomani date back to the sixth century.[81] The Golasecca thrived not just as intermediaries on trade moving between Italy and Europe but also as consumers themselves.[82]

Among the Golasecca and indeed for most of northern Italy, the eighth through the fifth centuries BCE were marked by general continuity, growth, and urbanization, as well as increasing commercial and cultural interaction with central Italy and Europe.[83] There were abrupt changes in the fourth century, as the number and distribution of the La Tène objects characteristic of central and western Europe increased.[84] This increase in characteristically "Celtic" material culture was accompanied by disruptions in Po Plain settlements. Sites throughout northern Italy were abandoned or saw contraction, and in the southern Po Plain there was an increasing preference for fortified hill settlements, which suggests security concerns.[85] In the Aemilia, Felsina (Bologna) became a stronghold of the Boii, and there was an accompanying shift in the types of burials and grave goods, while at Marzabotto the new inhabitants buried their dead within the town, in contrast to the extraurban burials of the Etruscans.[86]

There were important limits to the transformation. Even in the southern Po Plain, newer Celtic-speaking inhabitants did not totally displace the earlier inhabitants or their customs.[87] Most famously, at the necropolis of Monte Bibele, near Bologna, fourth- and third-century tombs contain mixtures of La Tène armaments and Etruscan ceramic goods, indicating a cosmopolitan population and a cultural middle ground similar to that seen at Greco-Etruscan Spina.[88] Nor did the La Tène practice of inhumation entirely displace older Golaseccan style of cremation in Lombardy.[89] In Piedmont and Liguria, there seems to have been little disruption, and the characteristic La Tène material is largely absent from those regions.[90]

The changes of the fourth century are not necessarily the result of a large-scale

Celtic invasion, as imagined by later Greek and Roman authors. In the southeastern and central Po Plain, the invasion model may be appropriate, but in Lombardy internal political or economic pressure may be to blame for the disruptions among the Golasecca.[91] Even within individual regions there could be a diversity of migration models. In general in the Carnic Alps, a growing cultural interaction and migration by individuals or small groups from the Danube Basin in the fifth and early fourth centuries was followed by increased migration and internal mobility in the late fourth and third centuries.[92] Yet at Verzegnis, in the Carnia, the major shift in material culture and population seems to have happened at the beginning of the third century.[93]

Northern Italian changes ought also to be placed in the larger context of population movements across central and northwestern Europe, the coincidental spread of La Tène material culture, and fourth- and third-century raids in central Italy, Greece, and Anatolia.[94]

Analyses of haplotype distributions and strontium isotope studies of La Tène cemeteries across Europe—including the necropolis at Monte Bibele—show small groups of men moving long distances, a pattern that suggests raiding or mercenary activity.[95] Accordingly, some of northern Italy's new inhabitants likely migrated in military bands or worked as mercenaries. Rather than as a series of invasions, northern Italy's fourth-century transformation is perhaps more accurately described as a combination of large-scale migrations, raiding parties, and changes to transalpine trade networks and economic systems.

Northern Italy before the Romans

By the time the Roman army had moved north of the Apennines in the third century, the political map of northern Italy was a patchwork of federations, peoples, and independent settlements.[96] On the northern Po Plain, the most dominant powers were the Insubres, a large federation in Lombardy centered at Mediolanum; the Cenomani around Lake Garda, with centers at Brixia and Verona; and in the east, the Veneti. South of the Po were the Boii in the Emilia, Senones in the Romagna, and the Lingoni in the Po Delta.[97] The Ligurians in the western Apennines and along the coast were composed of many smaller tribes and communities.[98] In the Piedmont were the Taurisci, and in the Aosta Valley the Salassi. North of the Cenomani in the Alps were the peoples that the Romans called collectively the Raetians, and in the eastern Alps were the Carni.

Northern Italy was, for the entirety of the Bronze and Iron Ages, never unified politically or culturally. Some degree of cultural uniformity might be discerned in the spread of Urnfield cremation practices at the end of the Bronze Age, but there remained significant differences in settlement patterns and material culture across northern Italy.

Economically, the region's role in long-distance trade routes was remarkably consistent. Trade routes shifted over time, with different passes being favored at different times, and the volume and type of goods also fluctuated. Nevertheless, northern Italy continued to function as a point of exchange between continental Europe in the north and peninsular Italy and the Mediterranean in the south. How the Roman state affected those trade routes and created a hitherto unseen political and cultural unity in northern Italy is examined in the following chapters.

Chapter Two

The Roman Conquest

The Roman conquest of northern Italy began in the third century BCE and was largely completed, except for the Alps, by the middle of the second century BCE. Within just over a century, all the land between the Apennines and the Alps was under Roman control, either direct or indirect, and Roman Cisalpine Gaul was created, both as a concept and as a political reality (fig. 3). During the first century BCE, the region was given citizenship and then incorporated into Italy. This chapter examines those two transformations.

The narrative for the Roman conquest is conveyed largely by later writers, primarily Polybius and Livy. Neither writer is unproblematic. Polybius often falls back on Greek stereotypes of Celts as undisciplined and erratic nomads, and he sometimes does not distinguish between different states in northern Italy. Livy, from the old Venetic settlement of Patavium, presents the Veneti as Roman allies without fault and their Venetic neighbors Cenomani and Boii as backstabbing and troublesome.

With these caveats in mind, a broad narrative of the conquest can nevertheless be traced in five phases: (1) the defeat, conquest, and expulsion of the Senones in the southeastern Po Plain in the 290s and 280s, (2) the campaigns against the Boii and Insubres immediately before the Hannibalic war, (3) campaigns during and following the Hannibalic war aimed at protecting Roman colonies and punishing the Boii and Insubres for their Carthaginian alliance, (4) wars against the

Figure 3. Roman Northern Italy. Map by Ancient World Mapping Center.

Istrians and Ligurians ending in the mid-second century BCE, and (5) Augustan campaigns against various groups in the Alps at the end of the first century BCE.[1]

From Sentinum to Telamon

The first phase began with the alliance of the Senones, who lived in the far southeastern end of the Po Plain, with the Samnites, Etruscans, and Umbrians in the Third Samnite War against Rome. In 295 BCE this war culminated in the battle of Sentinum, perhaps more famous for the *devotio* of the Roman commander Decius Mus, in which the Samnites and their coalition of allies, including the Senones, were defeated.[2]

War between the Romans and Senones again in 284 BCE resulted in the expulsion and slaughter of many of the Senones, and the Romans occupied their territory, with the colony of Sena Gallica serving as a base.[3] The wars against the Senones were tied to wars fought by the Samnites, Etruscans, Picentines, and Umbrians against Roman and Latin expansion in central Italy and need not be tied with contemporary Celtic incursions into the Balkans and Greece in the 280s, since the wars in Italy stemmed more from an ad hoc system of alliances between central Italian peoples and their neighbors in southern Cisalpine Gaul and do not seem to be part of any larger "Celtic expansion."[4] During these wars the Senones called in allies from north of the Alps as mercenaries. That they did so shows the continuing ties between cisalpine and transalpine federations and also the not uncommon practice of hiring Celtic mercenaries in the Hellenistic Mediterranean.[5]

The Senones' neighbors to their north, the Boii, had also allied with the Etruscans against the Romans—at the battle of Lake Vadimon in 282 BCE and at another battle the following year—but these did not mark the start of any serious Roman attempt to move beyond the land of the Senones. Only after the Telamon campaign in 225 BCE did the Romans campaign against the Boii and Insubres in the central Po Plain.[6]

According to the historian Polybius, the cause of the Telamon campaign, in which the Boii and Insubres hired transalpine mercenaries for an attack on Roman territory, was resentment against the Roman distribution of the former land of the Senones and a conviction that the Flaminian distributions signaled Roman intent to expel all the Celts; but these distributions had taken place years earlier.[7] The Boii and Insubres moved south into Etruria, while the Romans, caught by surprise and with one consular army stationed in Sardinia, made a hasty treaty with the Carthaginians and mobilized their forces. During the campaign the Romans secured the alliance of the Cenomani and the Veneti, who were able to contribute twenty thousand men to the campaign. The two coalitions, Boii and Insubres on one side, and Romans, Cenomani, and Veneti on the other, met for battle at Telamon in Etruria, and the result was a clear Roman victory.[8]

Telamon's Legacy

Telamon marked a shift, and Roman campaigns afterwards were designed to establish a permanent presence in the central Po Plain. Campaigns after Telamon secured the alliance of the Anares, the defeat of the Insubres and Boii, and the placement of the Latin colonies at Cremona and Placentia.[9]

For the Romans, the most important victory was that at Clastidium in 222 BCE, which secured the defeat of the Insubres and mercenaries hired from north of the Alps. The battle was important not so much for what it achieved as for how it was won. During the battle, the Roman consul M. Claudius Marcellus killed the leader of the mercenaries fighting for the Insubres and took his armor.[10] Marcellus was only the third man in Roman memory—the first being their mythical founder Romulus—to obtain the *spolia opima*, spoils taken by a Roman commander from the leader of the enemy in single combat.[11] Marcellus mounted the spoils on a trimmed oak trunk and carried the trophy along with him in an extravagant triumph at Rome.[12] Shares of the war booty were sent to Rome's allies in Italy as well as to King Hiero of Syracuse; a golden bowl was sent to Delphi.[13] The defeated Insubres surrendered all their cities to Rome and obtained from the victors "a peace on fair terms."[14]

These Roman gains were temporary and undone by the Hannibalic war, which saw attacks on the new Latin colonies and the siding of nearly all of Cisalpine Gaul with the Carthaginians against the Romans.[15] The campaigns following the war, which were designed both to punish those who had sided with the Carthaginians and to protect the much-damaged colonies at Placentia and Cremona, returned the Cenomani and the Insubres to the Roman alliance and subjugated the Boii by 191.[16]

Following the defeats of the Boii and Insubres, the Romans waged war on the Ligurians in the west and the Istrians in the east. The wars with the Ligurians lasted well into the 150s, leading to Cicero's characterization of Liguria as a triumph factory for Roman generals.[17] In the east, wars with the Istrians are recorded for the 120s, although an attack of the Istrians on Tergeste is attested as late as 52 BCE.[18] While sporadic fighting continued in the far east and west in the second century, major Roman campaigns in northern Italy were largely finished by the 190s and did not resume until the Augustan conquest of the Alps at the end of the first century BCE.

The Nature of the Conquest

By then the Roman conquest had radically reshaped the physical and demographic landscape of the region, particularly in Liguria and the southern Po Plain, where the Roman government had moved entire populations, reordered landownership, altered patterns of urbanization, and reworked the routes of land and water transportation.[19] In the Transpadana, or Italy north of the Po, Roman involvement was less invasive, but nevertheless the Roman conquest and subsequent administration of the region dramatically reorganized local governments and settlement patterns. Even in areas like the Veneto, where the Roman government initially had little reason or incentive to meddle in local activities, second- and first-century BCE Roman politics dictated land divisions and redistributions.

Such intervention was greater and longer lasting than it was in almost every other part of Italy south of the Apennines and in most of the provinces of the eastern Mediterranean. Why was Roman involvement here relatively—but unevenly—invasive?

The agricultural wealth of the region in the Roman period was legendary. Polybius tells the story that in his time innkeepers in the region charged their guests per head rather than per item since food was so plentiful and cheap.[20] The antiquarian Varro, quoting Cato, says that the Insubres grew pigs so fat that they could barely stand, and both Polybius and Strabo say that Cisalpine pork fed all Italy.[21] Strabo further says that Cisalpine Gaul also produced the wool that clothed most of Italy's households and that the viticulture there was so prosperous that Cisalpine wine casks were as big as houses.[22]

For a political power situated in the center of the Italian peninsula, as Rome was, the land of Cisalpine Gaul thus provided a potentially great source of wealth but also one that by virtue of its geographic position was extremely vulnerable. The double-edged nature of Cisalpine wealth is apparent in Greek and Roman literary accounts. Polybius says that the Etruscans who once inhabited the Po Plain were defeated and expelled by their envious Celtic neighbors to the north, who wanted the rich and beautiful plain for themselves.[23] Likewise, one of the explanations that Livy provides for the Gallic migration into Italy is that the Gauls were enticed to cross the Alps by reports of the fruits and wine of Italy; that Livy dismisses the story as chronologically improbable does not disprove the idea that the story had been in circulation.[24] The story that Livy does accept, that overpopulation in Transalpine Gaul prompted migration south across the Alps, still follows the same theme of northern Italy being a source of agricultural wealth and promise, in this case for starving Gauls from north of the Alps.[25]

That the stories parlayed by Polybius and Livy provide a much distorted view of the reality of population movements in Iron Age northern Italy is beside the point; for Polybius, Livy, and their sources, northern Italy was a land of dangerous wealth: it could clothe and feed the entire peninsula but could also entice invaders from across the Alps. For Polybius, Roman governance offered stability, protection, and proper utilization of these agricultural riches, something that nomadic Celts could not provide; for Livy it was the natural alliance of similarly ex-Trojan Romans and Veneti that would be the north's best caretakers.

Whether such ideas dated back to the third century and the initial land confiscations from the Senones is difficult to say, but certainly by the second century conceptions of the region as vulnerable and potentially so productive were circulating and may have encouraged a more invasive Roman approach to governance.

There were other factors that inspired a more "hands-on" approach to Roman control of the region. Fear was predominant. One that stands out most clearly in literary sources is a collective Roman fear of Gallic incursions from the north, a fear stemming from the traumatic sacking of Rome in 390 BCE by an army of Gauls. Livy says that the perpetrators were Senones; he is uncertain whether they were accompanied by others.[26] The memory of this event was perpetuated at Rome on the religious calendar; in the *Fasti Antiates*, a surviving Roman calendar from the Late Republic, the two historical events commemorated are the founding of Rome on April 21 and the July 18 defeat of the Roman army at the Allia, which lead immediately to the sack of Rome.[27]

Lingering fears from the fourth-century sack were part of a larger context: movements of transalpine Celts into Italy are usually associated by Greek and Roman authors with the initiation of hostility with Rome. This had been the case with descriptions of the Telamon campaign and again with the Carthaginians under Hannibal in 218 BCE. The Boii and Insubres, who had just recently been subdued by Rome, quickly joined Hannibal's army, and Hannibal's early successes at Ticinus, Trebia, and Lake Trasimene demolished Roman authority in the region. Hannibal's crossing of the Alps reinforced the view of the Alps as a route that Rome's enemies could take into Cisalpine Gaul and from there central Italy and Rome.[28] The invasion of the Cimbri and the Teutones at the end of the second century again emphasized the vulnerability of the region to invasions from across the Alps, since the Cimbri made it as far south as Cisalpine Gaul, where they were finally defeated by C. Marius at Vercellae in 101.[29]

Roman reactions to this fear lead to drastic and empire-wide decisions: the charter of the Roman colony of Urso in southern Spain to withdraw local magistrates' exemptions from military service in the case of a *tumultus Gallicus* in Italy.[30] The fear of a Celtic incursion in the preliminaries to the Telamon campaign was so great that a rare human sacrifice was ordered: the burial alive of a Greek man and woman and a Gallic man and woman in the Forum Boarium.[31] This sacrifice seems to have been reserved for rare and terrifying moments in the Republican period, as after the battle of Cannae.[32] The Romans buried another Greek and Gallic couple alive in 113 BCE, during the invasion of the Cimbri and Teutones.[33]

The Romans' perception of northern Italy as a place that by its nature was vulnerable to foreign invaders was thus combined with an inherited fear of the Gauls reinforced by commemorations of the sack of Rome and by the invasion of Hannibal. In this way, northern Italy's perceived vulnerability to transalpine attacks was closely linked in Roman memory with danger to the Roman Empire and to the city of Rome itself.

Legions

Roman fears about Gallic invasions and northern Italy's vulnerability played a large part in Rome's military decisions not just during the conquest but also in the remainder of the second and first centuries BCE. During this period the region became significantly militarized. This meant that Roman armies were present in northern Italy for about one year in three for the middle and late Republican periods and also that the region was a major source of legionary and auxiliary recruitment. Civil wars increased the need for recruiting, and important incidents in these wars took place on northern Italian soil, with the unfortunate town of Mutina besieged twice, in 78 BCE and again in 43 BCE.[34] The region saw action again in 71 BCE, when Spartacus's army marched through Cisalpine Gaul and defeated a ten-thousand-man army stationed there under the proconsul C. Cassius Longinus.[35]

These campaigns required Roman armies to march through, winter in, and collect supplies from northern Italy. The region's inhabitants, especially in the settlements along the main trunk roads of the Via Aemilia (built 187 BCE) and the Via Postumia (148 BCE), became accustomed to accommodating large numbers of Roman and Italian soldiers, both passing through and wintering in the region. There is also evidence for the placement of garrisons in Cisalpine Gaul as support for campaigns in surrounding areas.[36] Supporting this militarization were recruitment drives in the region, since the populous Po Plain could furnish large numbers of, first, auxiliaries and then, as the region was enfranchised, legionaries, so much so that by the Julio-Claudian period roughly half of those legionaries serving in upper and lower Germany whose origins can be determined come from Cisalpine Gaul. The same proportion holds true for the Legio XI Claudia in Dalmatia and the Legio VII Claudia in Moesia.[37]

While these figures refer to the Early Empire, they nevertheless reflect a continuation of Republican-era recruitment practices that, during that period, were closely tied to the Roman military presence in the region, as well as to the use of the region as a base and launching pad for actions in Spain, Gaul, and Dalmatia.[38] The military presence in Cisalpine Gaul was intermittent, not as constant as it was to be on the Danube and Rhine borders under the empire, but nevertheless the frequent presence of the armies was a feature that was to distinguish the middle- and late-Republican periods in northern Italy from the early imperial period that followed, while the pattern of recruitment established and encouraged by this militarization was to continue into the Imperial period.

Populations

Supplementing the placement of legions in northern Italy and the integration of a growing portion of the population into the Roman army was the shuffling of native populations by the Roman government.[39]

The practice was especially pronounced in Liguria and the southern Po Plain. In 187 BCE, the consul M. Aemilius Lepidus defeated the Ligurian Freniates and had them brought down from the hills and resettled in the plains.[40] The Apuani were the most easterly dwelling of the Ligurians, and in the early second century they had been threatening Bononia and Pisae with their raids.[41] While Ligurians to the northwest along the coast were left as they were, the Romans treated the Apuani differently, and in 179 BCE, during the campaigns of Q. Fulvius Flaccus in Liguria, the Romans transferred 47,000 Apuani from Liguria to Taurasia in Samnium, where the communities they founded were still to be found in the reign of Trajan.[42] During the same campaign Flaccus had 3,200 Ligurians moved down from the mountains into the plains.[43] These transfers of population betray two distinct patterns: a Roman desire to move hill-dwelling peoples into the plains and, for the second century at least, the confinement of such intervention primarily to the Cispadane region, the area of northern Italy south of the Po River.

An exception to the latter rule is around Aquileia, where shortly before the colony's foundation a band of transalpine Gauls had requested permission to settle near the site of the future colony. Their request was denied, and the Romans sent ambassadors across the Alps to warn others not to cross the Alps.[44] Similarly, in 129 BCE, the consul C. Sempronius Tuditanus is recorded as bringing down the Taurisci and Carni, who lived in what is now the nexus between Italy, Austria, and Slovenia, into the plains by the sea.[45] Here, in the area of the Venetia around Aquileia, the Roman state seems to have been just as interested in controlling populations as it was in Liguria and in the Apennines. The reason for this seems to have been the vulnerability of Aquileia as an isolated and distant colony, whose inhabitants, even in 171 BCE, were complaining to Rome about their defenselessness in the face of attacks from the Istrians and Illyrians.[46] Aquileia was an exposed base for campaigns eastward against the Illyrians, and in this sense it existed outside the schemae set up for the rest of northern Italy for the second and the early first centuries BCE. With Aquileia excepted as a security risk, the confinement of Roman state intervention to the Cispadane suggests that for much of the second century the Po, and not the Alps, was seen by the Romans as the region's predominant border.[47]

While in southeastern Liguria and the Carnic Alps Roman generals relocated populations, in the southern Po Plain wholescale expulsion was practiced. When the Romans conquered the Senones, they confiscated a large portion of the Senones' land. Part was used for the foundation of colonies at Sena Gallica and Ariminum in 284 BCE and 268 BCE, respectively.[48] The rest, known by the Romans as the *Ager Gallicus*, was parceled up to be distributed under the instigation of the tribune Flaminius.[49] The Senones' neighbors, the Boii, suffered a similar confiscation of land immediately after their final defeat in 191 BCE, when the consul P. Scipio Nasica confiscated half of Boian territory, presumably the more desirable half.[50] These land confiscations expelled the Senones and Boii from much of their former territory; in the mid second century Polybius recorded that "not long afterwards I was to see these tribes [the Celts] completely expelled from the valley of the Po, except for a few districts at the foot of the Alps."[51]

The expulsion of the Boii and Senones presents a problem. Large transfers of populations by states were not uncommon in the Hellenistic eastern Mediterranean.[52] The Roman Republic of the second century BCE was, judging by the transfers in and from eastern Liguria, as capable as its counterparts in the eastern Mediterranean. Polybius's comment does indicate that the Boii and Senones were certainly no longer present in the Po Valley as political entities. In contrast, Cicero, in a 56 BCE speech, indicates that the Romans still recognized the Insubres and Cenomani, at least legally, as states holding valid treaties with Rome.[53] After the 280s for the Senones and the 180s for the Boii, no literary or epigraphic evidence for the continuation of either federation in Italy presents itself, and on the ground there is a sharp divide between pre- and postconquest phases.

This discontinuity is clear throughout the Aemilia, including the chief Boian settlement at Bologna, which, just prior to the 189 BCE establishment of a Roman colony, was already showing signs of stress in the form of burned and abandoned structures and a paucity of graves, particularly at the end of the third century—a sign, perhaps, of demographic losses following the battle of Telamon.[54] After the establishment of the Roman colony, the earlier sanctuary at Villa Cassarini was abandoned, and Boian fortifications around the settlement were destroyed.[55] The new Roman colony was located just to the north of the old Boian settlement and was further from the hills. It was also located on a site that had seen an influx of central Italian migrants in the later third century.[56] The situation of the new Roman colony, symbolically further from the hills, centered on a Latin core, and with its old Boian defenses destroyed, was thus both a cooption of the older settlement and a clear break with the past.

Boian communities at Parma and Mutina met similar fates in 183, when a pair of Roman colonies was established there.[57] At Parma a few cult places—including a river ford sanctuary, where offerings were made from the third century BCE to the second century CE, and a chthonic sanctuary dedicated to Ceres and Proserpina and dating from the later third century BCE—continued on into the Roman period, but otherwise as at Bologna the settlement was completely remade.[58] Roman colonists' remaking of Parma extended beyond the city into the fields. The landscape around Parma, changed also by the warmer and drier climate starting in the later third century BCE, was more intensively cultivated, with a largely open landscape of extensive cereal fields, grapevines, and flax and hemp fields in the plains and chestnuts in the hills.[59] The plant remains from colonial Parma, like the religious topography, do show connections with the pre-Roman past. Early Roman votive deposits in Parma's Piazza Garibaldi contained coriander, opium poppy, and strawberry seeds, the remains of gifts to the gods. While the poppy and especially the coriander are archetypically Roman offerings, the use of strawberry as an offering before the imperial period is exceedingly rare in Roman contexts but common in Celtic ones.[60] The offerings to the deities of the Piazza Garibaldi sanctuary therefore likely show an amalgamation of Roman and Celtic religious traditions.

Given the continuity of certain religious practices, it is likely that the Roman expulsion of the Boii from the southern Po Plain was not total and that some of the earlier inhabitants remained after the conquest.[61] Nevertheless, in comparison with Italy north of the Po, the changes brought about by the Romans to the human and natural landscape were sweeping.

To the north, the Insubres and Cenomani did not suffer significant land confiscations and, having concluded treaties with the Romans, continued to exist as independent entities under Roman protection. At Brixia and Mediolanum, the chief centers of the Insubres and Cenomani, respectively, the main areas of habitation remain the same from the fifth through the later second century, with only the later second and first centuries seeing expansion and reorganization.[62]

Inscribed ceramics in Insubrian and Cenomanic territory show the continuation of local languages and epigraphic practices from the fifth into the first century BCE.[63] The inhabitants of Mediolanum, Brixia, Verona, and Bergamo in the Late Republic and Early Empire had Celtic, Italic, and Latin names, and Celtic names in particular persisted among the local elite.[64] Locally produced coinage, the so-called Padane drachmas, continued to be minted until the early first century BCE—probably stopping with the Social War—and continued to circulate through the first century BCE.[65] In short, archaeological, epigraphic, literary, and numismatic evidence all suggest that the Insubres and Cenomani remained in control of their territories after the Roman conquest.

Why the Senones, particularly the Boii, lost their land and the Insubres and Cenomani did not deserves explanation. While the punishment of the Senones might be attributed to the circumstances following the Sentinum campaign, the Boii, Insubres, and Cenomani all joined Hannibal and all fought the Romans after the conclusion of the Second Punic War, and so the harsh treatment of the Boii is anomalous. The leniency displayed toward the Cenomani might be explained by their lateness in leaving their alliance with Rome as well as their quickness in returning to it; Livy has them literally stabbing their Insubrian allies in the backs in the midst of a battle against the Romans.[66] That they were one of Rome's first allies in northern Italy also worked to their advantage.[67] Yet the Insubres, who persisted in the war against the Romans after their Cenomanic allies had turned, were allowed to remain intact and independent as well, so why were the Boii punished? Certainly in literary accounts of their wars with Rome, the Boii appear in an extremely unfavorable light; they alone of the Cisalpine peoples were said to have turned a Roman commander's skull into a ritual vessel. Livy is the sole source for the story, although Cicero mentions the aftermath of the disaster.[68]

In 216 BCE the praetor and consul-elect L. Postumius Albinus was leading two Roman legions through a forested area in an unspecified area of the Po Valley. Waiting for him was a trap carefully placed by the Boii, who had laid their ambush with trees surrounding open areas cut to both entrap and crush the Romans caught by their fall.[69] The ambush was successful, and in the ensuing fight, Albinus and most of his men were killed. What distinguished this Roman defeat from others in northern Italy during the Second Punic War was what followed the battle: "As is their custom" (*ut mos iis est*) the victorious Boii cleaned out Albinus's severed head, covered it with gold, and turned the skull into a sacred drinking cup. While it may be easy to dismiss the colorful story as part of later—Polybius and after—Greek and Roman tradition of dismissing "Celts" and "Gauls" as barbarous headhunters, the practice of using heads as war trophies was widespread throughout Europe and the Roman world, as the Dacian heads on Trajan's column show and as Cicero himself was to find.[70] This is not to suggest any unified Celtic head cult, but rather to say that the posthumous adventures of Postumius's skull was in line with the diverse and widespread use of head trophies in Iron Age Italy and Europe.

In a different category may be Livy's claims that it was the Boii who offered to guide Hannibal over the Alps, and Polybius portrays them as luring the Insubres from their alliance with Rome.[71] And yet the evidence stacked up against the Boii suggests, as does the accusation that it was the Senones who sacked Rome, a certain amount of post facto justification of territorial acquisition, with claims of inciting the Insubres and volunteering to guide Hannibal being the kind of accusations that were easy to manufacture and hard to prove. Even allowing for these stories to be true, the intensive Roman intervention south of the Po, at least in terms of land confiscation, cannot be easily attributed to a Roman desire to punish the Senones and Boii. That the Insubres and the Boii, in particular, received such differing treatment by the Romans, although their history of conflict with Rome was roughly equivalent, shows that the Romans had far different goals north and south of the Po and that the Romans did not conceive of the region as a single indivisible unit.

Like the Cenomani and Insubres, the Veneti remained at least nominally independent. Whether they aided the Carthaginians during the Hannibalic war is unclear; their actions during the war are notably absent from Livy's account. They remain absent from literary sources until the late republic, when Venetic elites joined Rome's political and—in the case of the historian Livy—cultural elite. Between the earliest treaty with the Romans and their emergence in Late Republican prosopography lies over a century of cultural change. Yet it is misleading to conceptualize such change as adoption of Roman culture, just as it is misleading to characterize all continuity as a conscious rejection of Roman culture. Cultural change among the Veneti—as among the Insubres, Cenomani, Carni, Taurini, and other peoples north of the Po—was both connected to larger, often Roman-instigated changes in northern Italy and also primarily driven by local communities and individuals. The disappearance of a particularly extravagant form of animal sacrifice provides a good model for this locally instigated but broadly connected change.

Prior to the Roman conquest, the practice of ritual horse burial could be found among the Senones, Cenomani, Carni, and, most conspicuously, the Veneti.[72] While the Senones and Cenomani more frequently deposited harness and bits in symbolic burials, the Veneti buried entire horses, sometimes interspersed among human burials, sometimes together with a human burial in the same deposit, as in the horse and rider burial from the Piovego necropolis of Patavium.[73] At the Brustolade necropolis near Altinum, human inhumations and cremations beginning in the sixth century BCE were joined in the middle-fifth century by horse inhumations.[74] The necropolis eventually contained twenty-seven horses, all adult, almost exclusively male, and often buried in their harnesses. The greatest concentration dates from the late fifth to middle fourth century, but the practice continued at the Brustolade necropolis until the mid-third century and possibly into the second century BCE.

The appearance of horse burials in northeastern Italy in the sixth and fifth centuries coincided with increasing urbanization in the southern Veneto, when communities like Patavium and Ateste were expanding their nucleated settlements and were defining their boundaries with networks of sanctuaries and more complex and richer necropoleis. Indeed, horse burials in the Veneto are concentrated around more urbanized areas, including Patavium and Ateste; burials are largely absent in areas like the northern Veneto, which had low levels of urbanization until the second phase of Roman colonization and veteran settlement in the first century BCE.

The sacrifice and deposition of horses within these necropoleis, alongside and sometimes with elite families, may have been a way for the elites of those communities to advertise their status and wealth—enough to possess a horse and to kill it at its prime—and in doing so define both their own place within communities and also the boundary of their community against that of its neighbors.[75] Supporting this theory are those horse burials in which the deposit was placed at the boundary of a larger family tumulus, such as the Tiepolo–San Massimo double horse of the early sixth century.[76]

In Venetia the practice declined and disappeared in the third through first centuries BCE as the area came under Roman influence and control. In other parts of the empire, such as Pannonia, Britain, or the Dutch river system, horse burials continued on and, in the case of Britain, even increased in the Roman period. The Romans themselves, as the rituals of the October Horse sacrifice at Rome suggest, had no problem with horse sacrifice, nor is there any indication that land confiscations (largely confined to the first century in the Veneto), colonization (Aquileia was far beyond the major Venetic horse-burying areas), or *attributio* (Patavium and Ateste seem to have maintained constant control over their territories)—indeed, any of the Roman-influenced changes described above—had anything to do with this cultural shift.

Rather, the disappearance of horse burials may reflect a shift in how local elites chose to display their status. From the end of the fourth century in the southern Veneto around Este and Padova, necropoleis saw a shift from large, extended-clan tumuli to small burials focused on the nuclear family; external stone grave markers, such as squat obelisk-like markers from Este or stelai from Padova, ceased to be used, and the focus on display and commemoration moved to the interior of the tomb, with large quantities of bronze and ceramic vessels and with the inscriptions being placed on the ceramic pots containing the deceased's ashes.[77]

While Venetic tombs became less monumental and turned their focus inward, to a more private focus on the family, urban areas like Padova and Este developed further, with the appearance of public buildings, increasingly monumental, in the late fourth to first centuries BCE.[78] In this context, ritually killing and burying a horse as a means of establishing status seems to have fallen out of favor, as elites turned from a kind of equine potlatch toward the embellishment of urban areas and as necropoleis turned from a civic, communal space to a more private one.

While brought about by the needs of Venetic communities, the disappearance of horse burial is not unconnected to larger trends in urbanism in northern Italy, which in some cases were directly and in others indirectly influenced by Roman actions.

Colonization and Centuriation

The most direct Roman interventions were those of the late third and early second centuries BCE in which the Roman state confiscated land and divided it among Roman and Italian colonists. The foundations of Roman and Latin colonies in northern Italy could be quite generous in their allotments of such land. At the Latin colony of Bononia, founded over the old Boian settlement in 189 BCE, the three thousand colonists each received between fifty and seventy *iugera*—a *iugerum* being about three-fifths of an acre or one quarter of hectare—although at the other end of the scale was the 183 BCE citizen colony of Mutina, where colonists received only five *iugera* each.[79] Nevertheless, even at the minimum, two thousand colonists would take up a total ten thousand *iugera*. The foundation allotments of land from the three colonies at Parma, Mutina, and Bononia alone would amount to around 176,000 *iugera*, a substantial amount of land to change hands so quickly. In addition to these initial postconquest colonial foundations, there were other redistributions of land, made for veteran settlements, later urban foundations, or *ad viritim* distributions to individuals, as in the Ager Gallicus.

The physical marks of this process of land redistribution are visible across northern Italy and are seen most clearly in the rectilinear lines of centuriation, marks of land distributions organized by Roman committees set up for the purpose.[80] Nearly all of the settlements along the Via Aemilia show the marks of centuriation schemes; here the intervention of the Roman government in land management was at its most invasive.[81] At least before the veteran settlements of the triumviral period, there is less evidence for the practice north of the Po, although there is a concentration of centuriation schemes around the eastern end of the Via Postumia near Altinum and east of Aquileia.[82] Nevertheless, nearly all of the major settlements in northern Italy—even in areas of the northwest where the landscape was less amenable to such geometric parceling—show physical evidence of land redistributions dating to sometime in the Republican period.[83] All of these schemes required central planning and demonstrate that Roman magistrates were actively involved in reordering the landscape of Cisalpine Gaul in general and of the southern Po Valley in particular.

The centuriation in the Po Valley covers a much broader area, especially along the Via Aemilia. Even the original distribution of the Ager Campanus in southern Italy involved only 1,500 *iugera*, just 15% of the land distributed in the comparatively small citizen colony at Mutina, and while the Romans placed colonies throughout Italy during the middle and late Republic, the sheer extent of land divisions associated not just with colonies but also with other projects in the southern Po Valley was much greater than in central and southern Italy.[84] Out of approximately 764,900 *iugera* distributed in new Latin and Roman colonies founded in the first half of the second century, 559,000 were in Cisalpine Gaul, even though only six of the twenty-two new colonies were founded there.[85] Closer comparisons can be found in the western provinces, particularly in the lower Rhône Valley, which follows the Po Valley in its pattern of extensive centuriation accompanied by large drainage projects.[86] The reasons for this high distribution of land should be attributed to the confiscation of land from the Boii and Senones, itself stemming from the Romans' perceived need to secure the land between the Po and the Apennines.

Roads and Canals

All of these land distributions absolutely depended on the presence of towns, from which the surrounding countryside could be administered. Here, too, the Roman state influenced regional development.

That influence was greatest in the Aemilia, where the Via Aemilia, built in 187 BCE, so greatly dominated the commerce and urbanization of the region that it eventually lent its name to the entire region, the modern Emilia. The road ran from Ariminum to Piacenza, two early and important colonies, and ran as the *decumanus maximus*, the main east-west town street, through the colonies of Bononia, Mutina, and Regium Lepidum. Also along the great trunk road grew towns like Forum Corneli, Forum Popilii, and Forum Livi, whose names honored the individual important Romans—most often magistrates—who founded them.[87] The road linked all of Rome's colonial foundations between the Apennines and the

Po and was the major route for transit and trade, so much so that it discouraged urban growth in other areas of the Aemilia. Apart from Ravenna, which by 132 was linked to Ariminum by the Via Popilia, there were no major settlements in the southeast Po Plain that were not either on or just near the Via Aemilia.

In the north the main road was the Via Postumia (148 BCE), which ran east-west from Genova through Verona to Aquileia.[88] Along the Adriatic coast, the Via Annia (131 BCE) and the Via Popilia (132 BCE) ran north-south to connect Atria and Patavium with the Via Postumia and Via Aemilia.[89] The four roads created a triangle of roads outlining the Po Plain.

In Transpadane some of the most important settlements, like Mediolanum and Brixia, were not on the major road, and so while the Via Postumia facilitated transit between the Roman colonies at Piacenza, Cremona, and Aquileia, it did not remake the urban landscape as the Via Aemilia did in the south. The effects of the Annia and Popilia are harder to discern. Some settlements, like Spina, were bypassed by the two roads but had already begun to decline before the Roman conquest.

Ateste, which had been a major Venetic center in the Iron Age, was also bypassed by the major trunk roads but had its population supplemented during the region's second phase of Roman colonization, which occurred during the civil wars of the mid-first century BCE.[90] By then, the conceptual divisions between north and south had become less sharp, and veterans of Rome's civil wars were settled in communities north and south of the Po. Ateste received veterans from the fifth and eleventh legions after the 31 BCE Battle of Actium.[91] The notorious land confiscations of the triumviral period hit some cities in Cisalpine Gaul worse than others. Here farmland was confiscated and given to veterans returning from the wars of the 40s and 30s BCE, and as a result we find population movements of veterans into Cisalpine towns and of the disposed out, largely to neighboring towns or to Rome. Hence we find refugees from Cremona at Bononia.[92] Since by the first century BCE the Cisalpina was a major recruiting ground for the Roman army, many of the settlers receiving confiscated land were also from neighboring towns.[93] The land confiscations, like the initial colonial settlements of the second century, were the product of circumstances unique to their age, but both helped shape long-term urbanism in northern Italy.

Roman administrative practices and biases against mountain communities were also key. To facilitate the administration of the Transpadane after the region was given Latin rights by the *lex Pompeia* in 89, larger towns were assigned responsibility for governing smaller communities nearby.[94] This process of *attribu-*

tio was important for the development of the region, for it created cities—such as Verona, Brixia, and Mediolanum—with exceptionally large administrative territories while, in the process, encouraging the growth of those cities at the expense of smaller settlements.[95] In Liguria and Venetia the pattern was largely the same, with Genua and Aquileia especially benefiting.[96] Examined alongside the earlier movement of hill peoples into the plains and the encouragement of urban growth along the Via Aemilia, *attributio* is part of a pattern of Roman administrative behavior in Cisalpine Gaul, where the Roman magistrates promoted the growth of towns as a means to govern and secure the province.

In the Po Valley such agricultural and urban realignments were also accompanied by the development of the area's waterways. In 109 BCE M. Aemilius Scaurus oversaw one particularly expansive hydraulic project, which drained the plains around the confluence of the Po and Trebia Rivers with a series of navigable canals that stretched from the Po to the south as far as Parma, a distance of about twelve miles.[97] The prevalence of place names containing *fossa* suggests that Scaurus's project was not an anomaly, and indeed such projects are attested through to the Augustan period.[98] As with the centuriation schemes, these hydraulic projects required some sort of official sponsorship, since the creation of long canals meant dealing with fraught issues of landownership and organizing a large amount of labor.[99]

Such drainage schemes and centuriation certainly occurred south of the Apennines as well. M. Cornelius Cethegus's draining of the Pomptine marshes near Rome in 160 BCE was followed by the centuriation and distribution of that land, while the Ager Campanus near Naples was reorganized for distribution in 165.[100] Nevertheless, the scale of Roman land reorganization in Republican Cisalpine Gaul, especially in the southern Po Plain, was greater in scale and longer in duration than anywhere south of the Apennines. That hydraulic schemes there were more numerous is perhaps less surprising, given the size of the Po River system.

The Borders of Citizenship

By the beginning of the first century BCE the actions of Roman magistrates, soldiers, and colonists had transformed northern Italy. Patterns of urban settlement and agriculture had changed and populations been reordered, partly as a result of Roman perceptions of the region as inherently vulnerable. Guiding Roman actions in the region was a perceived distinction between northern Italy north and south of the Po. This boundary was not without its complications and ambiguities, and the consequences of Romans using the Po as the boundary of what they thought to be their Italy guided the political development of the region in the last decades of the Republic.

While settlers at citizen colonies had always had full citizen rights, those at Latin colonies like Bononia and Aquileia were only partially enfranchised, and the clear majority of northern Italy's population lacked any citizen rights. The civic status of immigrants to Cisalpine Gaul, especially in the southern Po, may have been a point of contention, but still there is no clear evidence that there was any serious demand in northern Italy for enfranchisement before the Social War. Whether during that war there was support in northern Italy for revolt against Rome, as there was in Picenum, Etruria, and Umbria, is unclear.[101]

One incident that might indicate such support, the slaughter of the town council of Mediolanum by troops of Pompey, is ambiguous and exceptionally problematic, since it is unclear whether the incident happened with Pompey Magnus or his father, Pompey Strabo. The first-century CE senator and writer Frontinus describes the incident: "After the senate of Mediolanum had been murdered by the army, Cn. Pompey, so as not to arouse a mutiny, as would have been the case had he only called out the guilty, also summoned some who were innocent to come intermixed with them."[102] Two questions here are crucial: which Pompey is the passage referring to, and why did the soldiers kill the Milanese senators? Both Pompey Strabo and Pompey Magnus are plausible. The senate of Mediolanum might have been pushing for war with Rome, in which case Strabo's purging of that body to eliminate the potential for revolt would be followed by a show trial of mutineers designed to shield Strabo from blame. If there were in fact some support for war with Rome in the Transpadana, then Strabo's subsequent granting of Latin rights to the region may have been a measure designed to appease the region and prevent serious revolt, a method similar to that used in Etruria and Umbria, regions appeased with the granting of citizen rights via the *lex Iulia*.[103] If, however, the Pompey in question is Strabo's son, Pompey Magnus, then the most plausible context is during Pompey's campaign against Brutus at Mutina.[104] It is possible that there was support at Mediolanum for Brutus, and the town's keeping of a statue of the son of that Brutus during the Augustan period might be taken as evidence of familial connections with the town.[105] The presence of the statue of Brutus at Mediolanum makes this later scenario more likely, although not decisively so, and so there is still little evidence for any agitation for the franchise among the inhabitants of Cisalpine Gaul, at least none inciting revolt against the state and requiring Roman military attention.[106] This lack of any clear northern Italian desire for enfranchisement makes the following events that much more surprising.

The *lex Iulia* granted citizenship to all Roman allied communities in Italy who wanted it, and it appears that such a grant—or possibly one of the slate of enfranchisement measures enacted during and immediately following the Social War—also included the inhabitants of the Cispadane region of Cisalpine Gaul.[107] Under the *lex Pompeia* of 89 BCE the Transpadani received "Latin rights, so that they might have the same rights that other Latin communities have, that is, upon achieving a magistracy they should obtain Roman citizenship."[108] These two actions of the Roman state, the full enfranchisement of the Cispadane and the partial enfranchisement of the Transpadana, reinforce the notion visible in the past century that Roman Italy ended at the Po River.

The reasons for these enfranchisement measures in northern Italy are unclear, especially in the light of any apparent dissatisfaction in Cisalpine Gaul over citizenship, agrarian laws, or other state matters. One possibility is the Roman desire for a uniform political treatment for Italy, so as to avoid legal complications over which Italians were citizens and which were not. The enfranchisement of Cispadane Gaul and Pompey Strabo's enfranchisement of the Transpadani might be seen as both a reward for loyalty and a bid for elite clients with voting power.[109]

The Rubicon

The Transpadani, however, were not long satisfied with this arrangement, and by the '60s and '50s they were demanding full Roman citizenship, probably because of a combination of factors: their elites were starting to make headway into magistracies at Rome; Transpadane writers were pushing for a more expansive notion of Italian identity, one that encompassed both cultural and political notions and that stretched to the Alps; and ambitious politicians saw the advantage of championing the enfranchisement of such a populous and wealthy area eager to join the high political circles at Rome.[110] Both Crassus and Caesar attempted unsuccessfully to grant their request during the 60s and 50s, and the latter was successful only in the context of a civil war.[111] With the *lex Roscia* Caesar enfranchised the Transpadani on March 11 in 49 BCE, just weeks after crossing the Rubicon, the boundary between the province of Cisalpine Gaul and Italy proper.[112]

That political boundary ceased to exist in 42 BCE, when the triumvirs, at Augustus's insistence, incorporated Cisalpine Gaul into Italy.[113] Although Roman commanders continued to operate in the region during the civil wars and in campaigns against Alpine peoples, northern Italy would no longer be assigned as a *provincia* or have a governor. The triumvirs' actions thus ended a seven-year period of administrative ambiguity for Cisalpine Gaul, well-illustrated by the *lex de Gallia Cisalpina*, which specifies that municipal magistrates may appeal before a praetor at Rome rather than the provincial governor, and by the related *fragmentum Atestinum*, which prescribes adjustments for the jurisdictions of local magistrates.[114] A desire to clean up the judicial ambiguity left by Caesar's actions probably motivated the triumvirs' decision less than the more pressing problem of having a provincial governor so close to Rome, a problem vividly demonstrated not only by Caesar's invasion but also by the dispute with Decimus Brutus and the Mutina campaign.

While the administrative incorporation of Cisalpine Gaul into Italy, finalized later in Augustus's creation of the Italian *regiones*, seems to have been dictated by a number of political and logistic demands—the need to remove governors from the region following an unusual period of civil wars, an inherited concern for Cisalpine Gaul in general, and possible intentions to raise the area's stature or simplify its administration prior to personal campaigns in Illyria and the Alps—this political move nevertheless marked a sharp change in the administration of the region.[115] The disappearance of provincial governors and their attendant staff meant the removal of the apparatus that had been the means for major road construction, hydraulic and agricultural projects, and urban development along the Via Aemilia. Likewise, the integration into Italy meant that Cisalpine Gaul was no longer a place that was different and strange but instead was part of the Italian homeland, itself an idea being developed in an Augustan cultural milieu in the aftermath of the Social and civil wars.[116]

Nevertheless, the period from the Roman conquest to Augustus's incorporation had made Cisalpine Gaul a somewhat un-Italian place. *Attributio*, ongoing even in the early imperial period, was encouraging the development of cities with much larger territories than was typical in central and southern Italy, while in the Cispadane and around the Veneto the Romans had created a manmade landscape of centuriation and increased canalization. It was also in the Po Plain that, following the pattern of the area's pre-Roman inhabitants, the language of Roman provincial architecture and urban design was being developed.[117] The integration of Cisalpine Gaul into Italy, then, both removed many of the institutional catalysts for the region's Republican-period development and also attached to Italy a decidedly provincial landscape. The effects of that development on local identities, cities, societies, and economies will be examined in following chapters.

Chapter Three

Citizenship and Identity

Conquests have consequences, as in the late 1790s, when French campaigns under Napoleon defeated Austrian, local Italian, Russian, and Piedmontese-Sardinian forces in northern Italy to claim the region as a client state. Napoleon's campaigns not so subtly recalled the Carthaginian general Hannibal's 218 BCE invasion, but the political settlement was made in ancient Roman terms. The republic of Genoa was made the Ligurian Republic. Duchies and papal legations in the Po Plain were turned into the similarly Latinized Cispadane Republic, which was later merged with the remnants of a transitional Transpadane republic to its north into a larger Cisalpine Republic, its names derived from the ancient Roman province. Mirroring the growth of Napoleon's ambitions, the Cisalpine Republic became part first of an Italian Republic and then a Kingdom of Italy. The republics and kingdom did not outlast Napoleon's own power—but their brief existence shows the potential power of even long-since-abandoned group identities.[1]

Two thousand years before, in Roman northern Italy, conquest had created a new territory, united as Cisalpine Gaul but bisected by the Po River and two vastly different approaches to administration. Celtic states south of the Po had largely disappeared as independent entities, while those to the north continued on. Male inhabitants of the whole region served as auxiliaries alongside the legions and other Roman allies in Italy. The Roman approach to northern Italy during the Middle Republic had been somewhat schizophrenic, both unifying and dividing.

In this new Roman northern Italy there were no northern Italians, at least none who either called themselves or were called by others as such. For Roman writers there were the inhabitants of Cisalpine Gaul, that is, "Gaul this (i.e., the Roman) side of the Alps." There were the *civitates*, *gentes*, and *nationes*, such as the Veneti, Gauls, Raeti, Camunni, Insubres, Cenomani, and Trumplini. On honorific inscriptions and epitaphs there were townspeople—the Veronenses of Verona, the Comenses of Comum, and the Bononienses of Bononia—and the people who lived around the region's larger lakes, like the Benacenses around the Lacus Benacus (Lake Garda). There were the people who lived north of the Po, the Transpadani, although the corresponding term for northern Italians living south of the Po, Cispadani, was not used. People from northern Italy also described themselves as Italians and Romans but never as northern Italians (the same was true for central and southern Italy). Why were there no northern Italians?

In answering that question, this chapter traces the effects of the Roman conquest and subsequent governance on expressions of group and individual identity in northern Italy up to the second century CE and the height of the Roman Empire. This formative period saw the development and elaboration of conceptual identities that were to echo in Napoleon's Italy—and again and again through the Risorgimento and beyond. The era also demonstrates how interaction with the Roman state changed how people conceived of their place in the world.

Identity from the Seventh Century BCE to the Roman Conquest

There were many ways for people in the Mediterranean to define and present themselves to the world, be it through their appearance, possessions, behavior, writing, or work, and when to these individual expressions are added collective works both performative and monumental, the potential avenues for exploring ancient identity can appear almost prohibitively numerous.[2] The full range of individual and collective expression in northern Italy cannot be adequately explored here, but a more focused exploration can be productive. For this task, literary and epigraphic texts are especially useful, since for northern Italy there is a continuous, if not uniform, supply of both from the Roman conquest through the Principate.

Greek and Roman literary sources describing northern Italy in the second century BCE divide the area's inhabitants into Gauls (or Celts), Veneti, and Ligurians, with the Celts further divided into independent states and chiefdoms, such as the Insubres, Boii, Cenomani, and Senones; little differentiation is made of the Veneti, although the Ligurians are often subdivided into smaller states.[3] That the terms for these smaller states most often find their first attestations in Greek and Roman authors should not mean that they were identities grafted onto northern Italy's inhabitants by its conquerors. The ethnonyms used by authors like Polybius and Cato have, for the most part, secure roots in the region's linguistic soil—hence the Celtic Caturigi ("the kings of battle"), Cenomani ("the far-going ones"), the Carni ("the horned ones"), the Boii ("the fighting ones"), the Lepontii ("the left-behind ones"), and the charmingly named Libici ("the amiable ones").[4]

These political affiliations were long-lived. In the Late Republic, Cicero could cite treaties made with the Cenomani and Insubres; Cicero's phrasing indicates that the treaties were still in effect, which in turn suggests that, at least nominally, the Cenomani and Insubres still continued as political bodies even into the 50s BCE.[5] The Trumplini, inhabiting the Val Trompia along the Mella River, were making collective dedications as Trumplini as late as the Flavian era (late first century CE).[6] While these terms lasted into the early Principate when used by communities acting as a whole, they were generally not used by individuals to describe themselves, a pattern seen in the region's epigraphic habits.

In Iron Age northern Italy there were three main groups of non-Latin inscriptions.[7] In the northeast, the Veneti inscribed funerary markers, votive dedications, and pots in the Venetic language and with a script derived from northern Etruria (fig. 4). In the northwest could be found Gallo-Lepontic inscriptions, sometimes called Lepontic or Gallo-Etruscan, written in Celtic using the Lugano script, also derived from a north Etruscan script.[8] In an early and typical Gallo-Lepontic example, a cup made at the end of the seventh century BCE (Golasecca IC) and found at Sesto Calende, a woman simply scratched her name: Iunϑanaχa.[9] Most Gallo-Lepontic inscriptions are short, often bearing only a name, and chronologically cluster in the seventh–fifth centuries, with a revival in the second and first centuries BCE.[10] Venetic inscriptions appeared in the sixth century and continued into the second, when the Veneti switched to writing their inscriptions in Latin letters but still in the Venetic language.[11] These Latino-Venetic inscriptions continued to be produced into the late first century BCE, with significant regional variation. Finally, dominating the Po Plain until the fourth century were Etruscan inscriptions.

In all three major epigraphic corpora, references to the larger political bodies mentioned by Polybius, Cato, and other ancient writers are almost nonexistent, and this absence is typical of epigraphic habits across archaic Italy. This is not to say that this kind of collective identification did not exist. One Venetic votive from Cadore was set up, as its inscription notes, by the *teuta*, that is, "the people,"

Figure 4. Stele from Vercelli. Front face of a bilingual inscription. Photograph by author.

or "community."[12] Yet these kinds of group identities appear epigraphically only in those cases in which the community was acting collectively, suggesting that these identifications were not seen as integral to individual commemoration.

There are a few rare cases of individuals identifying themselves by ethnic labels, as in the case of a bowl inscribed with *Keltie*—"The Celt"— from the necropolis at Valle Trebba near Spina in the Po Delta.[13] Similarly, a fifth-century ceramic lid from Marzabotto carries an inscription *Larisal Kraikalus* ("belonging to Laris the Greek"); the man had an Etruscan praenomen but identified himself as Greek, albeit with the *alu* ending peculiar to Etruscan contexts in the Po Plain.[14] Such cases are quite rare, and while they do further highlight the cosmopolitan nature of the trading settlements at Spina and Adria, their scarcity suggests that these ethnic identifications were not of primary importance to individual epitaphs and dedications.[15]

For the most part the emphasis in inscriptions is on preserving and advertising an individual's name. One mid-third-century tomb at Spina's neighbor Atria, for example, contained among its otherwise typically Etruscan funerary goods an iron spear point, bronze La Tène fibula, and multiple cups and plates inscribed solely with the man's Celtic name, Verkanthus.[16] The formulaic Venetic funerary and dedicatory inscriptions from Ateste, Cadore, Vicetia, and Patavium often added patronymics and sometimes avonymics (personal names based on grandfathers' names) or *gentilicia* (family names denoting the *gens*, or clan).[17] The epigraphic habit of preserving the name as the primary identifier would outlast the Cenomani, Insubres, and even the Trumplini, but otherwise the means by which that name was preserved changed suddenly and dramatically in the Late Republic.

Postconquest Inscriptions

The Roman conquest brought an end to most of the states south of the Po. As noted earlier, those north of the Po lingered on at least nominally into the first century BCE. The conquest brought Roman and Italian settlers into the region, colonists and migrants who brought with them their own ways of identifying themselves. The introduction of Latin, new epigraphic habits, and thousands of new settlers from the peninsula might be expected to bring about similarly dramatic change in how the Veneti and remaining Celtic-speaking peoples identified themselves on inscriptions. And indeed there was change. The Gallo-Lepontic epigraphic habit in the northwest was revitalized, and in the middle of the second century Venetic inscriptions switched from an Etruscan-derived alphabet to a

Latin one.[18] But there was no wholesale switch over to Latin until the Augustan era, and Latin inscriptions are exceptionally rare until the first century BCE, when bilingual inscriptions appear.[19] Why?

The inhabitants of northern Italy were not alone in their late switch to Latin in inscriptions (both in script and in language). In the central Etrurian cities of Arezzo, Chiusi, and Perugia, Etruscan scripts predominated in inscriptions before the first century, whose early decades saw a marked change: (1) inscriptions in Latin and Etruscan scripts began to be placed next to each other in the same tombs; (2) Etruscan families began using both Roman and Etruscan onomastic formulae; and (3) some individuals began to identify themselves with Etruscan and Roman names, the latter habit similar to the process in Ptolemaic and Roman Egypt of persons using both Egyptian and Greek names in documents and on mummy tags.[20] At Caere, in southern Etruria and just at Rome's doorstep, the change to Latin in both script and language occurred swiftly in the first decades of the first century BCE; the transition was so swift that it cannot be the end result of slow Latinization but rather indicates, as Benelli argues, a "cultural choice."[21] In Umbria the shift was earlier; Latin scripts began to be used in the mid second century BCE, but inscriptions in the Umbrian language declined more dramatically after the early first century BCE.[22] Dominated by Greek scripts, southern Italy shows different patterns of epigraphic change. In Hellenophone Naples, for example, the shift toward inscriptions in Latin script and language was much slower than in Etruria and dates largely to the first century CE, although the first few Latin inscriptions appearing in Naples date to the early first century BCE.[23]

The synchronism of the shift to Latin scripts and language across much—but not all—of central and northern Italy suggests that the cause of the shift was not the gradual but inexorable spread of a dominant language; rather, the epigraphic language shift was, like the disappearance in horse burials, the result of elites changing the ways they commemorated themselves.

Here the case of Celtic inscriptions in the Gallo-Lepontic script is particularly instructive. After a hiatus in Gallo-Lepontic inscriptions in the fourth through early third centuries, the third through first centuries BCE saw a revival, with both longer and more numerous inscriptions.[24] Bilingual and Latin inscriptions appeared in the early first century BCE, although Gallo-Lepontic continues on in graffiti and small votives until the first century CE.[25] There was a sharp division, however, in the types of inscriptions used for each language and script, with Latin the favored choice for public, monumental inscriptions, and Lepontic was set aside for the more private world of graffiti and small votives.[26] This change to Latin for civic monuments suggests a conscious choice made by the elites of northwestern Italy, and, given the synchronicity with change in Venetia and Etruria, a choice tied to events in the late second or more likely the early first century BCE.

Given the timing, the prime suspect for the catalyst of those changes might be the Social War, the war between Rome and many of its Italian allies that began late in 91 BCE and lasted through two hard years of fighting, until 88, when only the Samnites remained hostile. During the conflict Italian identity became a key element of the Italian war effort. The Romans' former allies set up a federal capital at Corfinium, in the territory of the Peligni in the Apennines near modern L'Aquila, and renamed the city Italia, or Italica.[27] The coins issued by the Italians at Corfinium presented images of Italy personified, a bull goring the Roman wolf, and Italy personified seated atop Roman shields and being crowned by victory; accompanying legends of *Italia* (often written in Oscan) hammered the point home.[28] The rebels' ostentatious identifications as Italians may have been politically motivated, but at the same time it was fairly novel, as indications of such group Italian identity being expressed by people living on the Italian peninsula are rare before this date.[29]

Roman efforts to end the Social War and placate their former allies had also brought about a series of enfranchisement measures, most important the *lex Iulia* of 89.[30] The end result of the war was that the Italian allies were given Roman citizenship.[31] In peninsular Italy, citizenship was not immediately or equitably distributed, in an attempt to maintain Roman and Latin control over the magistracies. In northern Italy, a sharp division was made again between the areas north and south of the Po. Northern Italy was given two levels of citizenship: full citizenship in the south and a type of half-citizenship in the north. In the north, citizenship became the privilege of the political elite, creating a perception that Roman citizenship itself was inherently valuable.

There is also little evidence that any communities in northern Italy rebelled against the Romans or that there was agitation or even desire for the franchise before 89 BCE. Nevertheless, Italian identity was now part of the political language, and citizenship had become a divisive political marker in the region.

In this context, the use of the Latin language and script in civic and monumental inscriptions may have been a way for local elites among the Veneti and Celts to express their belonging to a now more inclusive Roman Republic. They could present themselves not as allies in a lopsided alliance but as partners who had the opportunity (however slight at this point) to climb the *cursus honorum*—the highly competitive system of public magistracies—of the largest state in Europe and the Mediterranean.

In the bilingual inscriptions of the first century, a Roman audience might not have been the primary one. A monumental inscription in Gallo-Lepontic and Latin, for example, might have been more effectively directed at a local audience, particularly if viewers included those who had not yet obtained a magistracy. Alternatively, those elites who did not have Roman citizenship could use Latin in an inscription to create the appearance of belonging to this new political order. Even better if this new Italo-Roman identity could be tied with elite euergetism—charity and benefactions usually given in return for honors—as in a large stele from Vercelli (fig. 5). The stele prioritizes the Latin, which is placed above and in larger letters, while the Gallo-Lepontic is relegated to the bottom third of the stele. There is no attempt to Latinize either Akisios's name or to add Latin formulae, and since there is no indication of Roman settlement or immigration in Vercelli before the late first century BCE, it is likely that the primary audience here was a Celtic one.[32] Here on the Vercelli stone Latin is for elite display, a means for Akisios to show off not only his generosity but also his *Latinitas*.

> FINIS | CAMPO · QUEM | DEDIT · ACISIVS | ARGANTOCOMATER
> ECVS · COMVNEM | DEIS · ET · HOMINIB | VS · ITA · VTI · LAPID[es]
> IIII · STATVTI · SVNT
>
> (Latin) Border of the field that Acisius Argantocomaterecus has given communally to the gods and men, just as the four stones are posted.
>
> ᚨKISIOS · ᚨDKᚨXOKO<K> | MᚨXEDKOS · XOᴧO | KOXE · ᚨXOM
> XEVOY | XOM · XOᛚEV
>
> (Celtic) Akisios Arka(n)tokomaterekos has given the field communally to gods and men.[33]

This decorous function is underscored elsewhere by the division between bilingual monumental inscriptions and smaller private graffiti and votives still written in Venetic and Celtic languages. Graffiti might better represent how people in the region spoke in the early first century, but monumental civic inscriptions show how local elites wished to represent themselves, and in the early first century this was as Latinized Italians. The appearance of bilingual inscriptions allowed men like Akisios, who had both the ability and incentive to put up these

Figure 5. Venetic Inscription from via Acquette. Padua, Musei Civivi agli Eremetani. Photograph by author.

monumental inscriptions, the opportunity to mark themselves as Italian while still communicating to their communities in the way to which they were accustomed.

The Creation of the Transpadani

In Akisios's Vercelli and in towns throughout the northern half of Cisalpine Gaul, self-representation as Italian had an increasingly political edge, since by the mid first century BCE the Latin status of the people living between the Alps and the Po had become controversial at Rome. The potential windfall of clients made the enfranchisement of the newly termed *Transpadani* ("those across the *Padanus* / Po River") attractive to ambitious Roman senators, senators like M. Licinius Crassus, who tried as censor to give the Transpadani citizenship but who met with such opposition from his fellow censor that a stalemate was reached, and with neither able to accomplish anything else, both resigned.[34] In the spring and summer of 51 BCE the controversy, fueled by typical Roman aristocratic competition, was so heated that

> Caesar built the town of Novum Comum at the foot of the Alps and gave it the Latin rights, which included a provision that those who had exercised year by year the chief magistracy should become Roman citizens. One of these men, who had been in office and was consequently considered a Roman citizen, was beaten with rods for some reason by order of Marcellus in defiance of Caesar—a punishment that was never inflicted on Roman citizens. Marcellus in his passion revealed his real intention that the blows should be the brand of the alien, and he told the man to carry his scars and show them to Caesar.[35]

Marcellus's actions were directed at Caesar and were as much if not more derived from personal pique as from any ideological opposition to enfranchisement. This was at one level a game between Roman aristocrats, but it was nevertheless also a game based on the presumption that the Transpadani would be grateful for citizenship, that the franchise was something they wanted.

This game had played out before at Rome, with the attempts of Fulvius Flaccus and the younger M. Livius Drusus to give citizenship to the Italian allies in the late second century. The Romans must have remembered this, for in May of 51 BCE Cicero fearfully records rumors that Caesar was about to enfranchise the Transpadani and indeed had already ordered them to appoint magistrates and set up *municipia*.[36] Both the existence of the rumors and the panic that such rumors produced highlight the post–Social War association of enfranchisement activism with civil war and civic discord.

At Rome the enfranchisement question was politically charged, and adding to the friction was the steady integration of northern Italians into the Roman political elite. Aquileia, Verona, Brixia, and Cremona were the first Cisalpine towns to produce Roman magistrates, with products of the old colony of Aquileia making their way into Roman offices as early as ca. 100 BCE, and with men from other Cisalpine towns achieving minor Roman magistracies in the mid first century.[37] Verona could claim a *triumvir monetalis* of 80 BCE and a praetor of 67, while Brixia was probably the origin of C. Helvius Cinna, tribune of the plebs in 43, and Cremona that of a consul *suffectus* in 39.[38] Cinna's fellow poet and friend, the Veronese Catullus, also fit into this group of upwardly mobile Transpadani; his father was a friend of Caesar's, and he himself served on the propraetor Memmius's staff in Bithynia in 57 BCE.[39]

Catullus's poetry provides a useful look at how these new men might present themselves to Roman political cliques. In his poems, Catullus presents himself as inhabiting two main spheres: one local and one in Rome and its vicinity. Hence, in one poem, Catullus invites a friend from Comum to visit him in Verona, and in another he complains that because he lives mainly at Rome, he has only a few books with him in Verona.[40] He is familiar with gossip both from Rome and from Verona, and he gives the same attention to a set of Veronese siblings as to Pompey.[41] Likewise, his villas on Lake Garda and outside of Rome near Tivoli both merit a mention.[42] Local affairs are put on similar standing as those at Rome, a dichotomy that fits well with Cicero's observation that Romans had two *patriae*, one by nature and one by citizenship, just as Cato had his origin at Tusculum but was also a citizen of Rome.[43] Catullus does not hide his connections with northern Italy because such connections show him to be like many other Roman aristocrats: bound by political obligations at Rome and at home.

Catullus does however make a strong distinction between what he defines as Italian and non-Italian *patriae*. This is especially apparent in poem 39, where he writes:

> If you were a Roman or a Sabine or a Tiburtine
> or a chubby Umbrian or a rotund Etruscan
> or a dark and toothy Lanuvian
> or a Transpadane—so I might not leave my own people untouched—
> or anybody else who washes his teeth with pure water
> still I would not wish you to go grinning all over the place,
> for there is nothing more foolish than a foolish laugh.
> Now as matters stand you are a Celtiberian, and in Celtiberian territory
> everybody every morning brushes his teeth and red gums with urine.[44]

Here Catullus explicitly identifies himself with the Transpadani, whom he groups with other Italian peoples and sets in contrast to the non-Italian Celtiberians.[45] Catullus was writing just a generation after the Social War, and in the context of controversial attempts to enfranchise the Transpadani, his claiming Italian cultural status was politically charged.

In another poem Catullus ridicules Arrius, a man who speaks with a Celtiberian accent; again Catullus is grouping himself with people who speak "proper" Latin—i.e., with Italians.[46] As one of the Transpadani, Catullus's own linguistic *urbanitas* would not be entirely secure. Cicero, writing in the decade after Catullus's death, warns a young orator that in Cisalpine Gaul he would hear words and phrases that were not current in Rome; he also notes that the provincial speakers he has heard have in general lacked *urbanitas*.[47] The linguistic snobbery Catullus directs toward the Spanish Arrius is in part defensive, but it also forms part of a larger discussion, taking place among Roman, Italian, and Transpadane elites, about how the Transpadani fit, both culturally and politically, into Italy.[48]

In this discussion terminology mattered; when Caesar, a supporter and patron of the Transpadani, refers to the province of Cisalpine Gaul in his commentaries on the Gallic Wars, he generally uses *Italia* instead of *Gallia*.[49] *Italia* of course had the franchise; *Gallia* did not. Significantly, Catullus's only mention of "Italy" or "Italian" comes in poem 1, where he dedicates his book to the Transpadane Cornelius Nepos, who was "the only one of the Italians" to write a history of the world in three volumes. Here the inclusion of the Transpadana within Italy is unmistakable, and the choice of Cornelius Nepos as the dedicatee underscores the point.

As Catullus and other Transpadane elites were integrating into Roman politics and presenting themselves as Italian (itself an only recently important construction), the Transpadani were also building an identity as Transpadani, a category that was created almost by accident by the patchwork of enfranchisement measures of the Social War. While there is no indication that the Transpadani had sought citizenship before, or even during, the Social War, their exclusion from the full enfranchisement given to towns in Aemilia and the rest of the Cispadane meant that they spent the next few decades attempting to get full enfranchisement. That exclusion from full enfranchisement also meant that, for the first time, the Transpadani became a defined group, people who lived in a defined geographical area and had defined legal rights. This group identity was strengthened every time their status and rights came into dispute at Rome, as when Caesar denounced Piso, the former governor of Cisalpine Gaul, for unlawfully executing a Transpadanus, or when C. Scribonius Curio argued that, although the cause of the Transpadani was just, their enfranchisement would not be beneficial to the republic.[50]

In republican-era literature the word *Transpadanus* appears predominantly in connection with the enfranchisement question, as when Cicero comments on rumors that Caesar had ordered the Transpadani to elect *quattuorviri*—the "four men" traditionally the magistrates of Italian *municipia*—or when, before the battle of Pharsalus, Labienus says to Pompey's troops that they are about to face legions recruited from Transpadane—and thus implicitly illegally recruited—settlers.[51] The classification of inhabitants of Italy north of the Po as Transpadani was strengthened over time by the ongoing political dialogue about enfranchisement. That the creation of Transpadane identity is a consequence of the enfranchisement question finds strong confirmation in the almost total absence of any form of the word *Cispadanus* in surviving ancient Latin; its only attestation is in the name of a cohort in Moesia in the early third century CE.[52] In Greek it is also extremely rare; Strabo uses the term *Cispadana* in his description of Italy, but there the term is used solely for organizational purposes in dividing book 5 geographically.[53] The absence of a generally recognized Cispadane group identity suggests that there was no strong motivation either for Roman politicians or the inhabitants of Aemilia and southern Liguria to create such a term; there was no political or cultural stimulus to use that particular group identity. Just as striking is the absence of the concept of the Transpadana before the Social War, when the predominating geographic label used by Greek and Latin writers is "Cisalpine Gaul."[54] Similarly, areas within Cisalpine Gaul were identified by their predominant *ethnos*, with the Ager Gallicus of the Senones, or the Venetia of the Veneti. Transpadane group identity was therefore a relatively new innovation, remarkable in that it was largely free of ethnic markers.[55]

Transpadane identity was very much the product of the unique political circumstances following the Social War, a war that at the same time developed and enlarged the concept of Italian identity. With first the enfranchisement of the Transpadana by Caesar in 49 and then the incorporation of Cisalpine Gaul into Italy under the triumvirate, the political motivations for formulating an identity as Transpadani disappeared.[56]

After the civil wars, Augustus divided Italy into eleven regions (*regiones*), four of which—Aemilia, Liguria, Venetia et Istria, and Transpadana—were in northern Italy). The name of the Aemilia region, derived from the via Aemilia, reflected its history of intensive state intervention in the Middle Republic. Liguria, Aemilia's neighbor to the west, took the geographic name traditionally given to that region, although the borders of the Augustan region were slightly different. Why the third new *regio* was called *Transpadana* and not, along the lines of the other *regiones*, something like *Insubrica*, *Libicia*, or *Taurinum* is difficult to determine, but, in the context of the earlier *causa Transpadani*, it is possible that the use of the name *Transpadana* shows Augustus commemorating the success of himself and his adoptive father as patrons of the region and the inhabitants of the region defining themselves as "Italy across the Po" rather than as a Celtic toponym. In the Early Empire the term *Transpadana* came to be used in a technical sense, by the elder Pliny to describe a geographic region amenable to certain crops—and which Pliny sets in contrast to Venetia—or by Tacitus to describe the Augustan *regio* XI.[57] That Pliny contrasts the Transpadana with Venetia shows that this new conceptualization of the term was based on the more recent administrative division of Augustus rather than on the old geographical definition of *Transpadana* as being that part of Italy north of the Po, since Venetia was also north of the Po. The enfranchisement of the Transpadani had removed any political incentive for identifying them as a separate group, and now, with the Augustan age, the Transpadani disappeared in literature and were replaced by the conceptualization of the Transpadana primarily as a state-defined administrative unit.

Identity in the First and Early Second Century CE

As Transpadane identity lost its political significance, it was engulfed by the larger definition of Italian identity. No longer presenting themselves as those Italians north of the Po unfairly cut off from citizenship, the Transpadani were now simply Italians, but as Italians they occupied a privileged place in the ideology of the Early Empire.

The division between provincial and Italian had its roots in the political environment of the Late Republic and, from then on into the High Empire, was perpetuated by the language of edicts and decrees, which formulaically divide the empire into "Italy and the provinces," with Italy almost always listed first.[58] The Roman state's granting of the *Ius Italicum* ("the Italian right"), by which a provincial city's territory was treated as Italian land and therefore exempt from the taxes of the *tributum soli* (land tax) and *tributum capitis* (poll tax) also highlighted how "being Italian" was better than being provincial.[59] Through repeated actions of the emperor, the hierarchy of the Italian over the provincial was reinforced even in the provinces, through both official language and the granting of privileges explicitly associated with Italian status.

The division between Italy and the provinces was not just expressed in the language of imperial administration; it had permeated the thinking of local elites in the empire. Pliny the Younger describes how engrained such a dichotomy was: "He [the historian Tacitus] was describing how at the last races he sat next to a Roman knight who had engaged him in conversation on several learned subjects and then asked if he came from Italy or the provinces. 'You know me,' said Tacitus, 'from your reading.' At which the man said, 'Then are you Tacitus or Pliny?' I can't tell you how delighted I am to have our names assigned to literature as if they belonged there and not to individuals, and to learn that we are both known by our writing to people who would otherwise not have heard of us."[60] The very first question that the knight asks about Tacitus's identity is whether he is from Italy or the provinces, not which region or province he was from. Trying to establish his elite credentials through other means, Tacitus steered the conversation to his literary rather than geographic identity.[61]

Italy's privileged status might have encouraged Italians in the provinces to advertise their origins. One late second- or early third-century altar from Vindolanda in Britain reads:

> I(ovi) O(ptimo) M(aximo | ceterisque | diis immort(alibus) | et Gen(io) praetor(i) | Q(uintus) Petronius Q(uinti) f(ilius) Fab(ia tribu) Urbicus) | praef(ectus) coh(ortis) IIII | Gallorum | . . . | ex Italia | domo Brixia | votum solvit | pro se | ac suis

> To Jupiter the Best and Greatest and to the other immortals and to the *genius* of the commander's tent, Quintus Petronius Urbicus, the son of Quintus, prefect of the fourth Gallic cohort . . . from Brixia in Italy carried out his vow on behalf of himself and his family.[62]

Here Petronius identifies himself with three larger groups apart from his immediate family: with his military unit, with his hometown, and with Italy in general. Likewise, the dedicator in a later inscription from Lepcis Magna identified himself as being *Mediolanensis ex Italia*, a Milanese from Italy.[63]

This kind of self-identification by region was for the most part exceptional; far more typical was identification by town alone, which in itself suggests that municipal origin was considered more important than the regional and that merely listing the town simultaneously conveyed the region. Of those very few inscriptions that do specify an origin in Italy for the commemorated, the majority also list town origins in northern Italy, although this may reflect the fact that the inscriptions come from military contexts and that the legions recruited disproportionably from northern Italy in the first two centuries CE.[64] Nevertheless, other monuments show a noticeable eagerness to demonstrate Italian origins, as in the case of a couple setting up a dedication at Belgrade who went out of their way to specify that they were "living at Aquileia" in an attempt to provide a link with Italy, even if they could not persuasively claim an origin there.[65]

At Urbicus's home back in Brixia, there was certainly less need to prove Italian status. Rather, inhabitants at Brixia and other towns in northern Italy throughout the first two centuries CE attempted to mark themselves as more Italian than other Italians. Here this was not an attempt, as it was in the provinces, to claim for themselves a privileged status within the empire but rather an effort to claim a particular cultural identity, as belonging to a more authentic and morally undiluted Italy. A set of perceived old Italian virtues might be seen to be preserved in Italian *municipia* when they had long decayed at Rome. Hence Tacitus describes the Julio-Claudian period as one of extravagance and luxury, which came to an end when Vespasian came to power: "At the same time new men from the towns and colonies and even from the provinces progressively entered the senate and brought with them their native frugality. Although most came to moneyed maturity through hard work or good fortune, they maintained their earlier mentality. But the most conspicuous model of these mores was Vespasian, who himself had an old-fashioned way of living."[66]

Tacitus links both Italians and provincials to a native frugality and old-fashioned way of living, and Tacitus's contemporary and correspondent Pliny goes one step further and ascribes these municipal virtues particularly to other Cisalpine towns.[67] He praises the Patavian Thrasea Paetus and his family at length as *exempla virtutum* and also commends one woman by saying that she was a model of stern self-discipline (*severitas*) even to the Patavians.[68] Pliny sets out these old Italian virtues clearly in another letter in which he recommends his friend Minutius Aemilianus as a potential husband for another friend's niece. He praises the young man by saying that "his homeland is Brescia, from our Italy [*ex illa nostra Italia*], which still preserves and protects much of the old modesty [*verecundia*], frugality [*frugalitas*], and old-fashioned rusticity [*rusticitas antiqua*]."[69] These last three qualities formed a set of ideals that defined Italianness in a way that could be used to counterbalance notions that these Italian *municipia* were peripheral or boorish.

Why would the people of northern Italy wish to express their Italian identity in such a fashion? In part this ideology reflected a century of imperial messages defining Italy in these terms. Augustus had used the image of the virtuous and uncorrupted Italian in his speeches and in the imagery he cultivated around himself.[70] This imagery suited not just Augustus, whose political rivals criticized his municipal Italian origin, but also the many local Italian elites whom he brought into government. Some of Claudius's legislation, too, shows a concern for Italy: one of Claudius's edicts forbade anyone from passing through the towns of Italy unless by foot or in a chair or litter (presumably to avoid noise), while another prohibited the destruction of buildings in Italy unless they were to be immediately replaced.[71] These edicts were designed to maintain the physical and auditory appearance of Italy's—and not the provinces'—towns and, as the latter edict says, to safeguard the future of all of Italy (*totius Italiae aeternitas*).[72] Trajan's edict that candidates for office at Rome hold at least one third of their land in Italy seems to have been designed for similar effect, as do imperially instigated alimentary schemes.[73] Even if actual imperial intervention in Italy was quite minor during the first and second centuries, nevertheless emperors continued to stress, through speeches and edicts, their concern for Italy's future. This emphasis was not consistent from reign to reign, and certain emperors such as Claudius made it a theme of their reigns, while others, like his successor Nero, emphasized their concern for other parts of the empire.[74] Concern for Italy was one of a menu of important imperial virtues that emperors could and repeatedly did choose from in the first and second centuries CE.[75]

This stress was particularly pronounced in Vespasian's reign, since the emperor had not only to repair the damage done to his reputation by a civil war conducted on Italian soil but also to counteract being from "an unknown family without any ancestral family portraits."[76] At the same time Vespasian was criticized for his rustic pronunciation, and quite tellingly, stories were circulated that his paternal grandfather was a contractor for day laborers and came from the *regio Transpadana*.[77] While this ideology of Italian simplicity and morality had been closely linked with the imperial house, it was still possible to be seen as too rustic or even quasi-Italian, as the attribution of Vespasian's grandfather to the Transpadana seems to indicate. Northern Italy was part of a cultural world where a morally defined Italian identity was seen as valuable but also where northern Italians' status as real Italians was still a matter of question, even as late as the Flavian period at the end of the first century CE.[78] This place in cultural limbo incited northern Italians to associate themselves rather aggressively with the cultural Italian identity built up both by imperial propaganda and by other Italian elites.

Cities under the Emperor

This configuration of group identity in which northern Italians defined themselves was the byproduct of a struggle to achieve unity with a larger peninsular identity; it mirrors the Late Republic when the Transpadane identity was created, strengthened, and finally destroyed by a larger conflict over how Roman and Italian identities were defined. The crucial difference between the Republican and Imperial periods in this matter is the influence of the emperor in defining Italian identity, both through action, as in legislation designed to protect or to spread Italian privileges, and through the language of documents and speeches.[79] The imperial period also broadened the field in which these games of identity were being played out, as service in the army brought people from towns in northern Italy to provincial borders for long periods of time, long enough to set up dedications and even tombstones. The imperial period both centralized and expanded the ways in which Italian identity was defined, as connections to the emperor became a new way for Italians to define themselves, both individually and collectively.

Association with the emperor became a way by which people and entire towns could attempt to elevate their status. For towns in northern Italy in particular, association with imperial prestige was a way to regain status lost by the leveling that had occurred at the end of the Republic. While the former Cisalpine Gaul had acquired Roman citizenship and incorporation into a privileged Italian heartland, its towns at the beginning of the empire now had little to distinguish them from regional rivals. Petronius Urbicus's hometown of Brixia, for example, had gone from being the chief town of the Cenomani to being one Italian *municipium* among many in northern Italy. While the attribution of smaller communities into the territory of Brixia would ensure that the town would be populous and wealthy—indeed, it had the largest territory of all Italian towns—some greater distinction was desirable.[80]

Competition between towns in the Roman world could be fierce, and during civil war long-standing rivalries might erupt into violence, as happened at Vienne and Lyons in Gaul during the civil war of 69 CE, while during that war in Italy the people of Placentia blamed the destruction by fire of their great amphitheater on the jealousy of their neighbors.[81] The rivalry between towns around the bay of Naples produced scurrilous graffiti in some cases, and street violence in others.[82] These town rivalries could exist alongside strong social bonds, and anti-Nucerian grafitti at Pompeii exist alongside advertisements for gladiatorial fights and elections at Nuceria; the two towns were part of the same circle of regional markets.[83] Citizens from rival towns who traded insults in the theater were sharing the same social space, and towns that erected honorific statues to one another might later complain of the other's insults in petitions to the emperor.[84]

Even closely linked towns like Brixia and Verona, which shared elite families and long-standing social and cultural bonds, also shared a competitive drive to outrank each other, even if it did not, as it did at Pompeii and Lyons, erupt in violence. In such a competitive spirit did one *quattuorvir* from Verona set up a monument at Brixia: although the spot for the monument had been decreed by the Brixian *decurions* (two councilors), the *cursus honorum* on the inscription reads, "*IIIIvir(o) Veron(ae) q(uaestori) Veron(ae) et Brix(iae)*."[85] Even in Brixia, Verona came first. Similarly, Brixians holding office in Verona and Brixia all listed Brixia before Verona.[86] Such epigraphic games are not as clearly antagonistic as the rumors surrounding the burning of Placentia's amphitheater or the graffiti around the bay of Naples, but they do point to an ongoing concern with municipal rank. Imperial recognition would be one clear, external means of obtaining that rank, especially in a region where there was no provincial capital or base of imperial power.

One way of obtaining that recognition was through acquiring colonial status. Rivals and neighbors Brixia and Verona both became honorary *coloniae*, Brixia at least by the reign of Tiberius, Verona probably under Augustus and certainly by the early third century.[87] The inhabitants of Verona thought its colonial status important enough to advertise on the Porta Borsari, its most elaborate and important city gate, where the first words of the main inscription were "*colonia Augusta Verona*" (fig. 6.)[88] Here Verona's civic identity was defined by this imperially bestowed status as a colony.[89] In the absence of direct imperial benefactions, which were exceptionally rare in first- and second-century Italy, status as an imperial *colonia* was a key way of advertising imperial favor, which functioned as the most prestigious external confirmation of a town's—and by extension, the citizens'—worth. For those towns that were not large enough to attract imperial attention, like Bedriacum, just east of Cremona in the central Po Plain, lesser patrons would have to do, and a fragmentary tablet commemorating an unnamed patron of Bedriacum indicates that the competition for elite if not quite imperial patronage was still waged in smaller communities.[90]

The ongoing competition between towns extended to their physical appearance. Embellishments such as amphitheaters and city gates added to a town's prestige in relation to its neighbors, and these structures were such a source of local pride that they became part of the town's identity; in Verona, the theater was built with hillside porticoes that gave spectators a panoramic view of the walled town.[91] This competitive embellishment was not new, and in northern Italy this fad for urban public works dates back to at least the first century BCE.[92] What was new was the tendency toward associating these structures with an imperial name.[93] The entablature of the 73 CE *capitolium* at Brixia presented a rare opportunity to publicize imperial benefaction, and Vespasian's prominent title and name suited not only the emperor but also the town as a whole, which

Figure 6. Porta Borsari, Verona. Photograph by author.

could point now to imperial favor (fig. 7).[94] Likewise, statues of the imperial family set up in municipal fora, such as the Claudian family group set up in Verona, established a visual connection between the heart of a town and the imperial family, even when actual connections were few.[95] These processes were of course not peculiar to Verona or northern Italy during the empire, and the setting up of imperial statues in fora and agoras across the empire was standard practice.[96] These processes do however show how standardization in urban identity—wherein towns competed to outdo one another in ways that were relatively uniform across the empire—existed alongside attempts at regional differentiation, such as the Patavian emphasis on *severitas*.

Within a town, competition for social prestige might be just as fierce as it was between towns. Italian towns as a whole could not claim much prestige as centers of the imperial cult, since they could not, as provincial cities were able to, claim to represent an entire region in worship of the emperor.[97] Yet for individuals within towns, service to the imperial cult was a means of obtaining prestige, both through the municipal priesthood and through the sevirate.[98] At Verona, a *flamen*

Figure 7. Roman Capitolium, Brescia. Photograph by author.

(priest) of Rome and Augustus is described on an honorific base solely by his name, tribe, and his position as *flamen*; as such, his service as priest for the imperial cult has become a major part of his public identity. Augustales nearly always list that office first in their dedications and epitaphs, and the office was one of the primary ways in which elites solidified their social connections with other cities. Hence L. Cornelius Prosodicus was sevir augustalis at both Brixia and Verona.[99] Status as an augustalis was often immediately followed by the name of the town where that office was held, which strengthened the association between citizen, town, and the imperial cult. The augustales played an important role in Italian towns, and the patron of Caere in southern Etruria sanctioned the construction of a new meeting place for the town's *Augustales* in order to increase the *dignitas municipii*.[100] The augustales increased their own status and through their actions that of their towns as well, even if not to the degree possible in the provinces. That a higher proportion of augustales were *ingenui*, or freeborn citizens, in northern Italy as compared to peninsular Italy suggests that the same uncertainty about status that prompted northern Italians to emphasize their Italian legal status abroad and to advertise an idealized Italian morality also pushed the freeborn inhabitants of Verona, Brixia, and other northern Italian towns to join organizations that, south of the Apennines, might be considered too closely associated with freedmen.[101]

Yet while emperors, living or dead, lent additional prestige to towns and their citizens, in nearly all of these cases the actual effort extended by an emperor or his administration was minimal or even nonexistent. Action was instead made on the local level by individuals or towns, and the emperor's influence was largely indirect, as in Vespasian's cultivation of an image of Italian municipal virtues. Yet that influence would have been unmistakable to anyone visiting Brixia, Verona, or even Bedriacum. The emperor's family was visibly present in the statuary of a forum, while imperial names occurred on milestones leading to the town, as well as on the main gates of the town. Even the town's inhabitants defined themselves in relation to the emperor, through an elite *cursus honorum* listing imperial service or association with the imperial cult.

Northern Italy without Northern Italians

There were no northern Italians in Roman northern Italy because there was no need for the inhabitants to identify themselves as such. Why claim to be northern Italian when there were no benefits to being such a varietal of Italian? In this matter the inhabitants of Mediolanum, Aquileia, Bononia, and the other villages, towns, and cities of northern Italy were not alone. As there were no northern Italians, there were no central Italians or southern Italians; rather, there were Italians and provincials, citizens and noncitizens. The partial consolidation of these two divisions during the Social War and its aftermath had created the transient category of the Transpadani, who came and went within a century but whose imprint is still found in the era's literature. With the transition to the Principate, Italian identity took on new forms, and collective and individual identity became increasingly defined within an interconnected web of honors, offices, towns, and emperors. Mutual manipulation by ambitious elites in northern Italy and at Rome created the ideology and terminology, while old and new forms of expression provided the means of expressing this identity. The Roman conquest created the concept of northern Italy, and Roman governance removed it.

Northern Italy's incorporation into the Roman Empire changed and was to continue to change how people and towns in the region interacted with one another and with other regions, but in creating new identities it also altered how people conceived of those networks of interaction.

PART II / Northern Italy in the Roman World

Chapter Four

Governing Northern Italy

It is arguable that Rome's impact on northern Italy was greatest in the southeastern corner, along the segment of the Via Aemilia stretching from Ariminum on the Adriatic to Placentia in the center of the Po Plain. The intervention of the Roman state in this region—in building new canals, moving populations, or reorganizing land use—was frequent and invasive. As the most closely managed Republican-era region of Italy, with the possible exception of Campania, the Aemilia thus serves as an ideal place to examine the nature of the more hands-off administration of the Imperial period, since the contrast in the administration of Italy between the Republic and the Empire is at its starkest here.[1]

Imperial Magistrates

During the early imperial period, imperial magistrates allocated to northern Italy were few, and the types of magistrates assigned to the region suggests that the two major concerns for the imperial state were the maintenance of the most important roads and the collection of the relatively few taxes to which Italy was liable. To maintain the major roads, senatorial *curatores viarum* (superintendents of the roads) were appointed. This position, in charge of the construction and maintenance of major roads, had been an important political stepping-stone for ambitious Late Republican politicians such as Caesar and in the imperial period continued to be an important senatorial level position at Rome.[2] Throughout the imperial period few changes were made to the *curatores viarum*. Numbers fluctuated slightly in correspondence with the number of imperially sponsored building or restoration projects—there seems to have been a peak under Trajan—but the basic organizational structure remained the same, and actual work on roads seems still to have been overseen by contractors, or *mancipes*.[3] The responsibilities of the imperial *curatores viarum* did not extend much beyond the major roads, and in Aemilia the construction and upkeep of roads other than the Aemilia, and possibly the Annia and Popilia, were the responsibility of either municipal governments or local landowners.[4] Landowners along the Aemilia itself were thus liable for taxes when maintenance needed to be done, but beyond that the upkeep of roads was left to the region's *municipia* and to individual landowners.

Residents along the Aemilia were liable to other taxes that fell within a defined Italian tax bracket. The Republican-era *vicesima libertatis*, a 5% tax on slaves at the time of their manumission, still applied.[5] To fund the compensation and settlement of veterans from the civil wars, Augustus had enacted a 5% inheritance tax—the *vicesima hereditatium*—for Roman citizens, but with exemptions for beneficiaries who were closely related to the deceased and for testators who were poor.[6] In addition to the *vicesima hereditatium*, Augustus instituted two sales taxes, the *vicesima quinta venalium mancipiorum*, a 4% tax on the sale of slaves, and the *centesima rerum venalium*, a 1.5% tax on auctionable goods.[7] The people of Rome saw the latter as burdensome enough to ask Tiberius for the tax's remission, to which Tiberius replied that the tax's revenues were vital for the payment of the army.[8] This suggests that the revenues from the tax were fairly substantial and that the tax impacted a large section of society.[9] Nevertheless, as an imperial benefaction Tiberius's successor, Gaius, remitted the tax.[10] Until the reign of Nerva, Italians were also liable for the *vehiculatio*, the compulsion to provide vehicles of transport for state officials; Nerva remitted the *vehiculatio* for Italy but not for the provinces.[11] Additionally, goods passing through provincial borders were subject to customs duties, the *portoria*.[12] Italians were exempt, however, from the *tributum capitis* and *tributum solis* and were sometimes given further honorary tax exemptions by the emperors.[13] The tax rate for residents along the Via Aemilia and for the rest of Italy in the first century CE will have been roughly equivalent to the rate during the Republican era, as new taxes established in the Early Empire either allowed for substantial loopholes (the *vicesima hereditatium*) or were eventually remitted (*centesima rerum venalium*), while others were carryovers from the republican period (*vicesima libertatis*).

For most of the first century, few changes in the basic structure of Italian administration set up by Augustus are discernable. Those few changes that are attested—the remittances of the *vehiculatio* by Nerva and the *centesima rerum venalium* by Gaius—are in keeping with a general trend in the Early Empire of granting financial and honorific privileges to Italy.[14] It should be remembered, too, that self-government and low taxes were explicitly tied together as Italian privileges. For example, cities in the provinces possessing the prestigious *ius Italicum* shared Italy's lenient tax status and were also removed from the jurisdiction of provincial governors.[15]

Antonine Administration

With the second century, however, new administrative posts do appear in Italy. But do these new posts signal a change in what had been a fairly hands-off imperial policy? Among these new magistrates were the *curatores rei publicae*, officials selected by the emperor to oversee a *municipium*'s finances or local building projects.[16] These *curatores rei publicae*, appearing first under Nerva, appear throughout the empire, in both Italy and the provinces, although they appear more frequently in Italy.[17] Typical of the men who held the office was Clodius Sura, a Brixian of equestrian status, who went through the posts of military tribune and, in his hometown, *quaestor*, *pontifex*, and *duumvir quinquennalis*.[18] Under Trajan he was *curator rei publicae* at nearby Bergomum, and under Hadrian he became *curator rei publicae* at Comum. Sura's career as *curator* was exceptionally localized, and this regionalization is typical of the office in the second century.[19] Both in Italy and in the provinces these second-century *curatores* were generally local men, drawn from the same area in which they served as *curator*.[20] The *curatores rei publicae* were not appointed for every town, and more specialized *curatores* could be assigned as well, such as the *curator operum publicum* and *curator operis thermarum* appointed by Hadrian for the southern Italian towns of Venusia and Beneventum, respectively.[21] Just within *regio* VIII, *curatores* were appointed for individual towns—in the second century they are attested for Ariminum, Otesia, and Faventia—as well as for the region as a whole.[22] The flexibility of the office can be seen in the career of C. Arrius Antononius, a senator who held the offices of *curator Ariminiensium* and *curator civitatum per Aemiliam*.[23] Arrius's appointment as *curator civitatum per Aemiliam* was almost certainly connected with the incursion of the Marcomanni toward the northeastern borders of Italy and preparations made by the emperor Marcus Aurelius for the defense of Italy.[24] The *curatores* seem to have been assigned on a case-by-case basis, with local elites granted imperial approval and recognition for local building projects or reordering municipal finances. This gave the emperors the flexibility to deal with municipal problems and city petitions as they arose by delegating to local elites.

The appointment of the *curatores*, moreover, may have had as much to do with the rank and honor of individual senators—as well as the emperor's public image in maintaining the standing of the senate—as with actual problems, such as financial difficulties at Bergomum or the lack of a good public bathhouse at Beneventum. The *Historia Augusta* claims that "he [the emperor Marcus Aurelius] appointed *curatores* to many cities, so as to extend senatorial *dignitas*.[25] The appointment of locally connected *curatores* also suggests that the position was designed to enhance the prestige of local elites within their own regions. Within a senatorial or equestrian career that crossed the empire, the position of *curator* was unusual in that the location of service corresponded so closely to preexisting local connections.[26] That *curatores* generally did not serve in their home communities but rather in towns close to those communities also suggests that the position helped build or strengthen regional social bonds. Hence C. Cornelius Minicianus, the *curator rei publicae* of Otesia in Aemilia under Trajan or Hadrian, in addition to his service as military tribune with the *legio III Augusta* in Africa, also served locally as a *quottuorvir*, *flamen divi Claudii*, *flamen divi Traiani*, and patron of Bergomum and was honored as such by the people of nearby Mediolanum.[27] Those local offices, which exist alongside a traditionally wide-ranging—geographically speaking—equestrian career, signal regional social bonds that Minicianus certainly had. Micinianus's connections in the area around Bergomum and Mediolanum encompassed Comum's Pliny the Younger as well, who wrote for him a letter of recommendation praising him as "by rank and manners the jewel of my region."[28]

To these municipally based *curatores*, Hadrian added *quattuor consulares*, who had jurisdiction over four regions of Italy.[29] During the reign of Antoninus Pius these men were replaced by the *iuridici*, who also had jurisdiction over regions of Italy and who rendered judgment in cases brought to their attention.[30] Their authority was somewhat fluid, and in a pinch they could be appealed to as a generic imperial magistrate and representative of the emperor. One 177 CE senatorial edict on gladiatorial prices says that the edict is to be enforced in the provinces by governors and in Italy by the prefect of the *alimenta* (the program for feeding poor children in Italy) or, if he is unavailable, by a *curator viarum*, *iuridicus*, or prefect of the fleet.[31] Their regional jurisdictions fluctuated over time, and so one *iuridicus*'s district was Etruria and Aemilia, while another was described as the *iuridicus* for Aemilia and Liguria, while yet another claimed jurisdiction over

Aemilia, Etruria, and Tuscia.[32] Like the *curatores*, the *iuridici* acted as representatives of imperial authority and, like the *curatores*, they seem to have had some previous connections to the regions where they held authority. Serving as one of Hadrian's *quattuor consulares*, Antoninus had, according to the *Historia Augusta*, "been chosen to administer the part of Italy in which he had the most properties, as Hadrian took consideration both of the man's honor and his quiet life."[33] Likewise, C. Arrius Antoninus, the senator who served as curator both for the towns of Aemilia as a whole and for Ariminum in particular, although originally from north Africa, had also served as a *iuridicus regionis Transpadanae*.[34] Nevertheless, the post of *iuridicus* was not tied to the holder's place of origin, as was generally the case with the *curatores*. Hence, one late second-century *iuridicus* of Aemilia and Liguria seems to have come from north Africa, were he was *curator rei publicae* at Cirta.[35] The second-century *iuridici* of Italy thus fit more easily with the typical and geographically scattershot posts of senatorial careers than with the locally tied *curatores*, although some effort seems to have been made by emperors to assign *iuridici* to places where they had connections, either through previous offices held in the area or through landholdings.

The most conspicuous innovation of the second century was the introduction of alimentary projects in Italy. In these schemes, Italian landowners borrowed sums of money from the imperial *fiscus* (treasury); the landowners then paid the interest on these loans to the local children on the alimentary lists.[36] These *alimenta* are first attested under Nerva, and over the next century various alimentary schemes can be found in more than fifty Italian municipalities.[37] The attested schemes are concentrated in central and southern Italy, although it has been rightly noted that such a concentration reflects the epigraphic density of the Italian regions more than it does any preference of the emperors for setting up schemes south of the Apennines.[38] That imperial alimentary schemes—as opposed to private schemes—are attested primarily in Italy suggests that the *alimenta* were yet another means of privileging the Italian peninsula over the provinces.[39] Outside of Italy, alimentary schemes were privately run, although these privately run alimentary schemes are also attested in Italy. Pliny the Younger established one at his native Comum.[40] Like the appointment of the *curatores*, the alimentary schemes seem to have been implemented on a case-by-case basis, with some towns receiving imperially sponsored schemes and others establishing their own schemes, and both the dates of their implementation and organization vary considerably.

The question remains: Did these new posts and innovations mark a significant shift in the previously minimalist policy of state intervention practiced in the first century CE? To be certain, there were more imperial magistrates assigned to regions and town in Italy at the end of the second century CE then there were during the Augustan period. Were these new positions a response to a chronic undermanagement of Italy? There was at least one roughly contemporary suggestion that Italy needed more government. Cassius Dio, in an account of the Augustan period, has Maecenas advice Augustus to divide Italy into administrative districts similar to the provinces, since Italy was so heavily populated and since it could not be governed efficiently by the magistrates at Rome.[41] While Dio's account describes the Augustan period and not the second century, at the beginning of the third century Dio was clearly aware of the argument that Italy had an insufficient administrative apparatus. Yet such an argument does not appear in second-century explanations for the introduction of this new administration. Rather, the *alimenta* are made to aid Italian children, and the *iuridici* introduced to enhance senatorial dignity.[42] It is possible that these official rationales cloaked more pedestrian administrative concerns, but that these developments are presented as imperial beneficence and not as attempts to fix a broken system suggests that the perception of Italy as undergoverned was not widespread. Had that been the case one would expect imperial messages at least to attempt to counteract that perception.

Were these new magistrates instead an attempt to provincialize Italy, to update Italy's status in keeping with a world in which the provinces had usurped much of Italy's political and economic dominance? The *iuridici* had existed on the provincial level previously, and it is possible that their introduction into Italy, where they took on some of the legal responsibilities of their provincial counterparts, suggests an effort to provide Italy with more imperial governance. Yet the overwhelming concentration of the state-sponsored alimentary projects in Italy suggests that Italy continued to be treated as an exceptional, privileged entity within the empire; indeed, the sole certain provincial outlier in distribution of state alimentary schemes, Hadrian's favored Antinoöpolis in Egypt, confirms the notion that the alimentary projects were strongly linked to imperial favor.[43] Likewise, the creation of *curatores* seems more in line with continuing official privileges for Italy. The position of *curator* allowed emperors to honor Italian elites and give Italian localities the honor of imperial attention; the phrase *dato ab imperatore* used in inscriptions underlines this connection between the appointment of *curatores* and imperial care.[44] So the imposition of municipal *curatores* should not be seen as an erosion of Italy's privileged status but rather as a confirmation of that status. More importantly, Italy's tax burden remained roughly the same through the first two centuries CE; a few taxes dating to the Augustan period had even been removed. Should the Antonines have wished to bring Italy's administration more into line with the provinces, a gradual attenuation of Italy's tax exemptions would have proved tempting. Rather, Italy was able to maintain its privileged position within the empire despite any political or economic decline vis-à-vis the provinces.

These second century changes in imperial administration in Italy therefore do not signal a substantial change in imperial policy, which continued to emphasize traditional Italian privileges, respect for the senate, and imperial euergetism.[45] On the ground along the Aemilia, this stability in policy led to relative continuity in the relationship between state and citizen for most of the first and second centuries CE.

Ariminum and Bononia

In the region's largest cities, Ariminum (Rimini) and Bononia, this meant little change in the actual structures of government both over time and between towns.[46] At both Ariminum and Bononia, municipal magistrates consisted of *aediles*, *quaestores*, *decuriones*, and *duoviri*; together these offices created a basic political homogeneity found throughout Italy that allowed and encouraged office-holding in neighboring cities by local elites.[47] Similar municipal structures also meant that certain epigraphic abbreviations could be used and understood across the region; the use of abbreviations like *L(ocus) D(atum) D(ecreto) D(ecurionum)* could become standard only through the existence of standardized municipal magistracies over a broad area and for a long period of time.[48] This is not to say that there were no differences in municipal government; Ariminum, for example, was divided into seven urban *vici* with Roman topographical names, like *vicus Aventinus*, while there is no evidence for a similar division at Bononia.[49] Nevertheless, the basic and most important magistracies, as well as their correlation to the major magistracies at Rome, remained the same. One *curator rei publicae* is attested for Ariminum and none for Bononia, although as noted above the same *curator rei publicae* at Ariminum also served as *curator* for all the towns of Aemilia.[50] The *curatores viae Aemiliae* and their contractors would have responsibility for Bononia's main road, while within Ariminum's territory the *curatores viae Flaminiae* should be added; with both cities the empire's major concern was the maintenance of the important trunk roads. Taxes, and the relevant tax officials, were the same for both cities.

Nor do there seem to be any major discrepancies in their treatment by the emperor. Both towns received some imperial euergetism. In 53 CE, after a severe fire, a speech made on Bononia's behalf by a young Nero netted the city a grant of 10 million *sesterces*, while Ariminum benefited from road work done on the Via Aemilia and the Via Flaminia, which terminated at the city, by Augustus and by Gaius Caesar.[51] Smaller benefactions were also made on behalf of Ariminum by Domitian and Marcus Aurelius.[52] Imperial benefactions seem to have been infrequent, but they had the potential, as in the case of Bononia, to be a substantial safety net; this latter kind of disaster relief was also given to Cremona after its sacking in 69 CE and the cities around the Bay of Naples after the eruption of Vesuvius.[53] Thus while imperial benefactions were not frequent enough to make a substantial impact on daily life, they would be on hand in case of calamity.

More frequent than these forms of disaster relief were the edicts and decrees issued by the senate and emperor at Rome; how much would these decisions affect the local government and populace at Ariminum and Bononia? Claudius, for example, issued one edict banning anyone from traveling through the streets of Italian towns if not on foot, in a sedan, or in a litter.[54] For towns like Ariminum and Bononia, both large towns with major roads running through their city centers, the potential impact of this edict, if enforced, would have been great. Other edicts that applied equally to Italy and the provinces had similar potential. For example, the edict preserved on the Tabula Siarensis, a copy of a senatorial decree granting honors to the dead Germanicus, decrees that a day of mourning be observed throughout the empire's *municipia*, on which no weddings, shows, sales, or banquets be held.[55] Together with civic and military calendars from Praeneste near Rome and Dura-Europos in Mesopotamia, the honors for Germanicus show how much local calendars reacted to honors decreed for the imperial family at Rome.[56] Honors decreed at Rome needed to be enacted by local magistrates, and public holidays or days of mourning impacted daily life for people using the market, marrying, conducting business, or producing or enjoying entertainments—this would be nearly everyone in a *municipium* like Bononia or Ariminum and in their territories. Edicts issued from Rome sometimes came with the proviso that they be inscribed and displayed in visible places in towns in both Italy and the provinces, sometimes for a specified amount of time; this meant that the forums, town gates, and other public, frequently trafficked, highly visible places of Bononia and Ariminum were filled with visual reminders of the decisions of the imperial government, even if personal representatives of that government were few.[57]

In a different fashion *damnationes memoriae* also presented visual representations of the decisions of the central government; at Ariminum, Domitian's name was erased from one building inscription in a negative reminder of state power that outlasted the removal of the late emperor's statues from the Ariminum's public areas.[58] Actions such as *damnatio memoriae* were of course not specially mandated to Bononia or Ariminum but were instead meant to apply more broadly to the empire or occasionally just to Italy, but this broadly aimed legislation had the potential of affecting the otherwise undermanaged Bononia and Ariminum both frequently and substantially.

In theory the actions of the emperor and senate at Rome, even without a large support structure of imperial magistrates on the ground in municipalities like Bononia and Ariminum, could easily and often affect local governments and citizens. Yet how could these decisions be enforced? How well did the potential impact of imperial legislation correspond to actual impact? Petitioning imperial magistrates will have been one method; it was through complaint to various imperial officials that an imperial freedman having difficulty with the magistrates of Saepinum obtained redress.[59] Accused of abusing the lessees of imperial flocks, the magistrates of Saepinum were sent a strongly worded letter by a prefect in Rome, who had been petitioned by imperial freedmen. The letter threatened investigation and then possible punishment if the magistrates did not desist from abusing the lessees.

The letter sent to the magistrates of Saepinum seems to have been sufficient, but what if threatening letters were not enough? Prosecution initiated by private individuals might then be in order. In 21 CE Cn. Domitius Corbulo complained that the *mancipes* of the *curatores viarum* were swindling the state and that some of Italy's roads had been so neglected that they were now impassable; during the next eighteen years Corbulo initiated prosecutions against both the *curatores viarum* and the *mancipes*.[60] The potential for prosecution by local rivals may have encouraged a town's magistrates to enforce centrally issued regulations more rigorously. Although the number of imperial officials effectively prevented their active prosecution of decrees and edicts, these same decrees and edicts may have been self-policing, and at Ariminum and Bononia local magistrates could chose not to enforce imperial edicts only at risk of prosecution by others in their communities or at Rome. As such a magistrate at Ariminum under Claudius might be more responsive to complaints to people riding through the streets of Ariminum in wagons.

So at Ariminum and Bononia under the Early and High Empire we find a combination of consistently low number of imperial magistrates, a slate of imperial edicts enforced by complaints and prosecutions initiated not by officials but by private individuals, infrequent but potentially city-saving imperial benefactions, and a relative uniformity of political structures between towns. Yet Ariminum and Bononia were large towns, and their experience with the state might be claimed as exceptional, so an examination of smaller towns is thus in order.

Faventia and Caesena

For Faventia (Faenza) and Caesena (Cesena), two moderately sized towns on the Via Aemilia about halfway between Ariminum and Bononia, the relationship between town and government in Rome was remarkably similar.[61] Like their neighbors at Bononia and Ariminum, both towns saw the same lack of imperial oversight and administration. Caesena had a curator later in the third century, and both were presumably overseen briefly by C. Arrius Antononius, the *curator civitatum per Aemiliam* under Marcus Aurelius.[62] At the same time Antononius was overseeing the towns along the Aemilia, the Marcomanni were approaching the borders of northeastern Italy, both emperors were stationing themselves at Aquileia, and the future emperor Pertinax was made procurator of the alimenta in the Aemilia.[63] The year 168 CE was anomalous, and Caesena and Faventia—along with their neighbors at Ariminum and Bononia—were in less exciting years left with strikingly little imperial administration. The *curatores* of the Via Aemilia minded the main road, and the procurators for the handful of taxes saw that their contractors brought in money from the sale of slaves and from inheritances. Both towns were also subject to the same tax rates as Bononia and Ariminum.

One difference in these smaller towns is that imperial benefactions seem to have been rarer in Caesena and Faventia than in their larger counterparts at Ariminum and Bononia. Towns like Faventia, especially those which—unlike a handful of other smallish towns, like Ilium—had no major claims of historical merit, were not large or important enough to attract a great imperial benefaction. In the case of a major disaster, these towns might, like those around the Bay of Naples after Vesuvius, have received some aid. Faventia also benefited from the general upkeep done by the central government on the Via Aemilia, which in the imperial period, as in the Republican, was the town's main artery. Caesena received some imperial benefaction—the restoration of one structure by Hadrian is attested—although almost certainly not as much as its larger neighbors.[64] That a town like Caesena received any benefactions at all is perhaps a sign of well-placed connections. The similarly sized town of Vicetia in Venetia had representatives or patrons in Rome able to oppose a local landowner's request for a market, so it is not unreasonable to suppose the closer Caesena had similar connections at Rome.[65] In this manner even a smaller town like Caesena still had some access to the infrequent imperial largesse bestowed on Italian towns, and in terms of their administration and overall treatment by the emperor and the imperial government, these moderately sized *municipia* had essentially the same relationship with the state as did Bononia and Ariminum. Here what mattered in their treatment by the state was their status as Italian towns; from this fact they received preferential treatment—in comparison with provincial communities—by the emperor, and this preferential treatment was shared fairly equally among Italian *municipia*.

Flaventia and Caesena also demonstrate well how much impact the state could have on the individual inhabitants of towns in which its representatives were largely absent. At Caesena the tomb of one Iunia Thallia and her husband bears a warning that anyone who should open the tomb should pay into the imperial treasury 60,000 sesterces.[66] Such warnings were typical of the ancient Mediterranean, but the stipulation that the tomb violator pay to the *fiscus* implies that fines could be and were collected and sent; if this were not the case, then the threat would have been empty, and Iunia Thallia would have had better luck with the usual threats of divine retribution.[67] This would mean that anyone wishing to punish the violator of a familial burial plot would have to know who to take their case to—a local magistrate, a patron, or any available imperial magistrate all might be tried—and that person had to have either the authority or connections to a person with sufficient authority to resolve the matter, collect the money, and have the money delivered to the imperial treasury. The efficacy of Iunia Thallia's funerary imprecation thus relied on a system of personal and official connections between local authorities and the *fiscus* at Rome. For Iunia Thallia, the authority and perceived efficacy of the state were tools that could be used to protect the burial space of her *familia*; in this case the relationship between state and subject was at least partially reciprocal, for although Iunia Thallia was subject to imperial legislation like Claudius's edict on wagons and paid inheritance taxes, she could also manipulate the local perception of the state to her own advantage.

For the young men of Faventia, the state also offered opportunities, especially in the form of the military. The army formed the main means of mobility across the empire as a whole, and veterans and soldiers from Faventia can be found buried at Viroconium in Britain, in Mogontiacum in Germany, Carnuntum in Pannonia, at Scardona in Dalmatia, and at Rome, where they served in the prestigious and lucrative Praetorian Guard.[68] In contrast, Faventians abroad not associated with the state are rarer, even allowing for a more pronounced epigraphic habit in the army. Those Faventians not explicitly tied with the army still might have taken advantage of economic opportunities offered by military communities along the borders; this is probably the case with the fifty-year-old Faventian doctor commemorated in Moesia at Troesmis, a legionary base.[69] Service in the legions under the empire was no small commitment; Titus Flaminius, the Faventian buried at Viroconium, served roughly half of his life in the legions. The C. Pomponius Severus, a veteran commemorated at Flaventia, had held a decurionate in Luceria in Apulia and a sevirate at Flaventia.[70] Likewise, taking advantage of economic opportunities, as T. Rascanius Fortunatus the doctor at Troesmis did, also required serious life changes. Fortunatus was commemorated by two heirs, Rascania Phoebe and T. Rascanius Eutychus, which suggests either that his family accompanied him to Moesia or that he started a family there. Migration in the other direction was possible, too; one funerary marker at Caesena commemorates a Syrian veteran of the Ravenna fleet and his Syrian wife; the sole significant concentration of Roman troops in northern Italy, Ravenna was near enough to the southeastern Aemilia that men stationed there could and did develop connections with local towns.[71] Even excluding atypical Ravenna, it is clear that the military, and the opportunities that Roman military communities provided, directly influenced the lives of those along the Via Aemilia; for Caesenan Iunia Thallia and Faventians Pomponius Severus and Rascanius Fortunatus, in particular, an absent Roman state was never entirely so.

This was the case for nearly all of northern Italy, since earlier distinctions between Italy north and south of the Po and between peninsular and continental Italy had disappeared with the Republic. The imperial administration of northern Italy, and indeed most of Italy outside of Rome, was both uniform and minimal. The next three chapters will explore further the effects of that system.

Chapter Five

Novum Comum

Apart from wool, pigs, and wine, northern Italy's most conspicuous product in the Early Empire was Gaius Caecilius Plinius Secundus, Pliny the Younger. Pliny's uncle and adoptive father, Pliny the Elder, was commander of the Roman fleet at Misenum, a friend of the emperor Vespasian, an exceedingly prolific writer, and the most famous victim of the 79 CE eruption of Mount Vesuvius.

The birthplace of both men was an idyllic town at the southwestern end of Lake Como, which the Romans called the *Lacus Larius*. The area had been occupied regularly since the Paleolithic, and in the Bronze Age the lake's shores were ringed with pile-dwelling settlements. Growing rich with transalpine trade in the Iron Age, the *oppidum* (fortified Celtic settlement) at Comum reached its greatest extent in the fifth century BCE, but in the following centuries it fell under the control of the Insubres around Mediolanum and declined in wealth and importance.[1]

In 89 BCE the settlement at Como gained the status of a Latin colony, although it received no new colonists until 59, when Caesar, by virtue of the *lex Vatinia*, established five thousand colonists—including five hundred Greeks—at Comum, which took on the name Novum Comum.[2] The colonists established a new settlement, with an orthogonal street plan, surrounded by walls. By the time of the Pliny the Elder, the town had expanded almost to the lakeshore.[3] Further expansion and development took place during his nephew's lifetime.

This chapter examines how both Pliny the Younger and the town on Comum evolved in the late first to early second centuries CE and, in particular, it examines the role that elite benefactions played in the development of Comum during that period.[4] While these benefactions are attested—largely though inscriptions—across northern Italy, only in Comum do literary, archaeological, and epigraphic evidence combine to provide so thorough a picture of euergetism and urban development.

Adorning Comum

By the time Pliny the Younger entered the Roman senate at the end of the first century CE, Comum had a theater, baths, a nymphaeum, a temple to Rome and Augustus, and probably a basilica as well.[5] Local elites provided most of the money. Calpurnius Fabatus, grandfather of Pliny the Younger's wife and owner of estates throughout Italy, donated a public colonnade and provided for the decoration of the doors.[6] The *gens* of Pliny's father, the Caecilii, are well represented among these donors. L. Caecilius Cilo left 40,000 sesterces to the city to provide oil for the baths and the festival of Neptune, while L. Caecilius Secundus set up the temple to Rome and Augustus in honor of his daughter Caecilia.[7]

The younger Pliny himself provided a library and public baths to the city, as well as money for their furnishing and upkeep.[8] In a letter to fellow townsman Calvisius Rufus, Pliny says that he has given 1,600,000 sesterces to the town and that he intends to donate a further 400,000.[9] The later 400,000 sesterces Pliny's friend Saturninus, probably from Comum as well, had originally bequeathed to the town. That legacy had been disallowed as illegal, and some of the disallowed inheritance went to Saturninus's other heirs, including Pliny, who honored his friend's wishes and donated the same amount of money out of his own increased inheritance.[10] By the end of his life Pliny had given Comum an unspecified amount of money for the construction of the town's baths, 300,000 sesterces for their decoration, the interest on 200,000 sesterces for their upkeep, 1,866,666 sesterces for the maintenance of 100 of Pliny's freedman and for the provision of an annual dinner for the people of Comum, 100,000 sesterces for the upkeep of the library he donated, additional money for the hiring of teachers for Comum, and 500,000 sesterces for an alimentary scheme for Comum's girls and boys.[11] In sum, he donated at least 4,766,666 sesterces—and probably closer to 5 million sesterces when unspecified costs are factored in—of a probable fortune of around 20 million sesterces.[12]

The benefactions recorded in Pliny's *Letters* or in surviving inscriptions most likely do not represent the sum total of monumental construction and elite euergetism in Pliny's time in the later first century and early second century CE. Excavations in the piazza Cacciatori delle Alpi in 2001 and 2002 produced columns and marble bases from an otherwise unattested Trajanic temple, and cornice fragments from the excavations at San Fedele suggest another late first-century monumental structure.[13] The recently excavated bath complex of the Viale Lecco was constructed sometime during the late first or early second century; this does not necessarily indicate that these were the baths built with Pliny's gifts. While there is still much work to be done reconstructing the evolution of Roman Comum's monumental center, the architectural, epigraphic, and literary material points to a significant building boom in the mid first to early second century. Such monumentalization was mirrored in the Comum of the dead, as the city's two main necropoleis were decorated with urns and stelae. In addition, the *suburbium* beyond these necropoleis had itself by the Flavian era grown and become more defined.[14] The town that Pliny was born in was becoming increasingly monumentalized, with much of that monumentalization initiated and financed by his relatives.

Baths

Comum's new public buildings were typical of Early Empire in which the Late Republican emphasis on fortification building gave way to a preference for theaters, baths, and temples.[15] Thus, while euergetism itself was not a new phenomenon in northern Italy, as the campus that Akisios Arkantokomaterekos donated in Vercellae ably demonstrates, its physical manifestation on the urban fabric very much reflected empire-wide trends.[16]

Baths in particular were a benefaction of their time. In Rome under the Republic, when public bathing was too closely tied with *luxuria* and potential immorality, public baths were a rarity, and elite benefactors even rarer.[17] Outside of Rome, in Latium and southern Italy, baths were becoming more common, and by the early first century BCE duovirs at Praeneste and Grumentum were overseeing and funding the construction of public baths.[18] In Rome, only with the Augustan age and Agrippa's patronage of "170 free baths" did bathing gain acceptability.[19] In northern Italy, there are a few potential pre-Roman precedents for areas of ritual bathing, such as at Lagole in the upper Piave Valley in the northern Veneto, but there is little evidence for anything resembling the public baths of the Early Empire.[20]

In this context neither Comum nor Pliny was exceptional, even within northern Italy; 70 km to the southwest at Novaria, C. Valerius Pansa, the former governor of Britain, restored the town baths—destroyed by either fire or violence—on a grander scale, on a larger lot and within two years.[21] Bathhouses were a common form of benefaction across northern Italy during this period, and such private bathhouse euergetism is attested in the first through second centuries at Bergomum, Novaria, Altinum, Mediolanum, Brixia, Placentia, Verona, and Asola, in addition to Pliny's Comum.[22] An unknown donor at Altinum was particularly generous:

d(ecreto) d(ecurionum)
[h]ic rei p(ublicae) Altinatium HS XVI(milia) [n(ummum) ded(it)]
[i]ta ut balinea Sergium et Puti[nium]
HS DCCC(milia) n(ummum) refecta in usu mu[nicip(um?)]
essent et alia HS CCCC(milia) n(ummum) ut ex [eorum]
reditu cale[fier]ent et HS CC(milia) n(ummum) [in perp(etuam)]
tutelam eo[ru]ndem item HS [CC(milia) n(ummum)]
ut ex usuris eorum VII Idus [---]>
natali ipsius et VII Idus eas[dem]
natali Petroniae Magnar ma[tris]
suae XVII Kal(endas) Ian(uarias) natali L(uci) Fabii St[ellat(ina)]
Amminiani patris ui decurio[nes]
[Au]g(ustales) et seviri sportulas acci[perent]

. . . by decree of the decurions. This man gave to the city of Altinum 1,600,000 sesterces, in such a way that the Baths of Sergius and the Baths of Putinius be repaired with 800,000 sesterces for the use of the town; so that from the return on another 400,000 sesterces the baths be heated and that they be maintained in perpetuity with 200,000 sesterces. Likewise, he gave 200,000 sesterces so that from the return on this sum, the decurions, augustales, and sevirs receive cash handouts 7 days before the Ides of . . . his birthday, and on the same day of that month, the birthday of Petronia Magna, his mother, and on the birthday of his father, L. Fabius Amminianus, of the voting tribe Stellatina, 17 days before the kalends of December.[23]

Altinum's donor was keen to ensure that the baths be maintained and, like Pliny, made a donation for their upkeep and fuel. The inscription emphasizes that the benefaction is a permanent one.[24]

Other benefactors subsidized, either through one-time donations or the creation of more permanent funds, like the interest on the 400,000 sesterces that financed bath maintenance at Altinum and provided free admission for bathers. At Bononia, the price was the same:

Divus Aug(ustus) parens
Dedit
[[C(aius) Caesar]] Augustus
Germanicus [[p(ater) p(atriae)]]
refecit
in huius balinei lavation(em) HS CCCC(milia)
nomin(e) C(ai) Aviasi T(iti) f(ilii) Senecae f(ilii) sui T(itus) Aviasius Servandus
pater testament(o) legavit ut ex reditu eius summ(a)
in perpetuum viri et impuberes utriusq(ue) sex{s}us
gratis laventur

> The deified Augustus, father, dedicated (this). Gaius Caesar Augustus Germanicus (Caligula) [father of his country(?)] restored (it). In the name of his son Gaius Aviasius Seneca, the son of Titus, Aviasius Servandus his father bequeathed 400,000 sesterces so that out of the interest on this sum men and young people of either sex might bathe free of charge forever.[25]

Aviasius Secundus's benefaction points to perhaps the key mechanism for the diffusion of this particular form of euergetism: the model of the emperor. In the case of Bononia's baths, there may have been a special political reason for Augustus's benefaction, since in the Late Republic Bononia had been loyal to Marcus Antonius, and Augustus had specially exempted the city from the loyalty oath he administered to the whole of Italy before the Actium campaign.[26] Yet whatever the political motivations of the time, the Augustan baths at Bononia set an imperial precedent in northern Italy, and indeed Aviasius Secundus's gift followed not one but two imperial precedents. Pliny, most likely in Rome supervising the banks of the Tiber when construction began on Trajan's Oppian hill baths, may have followed a similar inspiration.

The *Alimenta*

Pliny's alimentary scheme too was a benefaction of its time. Private *alimenta*, in which funds were set up to maintain a set number of free children in the town, had existed since at least the late Julio-Claudian period but increased dramatically when first Nerva and then Trajan started imperial alimentary schemes in Italian towns.[27]

The details of one of these imperial *alimenta* are preserved in a large bronze inscription from Veleia in the western Aemilia just south of Placentia.[28] Here Trajan and the treasury provided a capital contribution that provided low-interest loans to local landowners; the interest on those loans then supported 263 orphan boys and 35 orphan girls of legitimate birth, along with an orphan boy and girl of spurious birth. The children received distributions in cash according to their status and sex: legitimate boys received 16 sesterces a month, legitimate girls 12, illegitimate boys 12, and illegitimate girls 10. The details of these schemes, particularly private ones, varied over Italy. At Ostia, for example, payments were made only to girls, while at Tarracina payments were made to equal numbers of boys and girls—compared to the 7:1 ratio at Veletia—but on a tiered scale of 5 denarii for males and 4 denarii for females.[29]

Pliny's own scheme differed from that of Trajan's at Veleia. Pliny donated property to the city at a valuation of 500,000 sesterces; Comum then rented it back to Pliny at a rate of 30,000 sesterces a year.[30] After his death the city could continue to rent out the property, and Pliny says that "the property will always find a tenant to cultivate it because its value greatly exceeds the rent charged."[31] Thirty thousand sesterces a year would provide the city with 2,500 sesterces a month for cash subsidies. At 14 sesterces a month per child, the fund would provide for 178 children, on a par with other attested schemes benefitting 100–300 children. These children represented a small proportion of Comum's population of around fifteen to twenty thousand.[32]

The effects of the *alimenta* on Comum must have been fairly limited, at least in terms of the welfare and nutrition of its children.[33] The program was, however, intended by Pliny to be permanent: "It is fitting to put public advantages before private ones and to put permanent (*aeternas*) advantages before transient ones."[34] The alimentary scheme was as much a permanent adornment to Comum as the temples and bathhouses, and such permanence was, like the preference for these buildings, an empire-wide obsession. From the Flavian dynasty to the early Severans, personifications of *Aeternitas* appeared frequently on imperial coinage, where it reinforced the messages of types celebrating *Abundantia*, *Concordia*, *Fortuna*, *Salus*, *Providentia*, and *Concordia*.[35] *Aeternitas* is common in Pliny's own vocabulary of virtues, for "what greater could be given to man than glory and praise and *aeternitas*?"[36] Permanence brought stability and continuity to the empire and safeguarded individual praise and glory.

Praeceptores and a *grammaticus latinus*

This concern for long-term benefits is echoed in Pliny's other main benefaction to Comum's children—the hiring of public teachers, to whose salaries Pliny contributed a third of the funds. In a letter to Tacitus, Pliny describes the rationale for this benefaction:

> I was visiting my native town a short time ago when the young son of a fellow-citizen came to pay his respects to me. "Do you go to school?" I asked. "Yes," he replies. "Where?" "In Mediolanum." "Why not here?" To this the boy's father (who had brought him and was standing by) replied: "Because we have no teachers here." "Why not? Surely it is a matter of great importance to you fathers (and luckily there were several fathers listening) that your children should study here on the spot? Where can they live more happily than in their native place? Where can they be brought up more strictly than under their parent's eye or with less expense than at home? If you put your money together, what would it cost you to engage teachers? And you could add to their salaries what you now spend on lodgings, traveling expenses, and all the things which cost money away from home—and that means everything. Now as I have no children of my own, I am prepared to contribute a third of whatever sum you decide to collect, as a present for our town such as I might give to a daughter or my mother. . . . So you should meet and come to some agreement; be encouraged by my generosity, for I want my own contribution to be as large as possible. You can do nothing better for your children, nothing more welcome for our town. The children born here should be brought up on their native soil, so that from their earliest years they may learn to love it and choose to stay at home. I hope that you will introduce teachers of repute, so that nearby towns will seek education here, and, instead of sending your children elsewhere as you do today, you will see other children flocking here to you."[37]

The letter, which ends with a request that Tacitus look for candidates for the teaching positions from among his own coterie of students, emphasizes how these new teachers will increase both Comum's standing among its neighboring towns and also the patriotism of its citizens.[38] Comum, Pliny, and Tacitus of course all garner honor from the transaction. Pliny's euergetism and scholarly self-portrait are promoted and his preeminence in his hometown confirmed, the reputation of Tacitus as scholar and patron is praised and memorialized, and

Comum receives teachers, a second senatorial patron, and an educational standing no longer secondary to Mediolanum's.

Teachers were no insubstantial ornament; sometime in the first or second century the *grammaticus* P. Atilius Septicianus was commemorated at Comum with the following inscription:

(side a):	
Morborum vitia et vitae mala maxima fugi nunc careo poenis pace fruor placida	The weakness of disease and the worst things in life I fled and now I am free from hardship and enjoy tranquil peace
(side b):	
P(ubli) Atili P(ubli) f(ilii) Ouf(entina) Septiciani grammat(ici) Latini cui ord(o) Comens(ium) ornamenta decur(ionalia) decrevit qui universam substantiam suam ad rem publ(icam) pertinere voluit[39]	Publius Atilius Septicianus, son of Publius, of voting tribe Oufentina, a teacher of Latin literature, to whom the council of the people of Comum decreed decurial honors and who willed his entire fortune to the community

Septicianus was most likely local, since his voting tribe suggests an origin either in Mediolanum or in Comum and since, while the Atilii, members of his adoptive *gens*, are distributed across the empire, attestations of the Septicii are concentrated in *regio* XI.[40] He had enough prestige as a Latin scholar and teacher to be given decurial honors, which was also the case with his fellow *grammaticus latinus* (instructor in Latin literature) at Verona, Q. Tuticanus Eros.[41] That Septicianus bequeathed his property to Comum suggests that he had no heirs, but it also points to Pliny's bequests as being conspicuous but not unique.

The Library

Also designed to enhance both Pliny and Comum's scholarly status was a library, most likely Pliny's first major gift to the city, probably in 97.[42] No certain identification has been made with any remains in Como, but the library forms a key part of the *Letters*.[43] Already in book 1, Pliny discusses the speech he gave to the local decurions about the upcoming dedication of his library, which Pliny delivered in the local curia and not in front of general public, so as not to seem to be courting public favor.[44] In light of his uncle's prolific career as an author, a library was an appropriate gift, perhaps standing as the benefaction his uncle would have given had he not died in the 79 CE Vesuvian eruption. In Pliny's career as a writer and benefactor, it served as the programmatic gift, one that emphasized his own scholarship and promoted himself as a benefactor concerned with gifts that provided a permanent benefit to the community and, in particular, for the future. In his discussion of the library speech, he contrasts his own generosity with those benefactions made from impulse and designed to garner the immediate praise of the people, such as through public games and gladiator shows. Pliny compares his own *beneficia* (benefactions) to diets recommended by doctors to their patients; they are more like "a beneficial service that is not immediately popular."[45]

Pliny certainly had the option of giving gladiatorial games or putting forward money for the construction of an amphitheater or a theater; there is ample evidence for the games' popularity in the amphitheaters that dotted northern Italy in Pliny's time.[46] There were amphitheaters at the far ends of Italy, at Augusta Praetoria in the west and Pola and Aquileia in the east, and closer to Comum was the amphitheater of Verona, where Pliny's correspondent Maximus gave games—minus the African panthers delayed by weather—in honor of his late wife.[47] Construction at the amphitheater at Mediolanum, just 41 km away from Comum, began at the end of the first century CE.[48] Amphitheaters and *ludi* (games) were established *beneficia*, just not *beneficia* suitable to the ideal benefactor envisaged by Pliny in 1.8. Pliny's introduction of the library and *alimenta* donations to his readers and his views on euergetism suggests that bread and books were fine, but bread and circuses were not.

Based on internal evidence, book 1 of the *Letters* dates to 96–98, the same time the amphitheater was being constructed at Mediolanum.[49] Mediolanum and Comum had close economic and social bonds, and the simultaneously friendly and competitive relationship mirrored others throughout Roman northern Italy.[50]

Pliny's slightly disparaging remark about the *ludi* was, if not a direct criticism of Mediolanum's amphitheater, then at least a form of euergetistic competition with the larger city to Comum's south.

The Great Comum Inscription

In addition to Pliny's letters, which provide the fullest evidence for his relationship with Comum, four inscriptions mentioning Pliny also survive from the Transpadana.[51] Three of these—*AE* 1972 372, *CIL* V 5667, *CIL* V 5263—are fairly simple dedications, including one from the people of Vercellae. The fourth is far more informative. The great Comum inscription, which Werner Eck has termed a *Res Gestae Plinii Secundi*, is a now fragmentary marble plaque recording Pliny's offices and benefactions.[52] The inscription was originally placed on a large building or monument in Comum but was transported to Milan by at least 950, when it was used to construct King Lothar II's sarcophagus in the Basilica of Sant'Ambrogio.[53] Drawings of four of six fragments are preserved in fifteenth- and sixteenth-century manuscripts, but between then and the nineteenth century all but one of the fragments were lost.[54] The upper left-hand section, now built into the walls of the basilica's portico, is the sole surviving fragment (fig. 8).

Given the size of the inscription, its most likely original location would have been a large public building in Comum, and for Pliny this would have meant either his library or baths.[55] An otherwise unidentified tomb would also be a possibility.[56] Given Pliny's insistent self-presentation as a man of letters—at seventeen he famously found Livy more compelling than the eruption of Mount Vesuvius and years later was quick to tell Tacitus so—the library is also a persuasive candidate, since such placement would allow Pliny to adorn further this carefully constructed self-representation.[57] Whether fronting a tomb or the library, the inscription should postdate 112 and Pliny's service as *legatus pro praetore* (provincial governor) in Bithynia and Pontus.[58]

The inscription, in its almost standard list of offices and benefactions, is similar to countless other honorific and funerary inscriptions from across the empire and accordingly serves as another testament to the standardization of elite culture in the High Roman Empire. Yet the inscription deviates from the more customary listing of offices in chronological order to showcase the consulship (as *consul suffectus* in 100 CE), placed first after Pliny's nomenclature.[59] The prominence of the consulship in the inscription is paralleled in Pliny's *Panegyricus* to the emperor Trajan, which linked Trajan's consulships with his own.[60] Pliny's emphasis of the consulship allowed him to portray his career as starting under

Figure 8. Fragment of the Great Pliny Inscription, Sant'Ambrogio, Milan. Photograph by author.

Trajan and minimized his success under the now-loathed Domitian. Pliny had undertaken a similar distancing of himself from Domitian in the *Letters*, whose first book commences just after Domitian's assassination in September of 96. His closeness to Trajan, so well promoted in the tenth book of the *Letters*, is similarly promoted in the not strictly necessary inclusion of Trajan's nomenclature, placed immediately following his consulship and governorship.[61] The reader thus encounters Trajan's name, and the two offices that Pliny tried so diligently to associate with Trajan, before encountering those offices held during Domitian's reign.

The benefactions that follow those offices again serve to reinforce the portrait established in the *Letters* and through the constructions and gifts themselves. That these benefactions seem to have started with the library in 97, just months after Domitian's assassination, perhaps explain Pliny's exceptional generosity to his hometown. These gifts, all designed to enhance a scholarly image and also one associated with a lasting and generous new dynasty, its representatives themselves patrons of alimentary schemes, were not entirely the typical offerings of local elites, given to the city in exchange for prestige within a larger economy of honor. They were part of a sustained effort across multiple venues to remake Pliny's image after the emperor whom he had begun and advanced his career under was assassinated. The urban development of Comum in the later first and early second century is thus partly typical of the era, one in which local elites donated bathhouses and provided for their maintenance in keeping with imperial precedents at Rome and with the messages promulgated in imperial edicts and coins. But the Younger Pliny, an innovator in the publication of letters and of political speeches, was also intensely atypical, and the amount of and type of benefactions given to Comum reflect both his unique circumstances and his innovative reaction.[62]

Lacus Larius

Moving beyond Comum's city center, although not away from Pliny, the suburban road leading south to Mediolanum was lined with funerary monuments, decorated with the same images found in Mediolanum's monuments.[63] To the east anther suburban road led to the area around Lecco, on Lake Como's eastern branch, and to Bergomum.

Lecco, occupying a position analogous to Comum, was never monumentalized to the extent that its western neighbor was. To its detriment, it was not made an independent *municipium* in the Republican or Augustan eras, and the territory was divided between the *municipia* of Comum, Mediolanum, and Bergomum.[64] Accordingly, there was no urban center where the modern town of Lecco stands, but rather the territory was composed of villas and small villages. Stone altars there were dedicated to Jupiter, Hercules, Mercury, Minerva, Diana, and Juno, a subset of a pantheon replicated across northern Italy, and locally attested family names, such as the Novelii, the Valerii, and the Vibii, are likewise widely dispersed across the region.[65] Lecco's lack of identity and development point to the importance of early imperial Italy's *municipia*, which grew at the expense of communities in their attributed territory.

Directly fronting Comum on the north was the western branch of Lake Como, a center of economic activity since the time of the Palafitte and continuing as such during the imperial era. Working on the lake, whether in harvesting fish or transporting goods, was a key part of the town's livelihood. At Comum there was a *collegium nautarum Comensium* (guild of sailors of Como), who could count a local sevir and augustalis, Gaius Messius Fortunatus, as a patron.[66] The collegium had another unnamed patron honored at Mediolanum, another sign of the close links between the two towns.[67] Work on the lake had its perils. The skeletal remains from the first- to second-century CE necropolis between via Benzi and viale Varese show signs of repetitive stress and injuries associated with the work of the boatmen.[68]

As was typical of the Early Empire, aristocratic maritime villas lined the lake.[69] Pliny mentions several ("*plures*") villas built by him on lake Como's shore, two of which he says were particularly charming and which he describes in further detail.[70] Pliny called one "Comedy" because it sat right at the edge of a lake like the low slippers of comedic actors; it was located along a gradually curving bay. The other was named "Tragedy" because it sat high on a ridge like the characteristic high boots of tragic actors; it was located on a ridge dividing bays. In the sixteenth century local antiquarians had already suggested Lenno as the site of Comedy and Bellagio as the site of Tragedy, although their exact locations have proved elusive.[71]

Comedy and Tragedy formed a pair, one to be matched with the more extensively described villas at Laurentium and Tusculum. According to Pliny, his Laurentine villa on the coast near Ostia was more suitable for winter and spring and for figs and rosemary; Tusculum, in the Tuscan hills, was more suited for summer, autumn, and wine.[72] The two pairs of villas formed the cardinal points in Pliny's carefully constructed portrait of himself, drawn in the rural landscape of Italy; they displayed his taste in good and ill fortune and in all seasons.

Pliny's villas, including the two on Lake Como, had an afterlife beyond his benefactions and beyond the empire itself, for the villa letters were, by the sixteenth century, influencing architectural design.[73] Paolo Giovio, the bishop of Nocera and the namesake of Como's archaeological museum, had at his Como villa a garden and lakeside study designed to mimic Pliny's villas.[74]

Pliny and Novum Comum

Comum's development in the Early Empire follows a trajectory not easily explained by models of Romanization, creolization, hybridity, or the middle ground.[75] Comum's baths, library, publicly hired teachers, all match Tacitus's famous description of baths and Latin education enslaving the Britons.[76] In the case of Pliny and Comum, these particular forms of development did not enslave the Comenses; they signified not so much *Romanitas* as much as a precise form of *urbanitas*, one dictated both by the broader tastes of the late first century and by the individual, even idiosyncratic, needs of regional elites.

Pliny the Younger was not a typical senator, nor was Comum a typical northern Italian *municipium*. Comum had a contested colonial history, unusual for the Transpadana, while Pliny, in both his success and his self-reinvention after Domitian's demise, should not stand as the standard early imperial senator, if such a creature ever existed. Nevertheless, both Pliny and Comum demonstrate the mechanisms, politicized and cultural, by which changes to the landscapes of northern Italy were made.

Chapter Six

The Tanaro Valley and Italian Networks

Ideology and government held Roman Italy together and gave it, respectively, its conceptual and administrative place within the empire. The next two chapters examine more mundane movements: how people and goods circulated through this system in the Early and High Empires. Circulation within Italy is examined first, while the subsequent chapter traces those networks linking northern Italy with the provinces.

The Valley of Sheep

The wealth that funded the ambitious states of Renaissance northern Italy was partially based on silkworms. While silk in Roman Italy had largely been imported from the island of Cos or from outside the empire (from India and China), beginning in the twelfth century CE and increasingly so in the fifteenth, Italian sericulture became a major business.[1]

In the process of supplying the wealthy of Europe and the Ottoman Empire with silks, velvets, and damasks, Italian silk firms and cities became specialized in both producing and marketing silk. In Milan the ruling clans of the Visconti and Sforza imported silk makers from rival cities, legally enforced the planting of mulberry trees, and patronized the industry to the point that 10%–20% of Milan's population was occupied in sericulture.[2] Genoa and Venice developed distinctive styles and attempted to brand their products with cloth seals, standard widths, and specially dyed selvedges to indicate the silk's place of origin and dye quality; rivals quickly produced counterfeit pieces to pass off Spanish silk as Genoese or Venetian.[3]

Similar specialization could be found in northern Italy during the first and second centuries CE, when towns in the region specialized in textiles. The Po Valley as a whole became famous for its excellent white fleeces, while Liguria clothed households across Italy in tunics and cloaks made from coarse wool.[4] Altinum, Parma, and Mutina vied with Apulia for the reputation of producing Italy's best white wool, while Pollentia produced wools in whites, greys, and most especially blacks.[5] By the end of the third century, Mutina was also producing wools in dark colors as well as wools with a golden sheen, 200 denarii a pound and 300 denarii a pound, respectively, in Diocletian's Edict on Maximum Prices.[6] Pliny the Elder ranked the linen from Retovium on the Via Aemilia the second-best in Europe, while that produced between the Po and Ticinus ranked third (Spanish Saetabis took first place).[7]

The specialization in textiles was not limited to the raw materials; finished clothing items were also produced. Workers in Patavium made clothes, including cloaks and overcoats, for export.[8] Martial could even celebrate Patavium's squared cloaks with an epigram:

> Lodices mittet docti tibi terra Catullu:
> nos Helicaonia de regione sumus.
>
> The land of learned Catullus will send you blankets/rugs
> We are from the area of Helicaon.[9]

Patavian tunics rated yet another of Martial's epigram:

> Vellera consumunt Patavinae multa trilices
> Et pingues tunicas serra secare potest.
>
> Patavian triply-spaced fabrics use many threads
> And a saw is able to cut the thick tunics.[10]

Just as Ligurian production concentrated on coarse wools and Pollentian on dark hues, Patavian workshops seem to have focused production on thick, heavy-weather clothes and so competed with the similarly sturdy cloaks produced by Canusium in Apulia.[11]

Inscriptions show the scale and intensity of the industry, in particular a high concentration of *centonarii* (producers and traders of non-luxury textiles), *vestiarii* (producers and traders of clothing, largely woolen), and the more specialized *sagarii* (producers and traders of cloaks) in northern Italy in comparison with the rest of the Empire.[12] A *collegium centonariorum* was established at Patavium by at least 69 CE; it is the earliest dated guild of *centonarii* outside of Rome. Other *collegia centonariorum* are attested at Alba Pompeia, Altinum, Aquileia, Ariminum, Augusta Taurinorum, Bergomum, Brixellum, Brixia, Cammuni, Clastidium, Comum, Concordia, Feltria, Forum Cornelii, Forum Fulvi, Industria, Mediolanum, Novaria, Parma, Patavium, Placentia, Ravenna, Regium Lepidum, Ticinum, Tridentum, Vardagate, Vicetia, Verona, and possibly Segusio.[13] In short, nearly every area of northern Italy showed signs of a thriving and specialized textile industry by the Julio-Claudian and Flavian eras, if not earlier.

In some respects the Roman-era textile industry represents a continuation of earlier economic patterns, themselves favored by the geography of the region. This seems to be particularly true with linen production. Flax was grown at Po Valley sites throughout the Bronze Age and Iron Age—indeed, the oldest attested flaxseed in Italy was found at the seventh–sixth millennium BCE site at Sammardenchia, near Udine—and plentiful Terramare finds of linen fragments point to a thriving Bronze Age industry.[14] Durable, breathable, and fast drying, linen was used in Iron Age Italy for religious books, sails, tents, food storage, bandages, paintings, wine strainers, curtains, tablecloths, fishing nets, and clothes; it was both practical and culturally important.[15] Linen finds at Palse, Montereale Valcellina, and Casale di Rivalta indicate that in the Po Valley the cultivation of flax and the production of linen continued throughout the Iron Age.[16] Furthermore, flax production requires water and fertile agricultural land, whereas sheep can be pastured on land otherwise unsuitable for farming.[17] Flax was, according to the Roman agricultural writer Columella, one of the most labor-intensive crops, but in northern Italy it could be sown in spring and harvested in summer.[18] With its abundance of alluvial and loamy soils, the Po Valley was naturally suited to flax cultivation.

The land also favored sheep production, since northern Italy's plains and foothills offered terrain, climate, and access to fresh water. This meant that, unlike in the central Apennines, there was no need for transhumance.[19] As with linen, there was a long history of wool production in the region; multiple textile and tool finds from the Early and Middle Bronze Age sites of Molino di Ledro and Fiavé Carera (both in the Trentino), Barche de Solferino (near Mantova), Valle delle Paiole (near Brescia), Castellaro del Vhò (near Cremona), and Castione dei Marchesi (near Parma) show the production and use of wool textiles in the Alto-Adige and central Po Plain.[20] Petroglyphs at Naquane in the Val Camonica portray looms and accompanying weavers and testify to weaving's cultural importance in the Bronze Age.[21] Wool production continued to play a key part in Iron Age economies in the north.[22] During the Early Empire, raising sheep for wool rather than for meat was much more common in southern and northern Italy than in central Italy, whose densely packed population required more meat.[23]

Sheep and flax both thrived on the Po Plain and indeed had done so for the Terramare and the Celts, and export outside of the region was no Roman novelty. The high degree of specialization, however, and possibly the scale of the industry, were unprecedented. The incentives for such specialization—and the concurrent development of textile production and trade—seem to have been as much cultural and historical as geographic. Large markets and an increasingly large elite class engaged in a uniform game of claiming rank through clothes—worn by their slaves as well as themselves—were necessary preconditions, as was the typically imperial habit of "brand-naming" textiles by town of origin.[24]

The Early Empire saw an explosion of new textiles and hues for clothing.[25] Apulian wool had a very good reputation and was exported across the empire and sold for high prices because of that reputation.[26] In an attempt to capitalize on the fame of cloaks from northern Gaul, textile producers in Asia Minor began making their own knock-offs of the Nervian cloaks.[27] Colors were important; the whitest wool took dye the best, while reds, greys, and blacks were valued for their particular hues, and producers went to great lengths to make those colors. Columella's uncle crossbred Spanish and Mauretanian sheep, and then the hybrid offspring of those sheep, with highly valued, imported Apulian sheep to produce a strain of sheep whose wool combined the fineness associated with Apulian sheep and the exotic colors of the Spanish-Mauretanian hybrids.[28] The security provided by the Roman state made long-distance trade in these textiles and sheep feasible.

The development of the textile industry in northern Italy was, moreover, not in response to the demands of the state. People in the region did not have to pay taxes in kind, and as taxes paid in coin were very minor, flock owners did not need to increase their textile production to pay taxes. The involvement of the state was instead indirect, in the maintenance of trade route security, the suppression of banditry, and the development of a large, relatively culturally homogenous elite, who emulated the clothing of the emperor and his household.

Workshops, Weights, and Gods

Surviving textile fragments from Roman northern Italy are, at least in comparison to more durable materials like ceramics, very few.[29] Yet ceramic loom weights testify to the presence of textile production across northern Italy.

At Mutina, famous for its high-quality and sometimes golden-sheened wool, loom weights were stamped with elaborate decorations and inscribed names, including those of the freeborn, freedmen, and possibly slaves who either supervised or owned the workshops making the weights.[30] These decorated weights show a marked change from their more utilitarian Bronze Age counterparts, which, while varied in terms of shape, were generally undecorated pieces of stone or terracotta.[31] A similar change, although with less elaborately decorated loom weights, took place in Roman Spain, where Latin inscriptions were used to denote ceramic workshops.[32] While weights continued to serve their basic purpose of keeping the warp threads of a loom taut, they now reflected a particularly Roman epigraphic habit, where short inscriptions and names assured quality and advertised individual workshops. This was a habit found across the empire, from such diverse contexts as barrels, bricks, weights, blocks of eye medicine, spoons, hand-mills, and—at Vindolanda in Britain—even a lady's slipper.[33]

The Modense loom weights also show a close and mutually beneficial relationship between textile and ceramics producers; the latter clearly knew the local market. In some instances ceramics and textile producers may have been the same, and at a Roman villa at Russi, just outside Ravenna, loom weights were found near a kiln, which suggests that the villa produced both pots and cloth, possibly to supply the local naval base.[34]

The high prices that good quality wool could fetch encouraged increased production. At Mutina the proportion of land devoted to pastoral usage increased in the first century CE, and the high proportion of caprovid bones indicate that sheep were the predominant livestock.[35] Oddly, forest cover in the *ager Mutinensis* increased slightly from the Late Republic to the Early Empire, although even at its Roman-era nadir in the Late Republic, the percentage of forest cover was still greater than it was when the Terramare were cultivating the land.[36] Mutina's pastoral landscape was religious as well, and spaces for votive offerings sacred to Heracles—particularly favored as a pastoral god—were found throughout the *ager Mutinensis*.[37]

Workers

Like their Renaissance counterparts, who organized into a variety of guilds, textile workers in the Roman era formed *collegia*, trade organizations that doubled as "social communities."[38] There were *collegia* for wool-washers (at Altinum), wool-combers (at Brixia, Regium Lepidum), wool-carders (at Regium Lepidum), and textile and clothing dealers (Alba Pompeia, Altinum, Aquileia, Ariminum,

Augusta Taurinorum, Bergomum, Brixellum, Brixia, Cammuni, Clastidium, Comum, Concordia, Feltria, Forum Cornelii, Industria, Mediolanum, Novaria, Parma, Patavium, Placentia, Pollentia, Ravenna, Regium Lepidum, Segusio, Tridentum, Vada Sabatia, Vardagate, Vicetia, and Verona).[39]

Members of *collegia* set up funerary monuments for other members, and membership in some *collegi* could provide a kind of funerary insurance.[40] This was the case with the *collegium* of Diana and Antinous at Lanuvium, whose members, as long as they paid their membership fees and paid again into the burial fund, would receive a decent burial. Members were also supposed to attend an annual dinner, and bad manners netted additional fines.[41] For northern Italy's textiles workers, *collegia* provided a venue for social mobility in addition to insurance against a pauper's grave, as *collegium* dinners were a chance to forge connections and display manners signifying their *urbanitas*.[42]

Gaius Pomponius's epitaph from Regium Lepidum illustrates another potential source of funding for collegial burial funds:

> C(aio) Pomponio
> Rufi lib(erto)
> Felici
> VIvir(o) Aug(ustali)
> Claud(iali)
> lanari(i) pect(inarii)
> et carmin(atores)
> ob merita eius
> quod testamento
> suo legaverit
> eius non sufficientib(us)
> sibi dationes et
> vestiarium quoq(ue)
> et si qui(s) defunctus
> esset certa summa
> funeraretur[43]

> To Gaius Pomponius Felix, the freedman of Rufus, *Sevir Augustalis* and *Claudialis*, the wool combers and wool carders (made this monument) on account of his merit, because he left as a legacy in his will donations and clothing for those not having sufficient resources and if anyone should die that he be buried with a fixed sum.

For patron Pomponius Felix, his donations allowed him to advertise his status, service as a sevir, and euergetism, and in return the wool workers gave him a monument that commemorated not only Pomponius Felix but also the collective wealth and position of the workers and their *collegia*. Felix's monument marked out a position for the textile workers in the public space of Regium Lepidum. That Felix gave his donations in clothes as well as cash suggests that Felix himself was a textile dealer, although the clothes themselves were valuable commodities.

Textile workers and dealers commemorated their place in the industry prominently on their tombs. Two middle-first-century-CE funerary stelai from Mediolanum show on their lower reliefs figures proudly holding up samples of fabric (figs. 9 and 10).[44] Four other Milanese epitaphs commemorate *sagarii*, dealers in *saga*, cloaks.[45] One, M. Cluvius Tertullus, was a *sagarius* and *negotiator* (merchant) from Apulia, a rival region in wool production. Tertullus's presence in Mediolanum suggests that such rivalry did not preclude but may have even encouraged economic or at least personal connections between regions that earlier had had few ties. These funerary monuments point to the key role played by the trade *collegia* in helping define social space in the Roman world. At Brixellum the *lanarii* (wool workers) had their own cemetery; at Aquileia the communal cemetery of the *vestiarii* dominated the town's largest necropolis.[46]

From Felt Maker to Emperor

Demand at Rome and across the empire for specific fabrics helped make towns not only specialize in textile production but also rich, and with wealth came social mobility. Even the earlier "triumph factory," Liguria, produced *equites* (members of the equestrian order; the second highest wealth classification after senators), governors, and senators. No Ligurian town could match the output of Brixia, Verona, or Patavium in terms of *equites*. The most came from Pollentia, an indication possibly of the town's woolen wealth, while at the port of Vada Sabatia only one senator is attested. One man from Albintimilium, after serving as an officer with at least four separate military units along the borders, then oversaw the census in Bithynia and Pontus, served as *epistrategos* ("overgeneral") in Pelusium and in the Thebaid in Egypt, and finally acted as procurator of the province of Judaea.[47]

By the end of their careers the most successful of these formerly local elites had served in a variety of posts with the legions or in administrative centers across the empire, and in some cases they had advanced to posts as provincial governors and to senatorial rank. That kind of status brought them into proximity

Figure 9. Roman funerary stele from Mediolanum, Museo Archeologico, Milan. Photograph by author.

Figure 10. Detail of Roman funerary stele from Mediolanum, Museo Archeologico, Milan. Photograph by author.

with the emperor; Pliny's correspondence with Trajan shows how this imperial service could put one of Comum's local elites into a position to ask for and receive favors from the emperor himself; this made these elites useful patrons and in turn increased their social standing. This kind of geographic and social mobility made these elites influential beyond their numbers.

An extreme example of this social mobility can be found with P. Helvius Pertinax, the first emperor born in northern Italy. Pertinax was born in Alba Pompeia in Liguria. His freedman father owned a *taberna coactiliaria*, a felt-makers' shop, which Pertinax himself later ran and expanded.[48] The lowly felt-maker's shop and freedman father might be invented taunts, but the predominance of the textile industry in the region and in the Tanaro Valley in particular argues against discounting the story. The potential economic boon from textiles should not be discounted; indeed, Patavium, most famous (apart from Livy) for its textiles, had 500 *equites* during the Augustan era.[49] Pertinax himself raised substantial sums of money upon his accession by auctioning off Commodus's clothes.[50]

His contemporary Cassius Dio says that while Pertinax was not from a well-born family, he nevertheless had through a combination of education and connections obtained a series of posts in the imperial service.[51] By the time he was made emperor, a position he held for less than three months in 193 CE, Pertinax had commanded a cavalry squadron, become prefect of a cohort in Syria, supervised the finances of Dacia, commanded the German fleet, overseen the distribution of the *alimenta* along the Via Aemilia, and served as governor of Dacia, Moesia, Syria, and Britain.[52] Pertinax serves as an example of the social and geographic mobility made possible by the Roman imperial system; his career in the imperial service took him to the empire's borders and eventually—albeit very briefly—to the top of the Roman political hierarchy. This career was very much the product of a system of imperial administration, both military and civil, that drew local elites into an empire-wide network of posts, concentrated along the borders and still largely controlled by an imperial bureaucracy at Rome and around the emperor.

As emperor, Pertinax took a harsh line against the Praetorian Guard, which killed him within three months of his accession.[53] The men who killed him were almost exclusively recruited from Italy.[54] Nearly a century earlier Tacitus had claimed that the guard recruited primarily from Latium, Etruria, and Umbria, but praetorians with hometowns in northern Italy show up regularly on first- and second-century CE inscriptions.[55] In one 136 CE list of praetorians recruited in 119/20 CE, there are men from Aquileia, Ateste, Atria, Augusta Praetoria, Bononia, Brixia, Cremona, Eporedia, Libarna, Mediolanum, Mutina, Patavium, Placentia, Ravenna, Regium Lepidum, Ticinum, Tridentum, and Verona.[56] Pertinax's hometown of Alba Pompeia produced Q. Manlius Severus, who served in the Legio XXII Primegenia in Mogontiacum until he was transferred to the Seventh Praetorian cohort, probably by the emperor Vitellius in 69 CE.[57] Italian dominance of the Praetorian Guard did not last long after Pertinax's murder. In revenge for the murder, the new emperor, Septimius Severus, opened up the praetorians to nontraditional sources of recruitment, an act that the historian Dio complained turned Italy's youth from useful work to banditry and gladiatorial combat.[58]

Q. Alfidius Hyla

Dio's complaint about Italian praetorians turning to gladiatorial work is hyperbolic but does point to another kind of mobility within Italy, that which came with gladiatorial or theatrical work. Gladiators, mimes, actors, and others associated with theaters and arenas moved throughout Italy and the empire. Gladiators from the Rhine border might perform in Spain, and gladiatorial *familia* were often highly mobile. A twenty-two-year-old gladiator from Placentia was commemorated outside of Corduba, where he likely performed.[59] "The foremost pantomime of his age," at least according to his honorific inscription, received civic honors at Verona, Vicetia, and Mediolanum.[60] A *retiarius* (a type of gladiator who specialized in net and trident fighting) appropriately named Rapidus, listed his hometown as Bellunum but seems to have made his career at Aquileia. His career later took him outside Italy, and he died at Salona, where his epitaph makes a point of saying that he was taken down by medicine and his doctor rather than by a fellow gladiator.[61]

The last word should go to the funerary altar of Q. Alfidius Hyla (found at Mutina):

D(is) M(anibus)
Q(uinto) Alfidio
Q(uinti) l(iberto) Hylae
VIvir(o) Foro Sem-
proni(i) colleg(ii) harena-
riorum Romae negot-
ianti lanario
Alfidia Severa pat-
[ri] pientissimo[62]

(Sacred) to the spirits of the Underworld.

To Quintus Alfidius Hyla, the freedman of Quintus, *sevir* at Forum Sempronii (in Picenum), of the *collegium* of the arena staff at Rome, wool-merchant, Alfidia Severa (made this) for a most devoted father.

Hyla's career epitomizes the ways in which intra-Italian networks were reconfigured in the Early Roman Empire. Old economic habits were intensified and became increasingly specialized, and Hyla's career as a wool merchant reflects northern Italy's peculiar economic place in a larger empire, in which particular types, weights, and colors of textiles became cultural necessities and in which such specialized products were part of a town's identity, as they were for Mutina and its wool with the golden sheen.

His connection with the *collegium* of arena workers suggests that Hyla may have been supplying either clothing or the awning used to shade game spectators. As the cultural demands of Roman life helped spur the development of the textile industry in northern Italy, Rome's sheer size and voracious demand for raw materials made it the great economic magnet of Italy and drew trade and traders toward it. The route between Rome and Mutina along the Via Flaminia and the Via Aemilia runs through Forum Sempronii, where Hyla held a sevirate. Here Hyla's economic interests also intersected with social ones, and a sevirate gave him—and his daughter Alfidia Severa, too—status and honor. Hyla's career showed social, economic, and geographic mobility, a mobility along lines specific to the Roman era and to the cultural and economic world of the Early Empire.

Chapter Seven

Aquileia and Imperial Networks

Around noon on a spring day in 238 CE (a year of civil war and six Roman emperors), a group of Roman soldiers, worn out by thirst and frustrated by an increasingly unsuccessful siege of the city of Aquileia, approached the tent of their emperor, Maximinus Thrax, just outside the city. Outside the tent, the conspirators, who included members of the emperor's bodyguard, began taking down the images of the emperor from the standards. When the emperor and his son came out of the tent, the soldiers quickly cut them down. The heads of the late emperor and his son were sent to Rome; their bodies were exposed to the scavenging birds and dogs of the northern Adriatic coast.[1]

The soldiers, thinking that with the emperor dead the city would now open its gates to them, were instead met with a surprise. The defenders inside Aquileia brought out the images of rival emperors and made a display on the city walls:

> And now the Aquileians set up a market on the walls, offering for sale a huge quantity of goods of all kinds, including ample supplies of food, drink, clothing, and shoes—in short, everything that a prosperous and flourishing city could provide for human consumption. At this the soldiers were even more amazed; they now realized that the Aquileians had enough of everything they needed even if the siege were prolonged, whereas they lacked all the necessities and would have perished to the last man before they captured a city so abundantly supplied. The army continued to remain in position around the city, while the

> soldiers purchased what they needed from the walls, each man buying as much as he chose.[2]

Aquileia's ample supplies and wealth had frustrated Maximinus Thrax's ambitions and brought about the end of his reign; there was little chance, as the defenders illustrated in their market, of his starving the city out.

The wall market was also the result of four centuries of urban development, in which the city's merchants and traders had built a network of connections stretching across the Roman Empire. Like Frattesina, Spina, and Adria before it and Venice after, Aquileia was the chief city of the Adriatic, the point at which Mediterranean and European trade networks connected.

Aquileia and Italy

Aquileia's origins were, however, less than auspicious. Such rocky beginnings were not atypical of Roman colonies in northern Italy. In their initial decades, for example, Cremona and Placentia had lost enough population through war and illness that both had to be resettled after the Hannibalic war, with six thousand new families divided between them.[3] Before Aquileia was even constructed, a group of transalpine Gauls that had settled near Aquileia's proposed site had to be expelled (183 BCE); in addition, the neighboring Istrians were trying to prevent the settlement of the colony, which even with the use of Roman military force took at least two years.[4] The Roman government had to provide greater incentives than usual for colonists, who received between 50 and 140 *iugera* per colonist, allocations that were at the high end even for northern Italian colonies, which were, as a rule, more generous in their distributions of land than those located south of the Apennines.[5] Even with such incentives, Aquileia struggled to maintain its population in its first decade, and in 169 BCE the colony received fifteen hundred more families as reinforcement for a city worn down by constant campaigns by the Istrians.[6]

In contrast to its troubled early history in the Republic, Aquileia in the Imperial period was one of the largest cities in the empire, with a population of around one hundred thousand.[7] The space within its walls was around forty hectares, about equal to that of Verona, itself a "big city" according to Strabo.[8] As the primary commercial center of the upper Adriatic, Aquileia dominated trade between the Adriatic, Istria, the Danube valley, and Dalmatia, and in the process its citizens accumulated a great deal of wealth. Hence the city possessed many of the characteristics of other northern Italian cities—a large population, an extensive urban area and *territoria*, position near a provincial border, agricultural and commercial wealth—but to an exaggerated degree. As such, the city and its territory offer an opportunity to examine northern Italy's reaction to its new place in the imperial system at an extreme.

Aquileia emerged from the Late Republic as one of a handful of populous, wealthy, and politically connected *municipia* in northern Italy. Elites from Aquileia had—along with citizens from Cremona, Brixia, Patavium, and Verona—been among the first northern Italians to integrate into the government at Rome; the first attested senator from northern Italy is a Q. Titius Mutto, a Roman *triumvir monetalis* from Aquileia in 90 BCE.[9] In 89 BCE Aquileia had become the first *municipium* north of the Po, and its citizens were enrolled in the Velina voting tribe.[10] The city's commercial importance can be seen in the placement there of *portaria* stations for collecting customs taxes in the Late Republic; these are the earliest attested for northern Italy.[11]

Roman commanders had used the city as a base for their operations throughout the Republic, extensively so during the Istrian Wars.[12] The city had served as winter quarters for Caesar's legions during the Gallic Wars and would, along with Mediolanum, serve as a base for Augustus during the Pannonian and German campaigns, and it was in this context that Herod I met Augustus at Aquileia in 12 BCE.[13] When Augustus created a base for the new Adriatic fleet at Ravenna, he stationed a detachment from that fleet at Aquileia, probably attached to the trireme *Crocodilus*; joining them were a small troop of praetorians.[14] The stationing of the praetorians and sailors again suggests that Aquileia was seen in the Late Republic and Principate as strategically the most important city in the northeast.

Augustus also created a string of colonies and *fora* around Aquileia and along the Illyrian border; these included Julia Concordia, Julia Parentium, Pietas Julia (Pola), Forum Julii, and Julium Carnicum.[15] These settlements were primarily useful to Augustus in two ways: they provided opportunities for the settlement of veterans and secured advances made by recent Roman military campaigns in Noricum, Illyria, and in the Alps.[16] At the same time they also constituted a major reorganization of the area, a reorganization that heavily favored Aquileia. The roads built connecting these cities all ran through Aquileia, now made the hub for land and sea transport in the region. So while veteran settlements could be highly disruptive to other Italian cities, as they were for Cremona, for Aquileia they only bolstered the city's position. The Augustan reorganization of the region was again based on the perception of Aquileia as the region's natural center, a perception that had become self-perpetuating in the Late Republic and Principate.

Aquileia now became the city through which smaller settlements in the region conducted their business. Aquileian merchants and businessmen dominated the commerce of Istria and the eastern Veneto, which in turn fed Aquileia's economy. Herodian, describing Aquileia under the siege by Maximinus Thrax, says:

> Aquileia was already a huge city, with a large permanent population. Situated on the sea and with all the provinces of Illyricum behind it, Aquileia served as a port of entry for Italy. The city thus made it possible for goods transported from the interior by land or by the rivers to be traded to the merchant mariners and also for the necessities brought by sea to the mainland, goods not produced there because of the cold climate, to be sent to the upland areas. Since the inland people farm a region that produces much wine, they export this in quantity to those who do not cultivate grapes. A huge number of people lived permanently in Aquileia, not only the native residents but also foreigners and merchants.[17]

Wine produced in the Veneto and in Istria depended on Aquileia's markets and merchants.[18] When Maximinus marched against the city in 238 CE, his army found—and burned—vines even in Aquileia's suburbs.[19] For wool too, Aquileia's *vestiarii* depended on its hinterland to the east and south for raw supplies, and with those supplies the *vestiarii* were able to acquire Aquileia's largest burial ground as their private necropolis.[20] Also represented in Aquileia's cemeteries were the *purpurarii* (dyers of purple), *fabri* (artisans), *linteones* (linen weavers), and *negotiatores* (merchants), all testifying to the size and variety of the merchant community in the city as well as to Aquileia's position as the center of exchange for the area's goods.[21]

That status as a commercial center meant that the city offered opportunities for social advancement and economic gain to inhabitants from neighboring towns. Freedmen in particular came to Aquileia, where some acted as business agents for the elite families of the region. Several freedmen of the Veronese Gavii, that city's most important elite family, are attested at Aquileia, and while the family has freedmen attested in other northern Italian towns outside Verona, the majority of attestations are from Aquileia.[22] Freedmen from neighboring towns built social ties at Aquileia, and Aquileia's freedmen returned the favor. About 15% of attested sevirs—mostly but not exclusively freedmen—at Aquileia also held the sevirate in another town (Ateste, Tergeste, and Concordia are attested).[23] Likewise, men holding the sevirate at Aquileia appear at Pola, Emona, and at Forum Iulii.[24] Nor was this pattern limited to Aquileia. Concordia, Aquileia's neighbor to the east, has sevirs appearing at Opitergium, Altinum, Patavium, Ateste, Aquileia, and Forum Cornelii in Aemilia.[25] This practice of holding office in multiple towns suggests that social ties often extended beyond city walls, and as a whole the pattern of dual officeholding suggests that the social network of Aquileia's sevirs encompassed most of the eastern Veneto and Istria.

Aquileia's size and population also meant that it offered services that its smaller satellite communities in *regio* X could not. Teachers and instructors of rhetoric are well attested in Aquileia, while these professions are rare elsewhere in the region.[26] Their presence in Aquileia would again mean that inhabitants from neighboring towns would have to go to Aquileia to go to school. For those families not wealthy enough to hire their own instructor or send their older sons abroad, this might be a problem. Even fairly sizeable towns like Concordia might lack schools.[27] Pliny the Younger discovered that Comum lacked teachers when he found one boy who went to Mediolanum for his schooling. That Pliny the Younger even felt the need to ask a local boy where he went to school suggests that the practice of sending children off to neighboring cities for their education was not uncommon.[28] Aquileia, then, with an established community of teachers, would be able to draw citizens, at least temporarily, from other communities in the region.

At the same time there were limits to Aquileia's influence in the region. While Aquileia seems to have had a greater supply of teachers, doctors in contrast are evenly dispersed throughout *regio* X, with even towns like Vicetia and Altinum possessing specialized doctors like veterinarians and eye doctors.[29] Aquileia's status as regional hegemon was also limited when it came to public entertainment venues. Patavium, Pola, and Verona had amphitheaters that were older and larger, while theaters could be found at Acelum, Altinum, Adria, Brixia, Concordia, Opitergium, Patavium, Pola, Tergeste, Tridentum, Verona, and Vicetia—Pola even had two; Aquileia had no monopoly on the games.[30] Politically, Aquileia's elites were well connected at Rome, but so were elites from Patavium, Brixia, Verona, and Mediolanum. Aquileia was one of Italy's largest and wealthiest cities, but as *regio* X was in general wealthy and populous, the distinctions between Aquileia and neighbors like Concordia and Trieste were lessened. The multipolar situation that developed in northern Italy during the Late Republic—with Brixia, Verona, Aquileia, and Patavium acquiring large quantities of wealth, land, and political connections through a combination of *attributio*, land redistribution, political climbing, and control of trade routes—also meant that Aquileia's influence was limited to the eastern Veneto and Istria, since Verona and Patavium created their own spheres of economic influence and social connections to the west and south.

Aquileia in the Empire

To the east and north, Aquileia's ambitions were less bounded. Territories in Pannonia, Raetia, and Noricum newly brought under Roman control were not as urbanized as northern Italy, and there was less economic competition. In Noricum merchants from Aquileia traded pottery, glass, oil, and wine from northern Italy for metal wares, including gold from the mines that had been discovered near Klagenfurt in the second century BCE.[31] Norican iron was the region's most famous product, and Aquileia's control of the trade is illustrated in the presence at Virunum of a *conductor ferriarum Noricarum* from Aquileia.[32] Noricum also functioned initially as a section of the amber road leading from the Baltic to the Mediterranean.[33] Since the Bronze Age, amber had made its way down from the Baltic and the Black Sea, over the Brenner and Resia Passes, down the Adige and Po Valleys, to the Adriatic ports, and then to markets in the eastern Mediterranean.[34] In the Republic, Aquileia gained control of the trade within northern Italy, and from the Late Republic to the second century, the city was the land terminus of the amber road as well as the point from which finished objects entered markets in Italy and the Mediterranean.[35]

By the reign of Tiberius, Aquileians had established a trading post on the Danube at Lauriacum, and, at the trading settlement of Magdelensburg in particular, Aquileians were active as merchants. Their presence in these communities proved to be long lasting. They married into the local population, creating business partnerships and sometimes obtaining for their new family members citizenship bestowed *ad viritim*. In one case the sons of a native father and Italian mother even took on their mother's citizenship and voting tribe, Velina, which suggests that the mother was from either Aquileia or Pola.[36] These merchants stayed long enough to be buried in Noricum, and when they died they had themselves commemorated in the funerary fashions of Aquileia. In the first century this meant elongated, rectangular funerary plaques topped with timpani; later in the second century, rectangular portrait niches began to be inserted between the text and the timpanum.[37] This style became popular in Noricum and remained the basic blueprint for Norican funerary art in the Roman period, even as the province's art evolved and, in the second and third centuries, adopted a few artistic elements, such as *clipeus* portraits (portraits on shields), which were exceptionally rare in Aquileia.[38]

Likewise, Aquileia and its merchants were active along the rest of the Danube frontier, in Pannonia and Moesia. From Aquileia came imports from the Mediterranean and goods manufactured in the Veneto and Istria—such as pottery from the kilns of C. Laecanius Bassus, near Pola—and from Pannonia and Moesia in return came hides, metal goods, and slaves.[39] Aquileia's economic power along the Danube provinces in general was great enough that much of the trade from Germany to Dacia went through Aquileia, even though the city required a detour far to the south.[40] In Pannonia and Moesia, as in Noricum, people claiming Aquileia as their home appear primarily as civilians; in contrast, representatives from other large northern Italian towns are almost exclusively veterans and legionaries (table 1). The contrast underlines the great extent and intensity of Aquileia's commercial activities and at the same time illustrates the different ways in which the Roman Empire guided the movement of people within its territory. With Aquileia, a combination of the Roman control of mines, the stationing of legions along a new border, and the military control of important roads encouraged the city's merchants to move into the Danube provinces; for the rest of northern Italy, the army, which recruited heavily in the region, was the main mover of people. Accordingly, along the Danube border, inhabitants of one northern Italian town were trading alongside soldiers recruited primarily from their neighbors.[41]

Northeastern Italy had, of course, longstanding trade links with central Europe, and the trade in metals from central Europe through the Adriatic ports to the Mediterranean is well attested even in the Bronze Age. The amber trade, too, long predated even the earliest Roman expansion into northern Italy. What made the Imperial period different was the impact of the state, through the perennial presence of armies, imperial control of mining, and the taxation and control of trade between Italy and the provinces via the use of customs stations. These conditions helped direct Aquileia's commercial activities along Roman roads to the Danube frontier, as such conditions provided merchants from Aquileia with patrolled roads, a stable source of metal goods, and a large market of consumers in the legions and auxiliaries.

A similar impact of the state can be seen in Aquileia's relationship with Illyricum. Perhaps even more so than with the Danube provinces, northeastern Italy had a long history of strong connections with the Dalmatian coast and with the Illyrians.[42] Commerce between the two areas continued into the Empire, when trade in Dalmatian metals became important; the Neronian period saw an increased exploitation of Dalmatian mines, and Dalmatian miners became so proficient that in the second century they were exported en masse to Dacia when the Romans began systematic mining there.[43] Copper from Dalmatian mines was used by Aquileia's numerous metal workshops; at least fourteen indepen-

Table 1 Northern Italians in Noricum, Pannonia, Moesia, and Dacia

Town of origin	Place commemorated	Status, if known	References
Aquileia	Pannonia: Carnuntum	centurion	*CIL* III 14358.15
Aquileia	Pannonia: Dunafoldvar		*CIL* III 10300
Aquileia	Pannonia: Emona	*sevir Aquileiae*	*AE* 1998: 548 + *AE* 1936: 159
Aquileia	Pannonia: Emona	*sevir Aquileiae*	*CIL* III 3836a
Aquileia	Pannonia: Emona	*sevir Aquileiae*	*CIL* III 3836b
Aquileia	Pannonia: Emona		*CIL* III 404
Aquileia	Pannonia: Heteny	legionary	*CIL* III 4351
Aquileia	Pannonia: Poetovio		*ILJug* 2.1153
Aquileia	Pannonia: Sirmium		*CIL* III 10232
Aquileia	Noricum: Lentia (Linz)		*AE* 1999: 1214a (= *AE* 1955: 101)
Aquileia	Noricum: Virunum	*conductor ferriarum Noricarum; praefectus iure dicundo*	*CIL* III 4788
Aquileia	Noricum: Virunum		*CIL* III 4869
Aquileia	Noricum: Celeia		*CIL* III 5217
Aquileia	Moesia: Singidunum	"*consistentes Aquileiae*"	*AE* 1956: 233
Aquileia	Moesia: Skupi	veteran	*AE* 1977: 725 + *AE* 1975: 737
Aquileia	Dacia: Alba Iulia	centurion	*AE* 1977: 653
Augusta Taurinorum	Pannonia: Bolcske	veteran	*AE* 2003: 1436+1437
Brixia	Pannonia: Carnuntum	legionary	*AE* 1982: 81
Brixia	Pannonia: Carnuntum	legionary	Hild 211
Brixia	Pannonia: Carnuntum	legionary trumpeter	*AE* 1979: 463
Brixia	Pannonia: Emona	legionary	*AE* 1958: 1
Brixia	Moesia: Oescus	veteran	*CIL* III 12348
Bononia	Pannonia: Carnuntum	legionary	*AE* 1900: 223
Cremona	Pannonia: Carnuntum	legionary	*AE* 1900: 217
Cremona	Pannonia: Carnuntum	veteran	*CIL* III 11229 = *CLE* 1011
Cremona	Pannonia: Carnuntum	legionary	*CIL* III 13485
Cremona	Pannonia: Carnuntum	legionary	*AE* 2002: 1151

Table 1 Continued

Town of origin	Place commemorated	Status, if known	References
Cremona	Pannonia: Carnuntum	legionary	*LegioXVApo.* 107
Cremona	Pannonia: Carnuntum	legionary	*CIL* III 14358.15a
Cremona	Pannonia: Poetovio	veteran	*CIL* III 10878
Cremona	Pannona: Poetovio	legionary	*CIL* III 10879
Iulium Carnicum	Noricum: Voitsberg (near Graz)	decurion	*CIL* III 11739
Mediolanum	Pannonia: Andautonia	veteran	*ILJug* 2.1133
Mediolanum	Pannonia: Carnuntum	legionary	*AE* 1934: 270
Mediolanum	Pannonia: Poetovio	legionary	*CIL* III 4061
Mediolanum	Pannonia: Savaria	veteran	*AE* 1972: 414
Mediolanum	Pannonia: Savaria	veteran	*LegioXVApo.* 32
Mediolanum	Dacia: Potaissa	centurion	*AE* 1992: 1470 + *AE* 1993: 1332
Patavium	Pannonia: Carnuntum	veteran	*CIL* III 11220
Patavium	Pannonia: Carnuntum		*CIL* III 11259
Patavium	Pannonia: Carnuntum	legionary	*LegioXVApo.* 91
Tergeste	Pannonia: Carnuntum	legionary	*AE* 1978: 627
Tergeste	Pannonia: Siscia		*AE* 1935: 162
Vercellae	Pannonia: Aquincum	legionary	*CIL* III 3567
Verona	Pannonia: Aquincum	legionary	*AE* 1990: 813
Verona	Pannonia: Carnuntum	veteran	*AE* 1929: 200
Verona	Pannonia: Carnuntum		*AE* 1938: 164
Verona	Pannonia: Carnuntum	legionary	*AE* 1973: 426
Verona	Pannonia: Savaria	veteran	*CIL* III 5220
Verona	Moesia: Scupi	decurion, *quaestor*, duovir	*AE* 1984: 747
Vicetia	Pannonia: Carnuntum	legionary	*AE* 1973: 424
Vicetia	Pannonia: Carnuntum	legionary	*AE* 1907: 177
Vicetia	Noricum: Rosegg		Lupa 11651
Vicetia	Moesia: Scupi	legionary	*AE* 1984: 762

dent bronze workshops are attested in Aquileia, and Aquileian metalwork—in vases, fibulae, or even Medusa head appliqués—is distributed through the upper Adriatic, in Pannonia along the road to Carnuntum, and along the Rhine and Danube *limes*.[44] The Dalmatian coast also exported wine and oil to Aquileia, which then traded those goods to Pannonia.[45] Returning though Pannonia were amber pieces, which, after being worked at Aquileia, were then traded as luxury items in Dalmatia.[46] This kind of triangular trade was dependent not just on the state-controlled mining complexes in Dalmatia but also on Roman military control of the Danube provinces and the main roads leading through them.

The close relationship between Aquileia and these provinces is epitomized in the history of one of Aquileia's largest merchant families, the Barbii.[47] At Aquileia the inscriptions of the Barbii are concentrated in the first century, but attestations continue into the third century.[48] Their most conspicuous member, a Barbius Fulvius Aemilianus, obtained the praetorship and was eventually *quaestor pro praetore provinciae*, although the identity of the province is unknown.[49] The *familia* included a large number of freedmen, and both freeborn and freedmen can be found in roughly similar distributions outside Aquileia, which suggests that the family's commercial interests were largely unified and that the family acted as a kind of commercial firm at Aquileia. At Aquileia they were members of *collegia*, veterans, and probably heavily involved in trade.[50] In northern Italy they are attested at Altinum, Ateste, Atria, Bellunum, Concordia, Forum Iulii, Opitergium, Pola, Tergeste, Vicetia, and Ravenna, corresponding almost perfectly to Aquileia's sphere of influence in northeastern Italy.[51] This is confirmed by the fact that westernmost examples from northern Italy are from Brixia and Cremona; there are none from Mediolanum.[52] In central and southern Italy the family appears in Rome and Puteoli, the latter not surprising considering Aquileia's maritime connections.[53] In the provinces, the name is most prevalent in Noricum—where it appears in various inscriptions along the route from Aquileia to Magdelensburg—but is also found with frequency in Pannonia along the Danube and in towns along the Dalmatian coast.[54] The Barbii became a permanent presence in some provincial towns; in the Pannonian town of Savaria, along the amber road, they even rose to the decurionate.[55] The Aquileian Barbii, their freedmen, and their descendants thus spread throughout the empire in a pattern that mimicked almost perfectly Aquileia's major commercial connections.

Aquileia was able to trade in these provinces because of the access the city had not only to goods from the Veneto and Istria but also to imports from the rest of the Mediterranean, which the city obtained from its Adriatic port at Grado and

Figure 11. Surviving section of river port of Aquileia. Photograph by author.

from the river port just south of the city (fig. 11).[56] As Aquileia turned its commercial efforts toward Noricum, Pannonia, and Dalmatia, other trading contacts seem to have been dropped; at Corinth, for example, northern Italian amphorae begin to disappear in the early Augustan period.[57] Nevertheless, Aquileia conducted trade with Cyrene, Egypt, Syria, and even the western provinces throughout the Imperial period, with pottery and glass wares from northeastern Italy appearing in Carthage, Gaul, Cyrene, Syria, and Britain, while Aquileia's specialized luxury industry in the production of amber pieces and engraved gemstones found consumers on the Black Sea, Athens, and Cyrene.[58] Not all trade was a luxury, and Aquileia, despite its proximity to the fertile Po Valley, imported some of its grain from Cyrene.[59]

The variety of these trade connections may account for the large pantheon of gods worshipped at Aquileia, with dedications to the Bithynian Attis, Mithra, the Celtic Iunones, the local Bellenus, and Anubis Augustus; worship of Isis at Aquileia is particularly well attested and seems, judging from the nomenclature employed in dedications, to have spread to the rest of northern Italy and Raetia from Aquileia, rather than from Rome through the peninsula.[60] The presence of the imperial fleet at Ravenna, with a detachment in the later first century at Salona on the Dalmatian coast, made commerce on the Adriatic safer and also encouraged trade to other parts of the Mediterranean. Again, while trade connections between northeastern Italy and the southern and eastern Mediterranean had existed previously—the presence of ivory and ostrich egg pieces at Frattesina in the LHIIIC period is one of the more striking illustrations of these connections—the scope and configuration of these connections were now reactions to the structure of the Roman imperial system, and the impact of those connections was now more extensive and more permanent.[61]

While Aquileia had a fairly strong influence over Istria and the Veneto and close connections with Noricum, Illyrium, Pannonia, and to a lesser extent the eastern Mediterranean, connections with Italy outside the northeast corner are surprisingly limited. Aquileian glassware was traded across the width of northern Italy, but the trade does not seem to have had the impact it did in the Danube provinces, and Aquileian origins are rarely found on tombstones in the rest of northern Italy, even less so in Italy south of the Apennines.[62] Also rare are cases of office-holding or *collegia* membership in Aquileia and towns outside the northeast corner. One freedman's epitaph from Placentia boasts of membership in both the Placentian and Aquileian colleges of augustales, and another man interred at Hasta in Liguria was a decurion in both Hasta and Aquileia, but these kinds of political connection are remarkable primarily for their rarity.[63] Rather, political and social connections within northern Italy are limited to smaller, subregional networks.[64]

Likewise, connections with central and southern Italy are rare. The major exception to this rule is, of course, Rome, where Aquileians can be found in a number of capacities from the Late Republic onward. Along with other northern Italians, they dominated the rosters of the Praetorian Guard and urban cohorts at Rome.[65] Aquileians were also active politically at Rome; the Caesernii were particularly successful at Rome, with members of the family obtaining the offices of *consul suffectus*, curator of Nicomedia, and proconsul of Cyprus.[66] The appearance of elites from Aquileia in the government at Rome shows a continuation of Late Republican–era trends.

In Aquileia itself these patterns of interaction with Italy and the rest of the empire are mirrored in the city's population.. Of the twenty-six epitaphs and dedications in which one of the inscribed is noted as originating from outside Aquileia, half mention cities within Italy, while the remainder are from the provinces. The proportion of provincials to Italians is relatively high, and of those Italian cities represented, not one is south of Latium, and only one, Album Intimilium (Ventimiglia), is located outside of the corridor running southwest from Aquileia through Umbria to Rome. It is worth noting that even the one outlier, Album Intimilium, is primarily a port city and as such connected to Aquileia by maritime trade.

The Empire in Aquileia

Aquileia's larger position within the Roman empire can thus be seen in miniature in Aquileia's population. That position could also be physically seen in Aquileia, since the city's urban plan—though in its basic orthogonal layout typical of other colonies in northern Italy—evolved to adapt to the city's growing commercial interests. In the Middle Republic this meant the construction of the large *macellum*, or market building, northwest of the forum, while during the Empire, at Aquileia's river port the city constructed and, more important, repeatedly renovated a nearly 300 m–long complex of magazines to hold goods being shipped and received.[67] The importance of the city's craftsmen could be seen in the funerary monuments lining the roads to Aquileia, and the dedications made by the city's residents showed a broad pantheon, behind which were broad trading connections and the large population of resident aliens those connections brought. Likewise, local politics reflected Aquileia's commercial identity, and Aquileia commemorated one of its elites for successfully lobbying the emperor to impose the same *munera* (obligations) on the city's resident aliens as were owed by Aquileia's citizens (table 2).[68]

Aquileia's experience, and even its physical appearance in the Early Empire, was heavily dependent on its position within that empire, which in turn depended greatly on the actions of the Roman state. Through the Roman acquisition and militarization of Danubian provinces, a boom in state-controlled mining, and the pacification of the Adriatic, Aquileia became the hub of the trading network in south-central Europe, and through Adriatic shipping it maintained trading contacts with most of the provinces of the Roman Empire, including Britain, with which contact prior to the Roman period had been nonexistent. Although the Roman state largely left northern Italy at the end of the Republic, with the removal of governors and armies, the Roman state continued to have a strong impact on Aquileia's development and on the city's place within the empire.

Aquileia's position in the empire remained relatively stable until the 160s, when the Roman military border came back to Aquileia with the invasion of Pannonia by the Marcomanni. Leading a punitive expedition against the Mar-

Table 2 Resident Aliens at Aquileia

Name	Profession	Provenance	Reference
M. Fabius L. f.		Ateste (Venetia)	*CIL* V 1029 = *IAquil* 1091
L. Iunius Successus		Altinum (Venetia)	*CIL* V 745 = *IAquil* 144
M. Cato M. f.	veteran	Cremona (Venetia)	*CIL* V 8274 = *IAquil* 2834
Macerus L. f.	veteran	Bergomum (Transpadana)	*IAquil* 2760
L. Decimus Aprus	veteran	Bononia (Aemilia)	*IAquil* 2829
M. Miledius M. f.	veteran	Mutina (Aemilia)	*IAquil* 2755a
P. Maenelius St. f.	veteran	Mutina (Aemilia)	*IAquil* 2836
C. Manlius Valerianus	*iudex*	Sarsina (Aemilia)	*CIL* V 923 = *IAquil* 2842
		Sentinum (Picenum)	*IAquil* 3537
T. f.	veteran	Perusia (Umbria)	*IAquil* 2843
L. Sallustius	veteran	Urbino (Umbria)	*CIL* V 8283 = *IAquil* 2841
C. Albicius C. f.	veteran	Album Intimilium (Liguria)	*CIL* V 886 = *IAquil* 2844
P. Caesius P. f.	aedile, *publicanus*	Sora (Latium) and Rome	*CIL* V 976 = *IAquil* 519
L. Valerius Primus	*negotiator*, *margaritarius*	Rome	*IAquil* 718
Publicius Placidus	*negotiator*	Rome	*IAquil* 148 = *AE* 1898: 85
	veteran	Suessatium (Spain)	*CIL* V 926 = *IAquil* 2750
Q. Etuvius Sex. f. Capreolus	veteran	Vienne (Gaul)	*IAquil* 2744 = *AE* 1902: 41
M. Secundus Genialis	*negotiator*	Claudia Agrippinensis (Germany)	*CIL* V 1047 = *IAquil* 717
L. Atilius L. l. Saturninus		Flavia Scarbantia (Pannonia)	*ILS* 8507 = *IAquil* 861 = *AE* 2003: 1281
L. Valerius . L. f. Longinus	veteran	Savaria (Pannonia)	*CIL* V 1011 = *IAquil* 2856
Tib. Claudius Magnus	decurion	Ephesus	*IAquil* 182 = *AE* 2000: 605
Arnouphis	*ierogrammateus*	Egypt	*IAquil* 234; see also Birley 1987.
		Alexandria	*IG* XIV 2338
Eutychas		Tacheira (Africa)	*IG* XIV 2355
		Africa	*IAquil* 3508
Restulus		Africa	*CIL* V 1703; cf. *CIL* V 1662

comanni, the co-emperors Marcus Aurelius and Lucius Verus set up their base at Aquileia, as Augustus and numerous Republican-era commanders had done before.[69] The city at that point was so accustomed to peace that its walls had fallen into disrepair. This return of military action in response to the Marcomannic invasion was brief, but the calamitous year of civil war in 238, in which the Aquileians used their city's wares to undermine enemy resolve, inaugurated a half decade of crisis and transformation.

PART III / Northern Italy beyond the Romans

Chapter Eight

Late Antique Transformations

Northern Italy prospered during an extended period of internal peace during the Early Empire, peace that in the first and second centuries was broken only for brief periods: in 69 CE, in the civil wars following the collapse of the Julio-Claudians, and in 170 CE, with the invasion of the Marcomanni. For all their immediate damage,[1] the civil wars of 69 CE were brief and were followed by sustained recovery efforts.[2] Likewise, the incursion of the Marcomanni into northeastern Italy, while resulting in the sack of Opitergium, the siege of Aquileia, and the creation of a temporary *praetentura Italiae et Alpium* (a command guarding Italy and the Alps), nevertheless was also of limited consequence for northern Italy as a whole.[3] The civil war between Maximinus and the Senate in 238 CE seems to have been only temporarily disruptive, since Maximinus was assassinated by his men outside Aquileia before the completion of the siege.[4] Whether the civil war between Philip the Arab and Decius, which culminated in a battle outside Verona in 249, was substantially destructive is difficult to say, given the brevity of literary material about the war, and it is possible that the crucial battle did not take place at Verona at all but in Macedonia.[5]

Northern Italy in the Third Century CE: Problems and Reactions

The war between Philip and Decius was, however, followed by a period of sustained violence and upheaval, lasting from the 250s through the 260s, which saw repeated invasions of northern Italy.[6] In 254 the Marcomanni again invaded Italy and reached as far south as Ravenna, and just a few years later, in 258 and 259, the Alemanni invaded Italy and this time reached as far south as Rome, where they were turned back by a makeshift army assembled by the Senate; on their way back they were defeated outside Mediolanum by the junior emperor Gallienus.[7] That the senate at Rome had to supplement the Praetorian Guards with emergency conscripts from the city demonstrates how unprepared the city and Italy as a whole were for a foreign invasion. Previous incursions into Italy, as shocking as they were, had only gone as far south as Aquileia and Ravenna. The novelty of this situation and the consequent Roman lack of preparation were demonstrated again later that same year when the Juthungi, taking advantage of the confusion caused by the Alemanni and by imperial preoccupations in Syria, invaded and plundered Italy; only on their way back through Raetia in April of 260 were they defeated.[8] More telling, the Roman force that defeated the Juthungi near Augsburg was composed not just of soldiers from Raetia and Germany but also of conscripted local militia, a sign that the Roman officials and commanders did not have enough soldiers to confront the Juthungi and had to resort to enlisting local civilians.[9] The Juthungi seem to have been in Italy for some time as well, since by the time they reached Augsburg they are described as having taken several thousand Italian captives.[10]

A brief respite for northern Italy following the victory at Augsburg was interrupted by civil war in 268, when Aureolus, the commander of the cavalry at Mediolanum, revolted and was besieged for months by Gallienus.[11] In the winter of 270/71 the Alemanni and Juthungi were again moving through northern Italy, where they captured Placentia and defeated the emperor Aurelian's army in an ambush near the city. Aurelian turned back the Alemanni in a battle near Fanum Fortunae (Fano) on the Metaurus River; he then destroyed much of the retreating army in a second battle, near Ticinum.[12] By the time of Aurelian's decisive victory at Ticinum, northern Italy had experienced nearly two decades of wars and invasions, the effects of which were no doubt exacerbated by an epidemic, the Plague of Cyprian, which spread throughout the empire between 251 and at least 270, when it claimed the emperor Claudius II Gothicus as a victim.[13]

These repeated and serious threats to the security of Rome and the Italian peninsula compelled the Roman state to act. With the Danube borders proved porous and Italy proved vulnerable, the emperors Gallienus, Claudius, and Aurelian established a more flexible and responsive system of defense in northern Italy. In 268 we hear of a large, mobile cavalry force stationed—to guard against attacks from the breakaway Gallic empire—at Mediolanum, and according to Aurelius

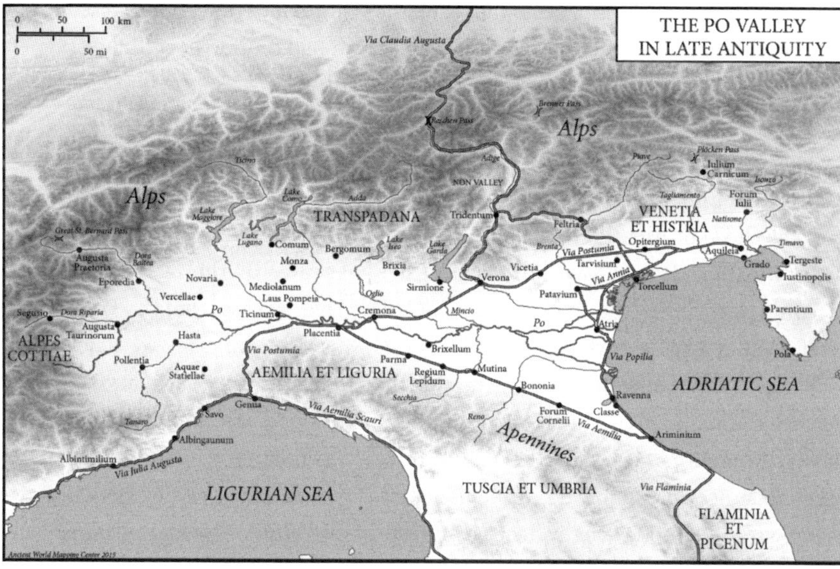

Figure 12. Northern Italy in Late Antiquity. Map by Ancient World Mapping Center.

Victor, Claudius II Gothicus was promoted to emperor that same year, while he was in command of a garrison at Ticinum.[14] The placement of mobile military forces in northern Italy, together with the creation of a front line actually in Italy, meant that a support structure for these troops needed to be put in place. These armies needed to be paid, and to ensure quicker and easier payment Gallienus established a mint at Mediolanum in 259.[15] To protect important individual cities, emperors ordered the construction of new defensive walls, such as those at Rome and Verona.[16] These measures, all undertaken in the 250s, 260s, and early 270s to counteract immediate security threats, represent the most dramatic change in state policy toward the region since the deprovincialization of the Augustan period. While many of the specific changes were temporary—the cavalry force at Mediolanum does not seem to have been stationed there under Diocletian, and the mint at Mediolanum was transferred—nevertheless, armed units continued to be kept in the region, the minting of coins continued, and the transformation of towns into defensive units continued through Late Antiquity (fig. 12).[17]

This chapter examines the evolution of northern Italy in Late Antiquity and in particular focuses on six towns—Ticinum, Iulium Carnicum, Forum Iulii, Mediolanum, Tergeste, and Ravenna—from the third century CE to the Lombard conquest of the sixth century. These six towns illustrate different aspects and phases of the long-lasting effects that the establishment of new imperial seats and the reorganization of the Roman imperial system had on northern Italy.

Ticinum: The Mint

Ticinum was a moderately sized town just south of Mediolanum.[18] The town's walled area under the empire was about half that of Mediolanum and nearly the same as those of Alba Pompeia and Placentia; this places it in the upper-middle tier of northern Italian towns in terms of size.[19] Located on the Ticino River near its conjunction with the Po, Ticinum controlled river access from the Po into the Ticino Valley and Lake Maggiore, and the town was also connected by major roads to Placentia, Mediolanum, Augusta Taurinorum, and Vercellae—and through Vercellae to Eporedia and the Aosta Valley. The town's economy depended on those connections, which tied Ticinum into larger northern Italian and transalpine trade networks, and the importance of the river network, in particular, to the town's livelihood was reflected in Ticinum's *collegium nautarum*, a private association of boatmen.[20] The town's social sphere seems to have been roughly the same radius as those of similarly sized north Italian towns, with local elites—including freedmen—holding office, receiving honors, and integrating into the social networks of nearby towns. Hence one man at Augusta Taurinorum also held office at Ticinum, and one elite Ticinensis could be found commemorated in Verona, where he set up a large funerary plot for himself and his wife.[21] Some of the town's elites also held office at Rome and in imperial posts throughout the Empire. The legions and the Praetorian Guard, which both recruited at Ticinum, similarly served to disperse Ticinenses throughout the empire, particularly at Rome and along the Rhine and Danube borders.[22]

The period of foreign invasions and strong government reactions to those invasions had a pronounced impact on Ticinum during the third and fourth centuries. In 274, the emperor Aurelian moved the minting operation based at Mediolanum to its neighbor Ticinum.[23] With the new mint, which became Aurelian's main producer of bronze coinage, Ticinum assumed a prominence that it had previously lacked, particularly since it replaced Mediolanum as Italy's primary mint, although minting continued at Mediolanum in the fourth century.[24]

While the emperors establishing these Late Antique mints had largely practical considerations in mind, nevertheless city encomia interpreted the mint as a mark of imperial benefaction.[25] Hence a late-fifth-century CE encomium of Narbo in Gaul lists mints with the forum, theater, baths, temples, walls, gates, and bridge as the praiseworthy attributes of that city.[26] Ticinum's claim to fame as Italy's major mint was not left uncontested, and in 294 the tetrarchs opened a mint at Aquileia.[27] Both mints were closed in the 320s, Aquileia in 324 and Ticinum at the end of 326, when Constantine reorganized the imperial mints.[28] Although Ticinum's period as an imperial mint was limited—its phase of high production lasted only from Aurelian's monetary reforms in 274 to Diocletian's reforms in 285—the establishment of the mint helped to raise the town's status.[29]

While the transfer of the mint to Ticinum gave the town prestige and a claim of superiority over neighboring towns, a claim that, unlike more standard urban structures like theaters and temples, was unique for the region, the day-to-day operations of the mint would have brought immediate changes to the town's economy and society. The mint's large output meant that large quantities of metal—especially copper, for the large productions of bullion currency—needed to be brought into Ticinum. This meant the establishment of supply lines leading from provincial mining centers. Since Ticinum's mint produced gold and silver coinage as well, small detachments of soldiers would probably have been sent to Ticinum for security purposes.[30] Skilled workers needed to be brought in to make the coins at Ticinum's mint; these included *argentarii, signatores, scalptores, malleatores, suppostores,* and *conductores*.[31] Supervising them were *procuratores* and *officinatores* of the individual *officinae*, or divisions.[32] Each of these officials required a further support staff, and a second-century CE inscription from Rome lists nine slaves assisting the *officinatores* of the mint.[33] The mint also required the supervision of quite high-ranking imperial officials, for example, C. Valerius Sabinus, Aurelian's *rationalis*, commemorated by Ticinum's decurions.[34] The operations at Ticinum were probably closely supervised by Sabinus and his subordinates because of concerns produced by the revolt of the mint workers at Rome in 271 CE, which had proved so disastrous and in which the mint workers had been suspected of rampant embezzlement.[35] The opening of an imperial mint at Ticinum thus required a substantial infusion of personnel—and the money they brought with them—into the town.

The mint also connected Ticinum more closely with other points of the empire with similar imperial interests. The opening of new mints, closing of others, and frequent reorganization of minting operations in the late third and early fourth centuries meant that specialized personnel were transferred among mints, and Ticinum received mint workers from Arles, Treviri, and possibly Lugdunum and Londinium.[36] Similarly, after the closing of the mint at Ticinum in 326 CE, the town's minting operations were transferred to the newly opened mint at Constantinople.[37] In this manner the Roman state transferred mint workers, much as it did men employed by the legions and the state administration, between particular points of the empire where the state was heavily involved; this process connected otherwise unrelated towns such as Londinium, Ticinum, and Constantinople.

Ticinum: Sarmatians, Treasuries, and Bows

The establishment of a mint at Ticinum was only one of a number of measures the state took to protect Italy and better supply the legions. Although by the 280s the borders had been reconstituted, breakaway parts of the empire recovered, and invasions of Italy halted, the changes that emperors such as Gallienus and Aurelian had instituted in northern Italy in response to those threats—better-fortified towns, mobile military units, and greater imperial presence—were continued by their successors. The results was that throughout the fourth century, northern Italy became more and more militarized, especially in comparison with central and southern Italy. The greater use of garrisons, such as that seen at Ticinum in 268 CE, has already been noted. The fourth century continued and increased this practice, to the point of resettling large groups of foreign auxiliaries in Italy. In 334 CE the emperor Constantine settled 300,000 Sarmatians in the Balkans and Italy, and prefects were assigned to monitor them.[38] The *Notitia Dignitatum*, describing state infrastructure in the early fifth century, lists the prefects in Italy:

Item in provincia Italia mediterranea:
Praefectus Sarmatarum gentilium Apulia et Calabriae.
Praefectus Sarmatarum gentilium Brutios et Lucaniam.
Praefectus Sarmatarum gentilium, Foro Fuluiensi [Liguria].
Praefectus Sarmatarum gentilium, Opittergii [Venetia].
Praefectus Sarmatarum gentilium, Patauio [Aemilia].
Praefectus Sarmatarum gentilium, . . .
Praefectus Sarmatarum gentilium, Cremonae [Venetia].
Praefectus Sarmatarum gentilium, Taurinis [Transpadana].
Praefectus Sarmatarum gentilium, Aquis siue Tertona [Liguria].
Praefectus Sarmatarum gentilium, Novariae [Transpadana].
Praefectus Sarmatarum gentilium, Vercellis [Transpadana].
Praefectus Sarmatarum gentilium, Regionis Samnitis.
Praefectus Sarmatarum gentilium, Bononiae in Aemilia.
Praefectus Sarmatarum gentilium, Quadratis et Eporizio [Transpadana].
Praefectus Sarmatarum gentilium, (in Liguria) Pollentia.[39]

The concentration of these prefects—and accordingly also the settlements of Sarmatians—was overwhelmingly in northern Italy.[40] There were three prefects who shared between them nearly all of southern Italy, while all the other prefects in Italy were assigned to individual northern towns.

Likewise, the placement of imperial treasuries in Italy, tied with the placement of earlier mints, shows those treasuries, essentially the financial support of the armies, concentrated in the north.[41] The *Notitia Dignitatum* lists:

Per Italiam:
Praepositus thesaurorum Aquileiensium, Venetiae.
Praepositus thesaurorum Mediolanensium, Liguriae.
Praepositus thesaurorum urbis Romae.
Praepositus thesaurorum Augustae Vindelicensis.[42]

Along with the settlement of barbarian auxiliaries and the establishment of the financial support structure for the armies, the location of arms factories within Italy further illustrates the reorientation of the region toward supporting the legions. The *Notitia Dignitatum*'s list of imperial arms factories in Italy reads:

Italiae:
Concordensis sagittaria.
Veronensis scutaria et armorum.
Mantuana loricaria.
Cremonensis scutaria.
Ticenensis arcuaria.
Lucensis spatharia.[43]

That these six factories were all located in northern towns along major roads again suggests that their purpose was to provide speedy and regular supply of arms to the army.[44] This redefinition of northern Italy into a support zone for the army is reflected in Diocletian's administrative division of Italy into two dioceses: *Italia annonaria*—consisting of the old Augustan regions of Picenum, Aemilia, Liguria, Venetia, Istria, and Transpadana, plus the Cottian Alps and Raetia—and *Italia suburbicaria*, which consisted of Etruria, Umbria, Campania, Apulia, Calabria, Lucania, Bruttium, Sicily, Corsica, and Sardinia.[45] The very names *Italia annonaria* and *Italia suburbicaria* implied different functions, with the wealthy north supplying the army and the capital and the center and south serving as extension of Rome's suburbs.[46]

The effects of these third-century changes on Ticinum and its inhabitants were pervasive and sustained. The bow factory at Ticinum, for example, affected the town's economy and society. This *fabrica* worked in concert with other arms factories in the region to supply the army. This meant, as it had with the mint, that specialized workers needed to be brought in to make the bows, procurement of raw materials organized, and a transportation system arranged to deliver the bows to the armies—in short, the creation of an entirely new industry as well as the incorporation of related industries, all of which were overseen by imperial officials.[47] This new industry would be visible even on the streets in Ticinum, since specialized arms makers, according to a 398 CE edict, were to be branded on their arms in the same way that military recruits were.[48]

The presence of these workers in the town had the potential to change the town's social dynamics: workers at similar *fabricae* at Caesarea and Adrianople were leading elements in late fourth-century riots in those towns, and even earlier in the 270s, the mint workers at Rome in their revolt had shown the potential danger to urban peace that large groups of imperial workers could pose.[49] Besides this potential for municipal violence, the presence of the guild of armorers in the town presented economic opportunities for Ticinum's inhabitants, who, providing that they could prove they were not of the decurial class and did not have any outstanding municipal debts, could join the guild of armorers and, tattoo aside, receive imperial pay and board courtesy of the *annona*.[50] A decree in the Theodosian Code recognizes the temptation that *fabrica* posed as a financial escape for a decurial class burdened by compulsory public benefactions and service. While the empire wanted to keep local decurions from fleeing their financial obligations, armorers once trained also needed to be kept in their positions, and once in the imperial service, neither armorers nor their children could change professions; anyone who took armorers or their children as farm overseers or tenants, for example, lost part of his land to the imperial fiscus.[51] The presence of this closely regulated imperial enterprise thus offered opportunities for the financially desperate but at the same time kept those who took advantage of those opportunities in something akin to imperial serfdom. The bow factory in Ticinum created stable but absolutely non-negotiable employment opportunities, an infusion of imperial and military officials, and a large, hereditary, and potentially disruptive class of bow makers.

Since Ticinum was part of a regionally based supply network for the court and the army, the town would also have seen goods from other state *fabricae* passing through on the roads connecting other towns with the army or the new imperial court at Mediolanum. For example, the state woolen factories, the *gynaecea*, produced clothing both for the court and for the armies.[52] In northern Italy there were two *procuratores gynaecii*, one for Mediolanum and Liguria and the other for Aquileia and Venetia.[53] Liguria, in particular, the Tanaro River Valley connecting to the Po about twenty miles west of Ticinum, had since at least the Early Empire been an important producer of woolen cloth, and most probably continued as such in the fourth century.[54] Ticinum would thus have been a natural transit point for wool and clothing traveling from Liguria to the court at Mediolanum and *gynaecea* throughout the region.

Proximity to the imperial court offered opportunities for advancement. Those connected with the court, the military, and the bureaucracy, as had been the case with the mint, were shuffled between the various places where the state had a strong controlling interest. One inscription at Ticinum, probably fourth-century, is an epitaph commemorating Valeria Vincentia, twenty-seven years old and for ten years, two months, and twenty-five days the wife of a Fabius Maianus, who brought her body back from Treviri for burial at her family home in Ticinum.[55] That she and her husband were in Treviri at all suggests that they were connected, either directly or indirectly, with the imperial bureaucracy or the court.[56]

Ticinum's proximity to the imperial seat at Mediolanum meant that the emperor's retinue, the *comitatus*, would have frequently passed through Ticinum.[57] Soldiers and officials attached to the *comitatus* had the right to quarter in homes, with a host of restrictions, such as bans on quartering in synagogues and prohibitions on quartering officials making demands for oil and wood.[58] Again this had a visual impact—if only temporary—on the town, as the names of those being quartered in each house were written on that home's doorposts.[59] The homes of armorers were, at least after 400 CE, exempt from compulsory quartering, although when the emperor and his *comitatus* were in town that exemption did not apply.[60] In civil war, such as that between Constantine and Maxentius in northern Italy in 312 CE, such restrictions may not have applied, especially for towns such as Augusta Taurinorum and Verona, which chose the losing side.[61] There is also the possibility that Ticinum, being close as it was to Mediolanum, would have had to house members of the imperial family or court who were out of favor, as nearby Comum did when the future emperor Julian was kept under guard there for several months in 354 and 355.[62]

Close connections with the centers of Roman power had their perils, too. The army mutiny following Honorius's arrival at Ticinum, in which Stilicho's supporters—Stilicho at the time was at Ticinum's equivalent in Aemilia, Bononia—and other high-ranking officials accompanying Honorius were killed; Zosimus records the emperor wandering in a panic through the streets of Ticinum without his imperial regalia.[63] The staging of the army at Ticinum in 408—it had been there in 405—also demonstrates why the town continued to be an important part of the state's support structure even after the western court transferred to Ravenna: the town's location on the Ticino River and on the roads leading across the western Alps made it an ideal location in which to prepare military operations in Gaul while still being relatively well-connected to the capital at Ravenna, and the existing infrastructure in Ticinum and in rest of the Po Valley facilitated supply of that army.[64] The importance that Ticinum acquired in the later third, fourth, and fifth centuries, an importance that was made possible by the greater military situation, also made it vulnerable. When Attila invaded northern Italy in 452, he sacked Ticinum along with the region's two most important towns, Mediolanum and Aquileia, the latter of which was so depopulated by the raid that Pope Leo was later asked to intercede on the matter of Aquileian men who had been taken into captivity by the Huns and returned to the city to find their wives remarried.[65]

Iulium Carnicum and Forum Iulii: The *Claustra Alpium Iuliarum*

Located in the foothills of the Carnic and Julian Alps north of Aquileia, Iulium Carnicum (Zuglio) and Forum Iulii (Cividale) had similar positions within the imperial system of the Early and High Empire. Both fell within Aquileia's economic orbit, and both were key posts on the trade between Aquileia and the Danube provinces. Iulium Carnicum, the more northerly, stood along a branch of the Tagliamento, the Bût, the valley of which created the Plöcken (1360 m).[66] This gave the settlement an important position along transalpine trade routes.

Natural passes like the Monte Croce Carnico / Plöcken Pass helped direct those routes and allowed favorably located communities such as Iulium Carnicum to prosper, but the Roman state had influence here as well. In order to facilitate transport of troops and supplies over the Alpine passes, co-emperors Valentinian and Valens reworked and resurfaced the route over the Plöcken Pass. A 373 CE inscription carved into the rock alongside the Roman road crossing the pass commemorates the construction:

> Munificentia D(ominorum trium) Aug(ustorum)que (duorum)
> n(ostrorum) hoc iter ubi homines et
> animalia cum periculo
> commeabant apertum est

curante Apinio Program-
matio cur(atore) r(ei) p(ublicae) Iul(iensium) Kar(norum)
D(ominis) n(ostris tribus) Valentiniano
Et Valente Aug(ustis duobus) IIII co(n)s(ulibus)[67]

By the munificence of the our three lords (Valentinian, Valens, and Gratian) and two *Augusti*, this route, where men and animals used to mix with danger, was opened, with Apinius Programmatius curator of Iulium Carnicum,[68] overseeing, with our three lords and two Augusti, Valentinian and Valens, as consuls for the fourth time.

This act of imperial roadbuilding as a benefaction was not a new phenomenon. In the first century CE the emperor Claudius had constructed the via Claudia Augusta over the Brenner Pass, partly to pay homage to his father, Drusus, partly to connect himself to the road-building Augustus, and partly to reinforce the political capital acquired from other boundary crossings.[69] Nor was this the first time the Roman state had turned its attention to this particular pass. In the later second century CE, Respectus, an imperial slave and official of the local customs station, in an inscription cut into the rock just to the side of the pass itself, commemorated a leveling and recutting of the road.[70]

What made Apinius Programmatus's work different from that of Respectus was that the fourth-century work was part of a larger program of fortification in the eastern Alps, the *Claustra Alpium Iuliarum*. Built to guard the passes in the vulnerable eastern Alps, third- and fourth- century emperors built three lines of forts and walls.[71] The largest fort and headquarters of the defensive system was at Ajdovščina, on the important road between Aquileia and Emona. Here work began in the 270s, during the first phase of construction for the Claustra.[72] This defensive system continued to be elaborated, with new forts, walls, and towers constructed throughout the fourth century.[73] At the southwestern end of this system was Forum Iulii, which received additional fortifications in the fourth century.[74]

Located on this new frontier, both Iulium Carnicum and Forum Iulii received some benefits from the imperial fortification and reorganization of the eastern Alps in the late third through fourth centuries. Iulium Carnicum had the Plöcken Pass, a major source for its earlier economic prosperity, renovated at the end of the fourth century, while the colony of Forum Iulii received fortifications similar to those built for much larger Italian cities.

The fortifications proved much more useful. Buildings at Iulium Carnicum show cycles of fire damage and rebuilding throughout the fourth century, and by the fifth century the population was shifting dramatically up to the nearby hilltop of Colle San Pietro.[75] The town's trade routes over the pass faced disruption from the civil wars of the later fourth century—the hazard of relying so heavily on one particular pass for economic livelihood. In contrast, Forum Iulii's walls helped ensure its continued importance in the fifth and sixth centuries, particularly after Attila's sack of Aquileia.[76]

The walls around Forum Iulii survived the dismantling of the Claustra Alpium Iuliarum as a whole. The Claustra proved to be a liability in civil wars of the later fourth century, when rival Roman armies were compelled to seize and hold the passes to gain control of Italy and the upper Danube. In the first decade of the fifth century, the fortifications were taken down, to the disastrous consequence in the Gothic invasions of the early fifth century.[77]

Yet while the Claustra, born out of the difficulties of the third century, did not last long into the fifth, its effects on the urban networks of the Friuli, as seen in the two towns of Iulium Carnicum and Forum Iulii, continued into at least the sixth century and the Lombard era. Luck played some role, since Attila could just have easily chosen to mete out to Forum Iulii the same destruction he gave similarly fortified Aquileia, but the infrastructure set up by the Roman state in the Friuli was just as decisive in establishing which towns continued on into the Gothic and Lombard eras and which towns retreated up the hills.

Mediolanum: Where the Men are Eloquent and the Houses Fine

In addition to demonstrating the need for defensive lines in the eastern Alps, the military difficulties of the 250s, 260s, and 270s proved the need for an emperor to be present with the army, as much for the psychological impact on the troops as for logistical advantage. Hence the emperor needed to be both more mobile and closer to the borders. Those needs lay behind the creation of the Tetrarchy, in which four emperors could better respond to military threats, and to the concurrent establishment of multiple imperial seats, not so much replacing Rome as supplementing it, creating places where the emperor and his *comitatus* could still be close to the borders and which could also supply the court.

In northern Italy Mediolanum—along with Sirmium, Antioch, and Treviri, in the provinces—became, beginning with Maximian at the end of the third century, a frequent imperial seat.[78] Mediolanum's selection as an imperial base was only part of a broader reorientation of northern Italy toward military security, and it is important to note that the city was part of a complicated regional network, with the emperor and court at Mediolanum supported by garrisons, arms factories, mints, and storehouses throughout towns along the roads of the Po Plain.[79]

Mediolanum remained an imperial seat from 286 to 402, during which time the city was transformed. The emperors based there built new city walls, new baths, a circus, and an imperial mausoleum.[80] Running through the city center was a two-storied, 600 m–long porticoed street, which linked the city walls to a triumphal arch.[81] Fourth-century writers gave special prominence to the monumental porticoed or colonnaded street in their orations, such as the late four-century *Ordo Urbium Nobilium*, in which the poet Ausonius described Mediolanum's urban virtues:

> And everything at Mediolanum is marvelous, and everything is plentiful;
> There are many fine houses, and the men are eloquent,
> Talented, and moral. Moreover the appearance of the place
> Is enhanced by double walls, a circus which is the delight of the people,
> The massive seats of the enclosed theater, temples, palaces, a wealthy mint,
> And an area of Hercules well known for its baths;
> And there are entire colonnades decorated with marble figures
> And encircling walls in the form of a fringed rampart.
> All the great works and enviable images there
> Are superior, nor is the nearness of Rome a burden.[82]

While Mediolanum was the more important imperial seat in four-century Italy, emperors and their courts could also be found, albeit much less frequently, at Aquileia, where a similar program of urban renovation occurred.[83]

At both Aquileia and Mediolanum, the effects of the emperor's court were not limited to the urban center. The presence of the emperor attracted a large group of elites, and elite culture required suitably picturesque country estates. Around Mediolanum the most suitable place was the shores of Lake Como, which had been home to the villas of elite Romans since the end of the first century BCE. The creation of an imperial capital at Mediolanum made that area more desirable, and consequently on lakes Como and Garda wealthy villas continued into the fifth century, when these villas saw decline and abandonment.[84] At the same time, the Roman government acted to ensure that productive agriculture was kept up so that the soldiers, officials, and bow makers could be fed, and the importation of barbarians to farm the land not only provided a ready-made militia but also made previously unfarmed land productive again.[85] Hence, in general in northern Italy, the fourth century saw a revival in rural agriculture;

areas subjected to field study have shown either stability or a relative increase in the number of rural sites.[86]

Ambrose's Mediolanum

Dramatic changes to Mediolanum were also brought about by the church, and particularly by its ambitious and vociferous fourth-century bishop, Ambrose.

Ambrose came from a senatorial family. His father was praetorian prefect of the Gauls when Ambrose was born at Trier; his brother managed the family estates in North Africa.[87] Ambrose received a typical elite education at Rome before being elected bishop of Mediolanum in 374.[88]

The bishopric that Ambrose occupied was one of political prominence. There is little evidence about bishops in third-century northern Italy, but by the 370s bishops are attested at Aquileia, Ariminum, Bononia, Brescia, Claterna, Comum, Mediolanum, Mutina, Parma, Patavium, Placentia, Ravenna, Ticinum, Tortona, Tridentum, and Vercellae—that is to say, nearly all of northern Italy's important towns.[89] These bishops—as well as the deacons, presbyters, monks, and other churchmen under them—constituted a new organized authority in the region, one paralleling that already established by the state.[90]

The elevation of Mediolanum to an imperial seat, for example, brought prestige to its religious leaders, and the bishops Auxentius and then Ambrose used their position in that town to influence church affairs in other towns.[91] An illustration can be found in the story of an unnamed bishop of Ticinum who found himself entrusted with a sum of cash by a local widow. When the widow went into debt, her creditor appealed to the secular authorities—to the *magister officiorum*—who then ordered the bishop to surrender the widow's money. The bishop in turn appealed to Ambrose, and after a conclave with Ambrose the bishop physically barred the authorities from retrieving the widow's money from its hiding place.[92] Worth noting in this story is that both parties, those in the church and in the imperial bureaucracy, appealed to their superiors—the *magister officiorum* to the emperor and the bishop at Ticinum to the more powerful bishop at Mediolanum. In the case of the former, the hierarchical relationship is clearly acknowledged by laws defining orders of precedence, but with the bishops the relationship is very much modeled on the perceived authority of their sees.

The hierarchical relationship between the two towns' churches is again demonstrated by Ambrose's ordination of bishops of other towns, including a bishop of Ticinum in 397 and Gaudentius in Brixia, the latter of whom, tellingly, brought back to his church saints' relics, both those that he picked up in Caesarea on pilgrimage and those of the saints of Mediolanum. Likewise, in Ticinum the basilicas of Saints Gervasius and Protasius and of Nazarius and Celsus were dedicated to Milanese martyrs.[93] That Ambrose found the relics of the first two martyrs in 386, in the midst of the bishop's quarrel with the emperor Valentinian over the latter's profession of Arianism, emphasizes the political nature of Ticinum's choice of new saints.[94] Relics of these saints given to Ticinum's churches were undoubtedly the personal gifts of Ambrose, and by accepting the relics the church authorities at Ticinum were showing loyalty to Ambrose at a time when the Milanese bishop was involved in a very public dispute with the emperor and his family. As with the Pavian widow's money, Ambrose used his position and authority to create and reinforce religious hierarchies, themselves highly politicized.[95]

As for the saints Nazarius and Celsus, found by Ambrose in Mediolanum in 395, around the time of the death of Theodosius, their exhumation provided a chance for Ambrose to demonstrate his authority—via an ability to produce miracle-making relics—at a time when his influence with the new emperor and court was not altogether certain.[96] For Ticinum, the acceptance of these latter two saints' relics illustrates the town's subordinate position within a regional religious hierarchy. This is not to say that that subsidiary position was never contested. The *Vita* of the bishop of Epiphanius, dating from the Ostrogothic period, claims that the people of Mediolanum were jealous that Ticinum had so pious and virtuous a bishop as Epiphanius.[97] This little taunt directed at Mediolanum suggests that, even in the Ostrogothic period more than a century after Mediolanum had ceased to be the imperial seat, the people of Ticinum still felt the need to assert their status against their neighbors at Mediolanum.

Ticinum was not the only town in Ambrose's sights. At Brixia, Ambrose secured the election of an otherwise unwilling Gaudentius as bishop by arranging for Brixia's Christian community to swear that they would accept only Gaudentius as their bishop.[98]

At Mediolanum itself, Ambrose was an enthusiastic church builder. Churches, such as that of San Tecla near the modern Duomo, had existed in Mediolanum before, but the scale of building under Ambrose was unprecedented.[99] The three great extramural churches of Sant'Ambrogio (originally the Basilica Martyrorum), San Simpliciano (originally the Basilica Virginum), and San Nazaro (Basilica Apostolorum), all started by Ambrose, laid claim to the older necropoleis outside the walls as Christian sacred spaces and highlighted Ambrose's use of martyrs' remains as political and religious capital. The Basilica Apostolorum, unattached to early Christian burials, was nevertheless connected to the great porticoed street linking the city gate to the triumphal arch and forum in the city center.[100] By its placement along this monumental *decumanus*, the church became part of the monumental entry into an imperial capital. The creation of large and elaborate churches along roads leading out of the city also paralleled the emperor Constantine's church-building activities in Rome at the beginning of the fourth century.[101]

Beneath the altar of Sant'Ambrogio, the bishop's first major project—and, by coincidence, the church into whose courtyard walls the surviving fragment of Pliny's great Como inscription was later embedded—Ambrose had placed Mediolanum's two newfound patron martyrs, Gervasius and Protasius. Gervasius and Protasius were key to Ambrose's ambitions for Mediolanum. In a letter he describes the June 386 discovery of the two martyrs:

> I ordered the area in front of the rails of Saints Felix and Nabor to be dug up. I found promising signs. When some persons were brought up on whom I was to perform the laying on of hands, the martyrs began to make their presence felt to such effect that instantly, without word from me, a woman was seized and flung headlong towards the site of the tomb. We found two men of amazing stature, such as were produced in the old days. All the bones were intact. There was an abundance of blood. There was a great thronging together of people throughout that two-day period . . . On the following day we transferred the relics to the basilica which is known as the Ambrosian. During the transfer a blind man was healed.[102]

The martyrs' usefulness extended beyond ophthalmology because, as Ambrose says, the new martyrs had "caused the church of Milan, once barren of martyrs, now the mother of numerous sons, to rejoice in the glory and examples of their passion."[103] Ambrose then declared, not without some subsequent public outcry, that he himself would be buried alongside Gervasius and Protasius underneath Sant'Ambrogio's altar.[104]

Ambrose's promotion of Gervasius and Protasius was not entirely self-serving. At Rome, Pope Damasus had also promoted the cults of martyrs, and Rome had far more martyrs' bones to capitalize on than did Mediolanum.[105] Rome, moreover, had the benefactions of Constantine, who had been stingy in gifts to Mediolanum. Ambrose and Mediolanum were competing with Rome and its similarly ambitious bishops. Such interurban competition had been the outstanding feature of the Roman Empire, and in Late Antiquity it took new form in competitive church construction and martyr promotion. Like the Younger Pliny's euergetism in Como 250 years earlier, Ambrose's construction program was a product both of his time and of his own particular political ambitions and forceful personality.

Tergeste: Urban Reactions

Urban development in four-century Mediolanum was politicized, but it could be argued that Mediolanum and Ambrose were exceptions, uniquely successful in establishing their authority and preeminence. How, therefore, did a town with less forceful advocates or with less access to the imperial court fare in the fourth century?

The town of Tergeste, located at the border of Istria, provides one example. During the Early Empire Tergeste, otherwise remarkable mostly for being a pun in a satirical pig's will, followed a developmental pattern typical of northern Italy.[106] As a base for Augustus's campaigns in Illyria, the town received a new set of walls from the triumvir in 33–32 BCE.[107] In the late Augustan or early Tiberian period, the town began to develop past the limits of those walls, and by the end of the first century CE parts of the triumviral-era walls were already in disuse.[108] Throughout the first and second centuries the town expanded and became increasingly monumental. A theater, a temple to Magna Mater, and port facilities increased the town's profile, although it remained in the shadow of its more prosperous neighbor at Aquileia, just 41 km away.[109] Unlike most other towns in northern Italy, Tergeste occupied the summit of a hill, and efforts were made in the early empire to shore up and terrace the Colle San Giusto, at the top of which was the town's forum. Around the same time, maritime villas were built along the coast between Tergeste and Aquileia.[110]

In the third century, the town's urban area contracted. Terraced structures leading up to the Colle San Giusto were abandoned, and in their place were burials.[111] There are signs of revival at the end of the fourth century, when northern Italy was reconfigured as a defensive and administrative zone. Statues of the tetrarchs and their *numines*, or their divine power, were set up at Miramare, on the outskirts of Tergeste.[112] Later in the fourth century Tergeste received a new set of walls.[113]

In the middle of the fifth century a church was built on the Colle San Giusto next to the Roman forum.[114] In contrast with Mediolanum's churches, it is unclear who built Tergeste's early church. There are no bishops recorded before the sixth century, although priests are attested as leaders of the Christian community.[115] While invasions and wars greatly damaged Aquileia, Tergeste seems to have weathered the tumult of the fifth century relatively well. Construction and maintenance of the town's defenses, churches, and port facilities continued on a consistent level from the fourth to the early sixth century.[116]

Tergeste did not benefit as greatly as did Mediolanum or Aquileia from imperial attention in the fourth century, nor is there evidence of any active episcopal presence promoting the town. Tergeste could not dig up a pair of martyrs like Gervasius and Protasius to lend the city luster; of Tergeste's two patron saints, Justus and Sergius, one was imported. Yet as part of a larger defensive network, Tergeste's urban fabric was developed and maintained in Late Antiquity.

Ravenna

Back on the western shores of the Adriatic, Ravenna's infrastructure was similarly developed. In the fifth century, the town became a frequent base for the Roman emperors. This is not to say that Ravenna became the new capital in the west, as has sometimes been claimed.[117] Emperors continued to spend time and hold celebrations in Rome, still important as the symbolic heart of the empire. Emperors and their courts are still attested as visiting other northern Italian cities: Mediolanum, Ticinum, Placentia, and Dertona.[118] These visits, however, were mostly made in a military context. Even Mediolanum, which had been so important in the fourth century as a center of the imperial court, witnessed no significant imperial ceremonies.[119]

The emperors based at Ravenna protected it further. New walls were built and the port renovated.[120] The fifth-century city benefitted from imperial patronage. Ravenna became the chief city of the northern Adriatic as Aquileia, no longer an imperial base and still suffering from its disastrous sack by Attila in 452, declined. By the sixth century even Aquileia's episcopal seat had been moved to Grado, the island just to Aquileia's south, where many of the town's refugees had fled.[121]

At Ravenna the imperial court glorified themselves in the mosaics of new churches, such as that of San Giovanni Evangelista, which before its sixteenth-century renovation bore portraits of the emperors Arcadius and Theodosius II and their wives, Eudoxia and Eudocia, on its apse and of Saint John the Evangelist saving Galla Placidia and her children at sea on the apse arch.[122] As with Ambrose's church-building at Mediolanum, Galla Placidia's construction of San Giovanni Evangelista at Ravenna had political benefits. The mosaic program highlighted her generosity and symbolically elevated her place within the imperial family, and the inclusion of Eudocia and Eudoxia made a claim for the importance of the women of the imperial family. These politicized mosaics highlight a key difference between Ravenna and towns like Tergeste, which, while important to the overall defensive network, were not bastions of the imperial court. While both Tergeste and Ravenna were fortified and protected, Ravenna's churches were more generously endowed and were adorned as much as political monuments as religious structures.

As imperial power in the Western Roman Empire collapsed in the second half of the fifth century, Ravenna found new patrons in post-Roman Italy's new Gothic rulers. In 490 CE King Odoacer took refuge in the city as Ostrogothic king Theoderic invaded Italy from the Balkans.[123] After three years of siege, Odoacer and Theoderic reached a settlement, mediated by Ravenna's local bishop, and Theoderic entered Ravenna to begin a joint and equal rule with Odoacer.[124] Days later, Theoderic invited Odoacer to a banquet and killed him with his own hands.[125]

After further conquests in the 490s and early 500s, Theoderic was in control of most of Italy and the Balkans. He embarked upon a building program in Rome and a few strategic Italian cities, including Ravenna, Verona, and Ticinum, all of which were important centers associated with late Roman imperial power.[126] Theodoric was, at least in terms of his euergetism, portraying himself in the mold of Late Roman emperors, but there were limits to that emulation.[127] He chose to use the title *rex* ("king") instead of *imperator* ("emperor") and, with the exception of one special issue, minted coins in the name of the emperors of the Eastern Roman Empire.[128] While he gave benefactions to Rome, he chose Verona, Ticinum, and especially Ravenna as royal seats.[129] He set foot in Rome only once.[130]

At Ravenna, Theoderic rebuilt a fourth-century palace to act as the center of his court. This redecorated palace included a large audience hall, a *triclinium* (dining room) whose mosaic floor showed Bellerophon and the Chimaera, and an equestrian statue of Theoderic in front of the entrance.[131] Another palace mosaic showed female personifications of Rome and Ravenna, the latter with one foot on land and one in the sea.[132] Next to the palace was Sant'Apollinare Nuovo, whose magnificent sixth-century mosaic decorations on the nave walls still survive. Among scenes from the New Testament and processions of martyrs and saints, the mosaics show Ravenna's port at Classe and the palace of Theoderic. The mosaic depiction of the palace was originally filled with figures of the court and altered after the city's reconquest by the Eastern Roman Empire to remove traces of Ostrogothic rule.[133] Of Theoderic's mosaic court only disembodied hands remain (fig. 13).

In addition to his patronage of Ravenna's churches, Theoderic built new porticoes and restored an aqueduct built under Trajan.[134] Just outside the city he

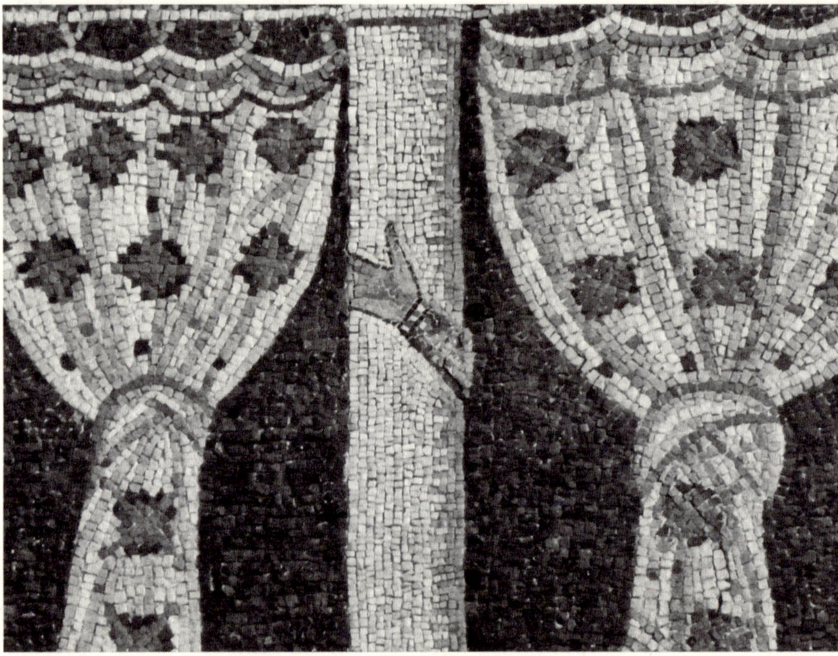

Figure 13. Detail of mosaic from Sant'Apollinare Nuovo. Depiction of Theoderic's palace. Photograph by author.

drained marshes and installed orchards.[135] In emulation of imperial mausolea at Rome, Constantinople, Thessalonica, and Mediolanum, he built a mausoleum for himself in a Roman necropolis near Ravenna's lighthouse, which had most likely been built under Augustus or Claudius, two rulers who, like Theoderic, stressed their dominance of land and sea.[136]

Theoderic's patronage of Ravenna and his placement there of his personal mausoleum was matched by inattention to Rome. While Theoderic sponsored building projects in the city, these were overmatched by his benefactions in Ravenna, Verona, Ticinum, and Parma.[137] While Rome had in the Republic and Empire been the city that most influenced development in northern Italy, now northern Italian cities diverted imperial patronage from Rome and influenced that city's development. Theoderic's reign was yet another step in the dissolution of an Italy ruled from Rome. Even Honorius, whom contemporary historians criticized for retreating to Ravenna while Rome was under threat in 408, chose to build his mausoleum in Rome, not Ravenna.[138]

Yet while Theoderic's choice of Ravenna as the site of his mausoleum suggests that city's primacy, other cities in the older Late Antique network of imperial cities served as bases for Theoderic's wandering court. Mediolanum was an important minting center, and Dertona's warehouses served an important resource for the Gothic court.[139] Verona seems to have had particularly strong connections to the court; Theoderic strengthened the city's defenses and for a time, between 519 and 524, ruled there.[140] Theoderic's *magister officiorum* (the high-ranking "master of offices") Boethius was tried in Verona and imprisoned just outside Ticinum.[141] Thus, while primacy in northern Italy was contested by Mediolanum, Ravenna, and Ticinum from the third to the early sixth century, the network of towns and cities set up by the Roman state in response to the challenges of the third century proved remarkably durable.

After the Ostrogoths

War between the Ostrogoths and the Eastern Roman Empire followed Theoderic's death. To illustrate the destructiveness of these sixth-century CE wars, Procopius—panegyrist, scholar, and extremely disgruntled courtier—recounted the story of the Ostrogothic king Theodohad, who, upon the advice of a Jewish astrologer, shut up three groups of ten pigs in three huts for days without food. In order to predict how the war with the Byzantines would go, Theodohad was advised to label one of the porcine groups as Byzantines, the second as Ostrogoths, and the third as Italians. Upon reopening the huts it was discovered that most of the Byzantine pigs had survived, all but two of the Gothic pigs had died, and of the Italian pigs half had died and the surviving half had shed their bristles.[142]

For Procopius the fate of the "Italian" pigs predicted the devastating impact of the extended wars of reconquest on Italy.[143] Many smaller communities, such as Aquae Statiellae, had shrunk considerably during the sixth century, while even larger, fortified towns, like Verona, showed widespread abandonment of buildings.[144] As in the earlier wars of the late third century, and even earlier in the Alemannic incursion during the reign of Marcus Aurelius, plague accompanied warfare and came in waves in the early 540s (the Justinianic Plague), the 570s, the 580s, and again at the beginning of the seventh century.[145] To this Paul the Deacon adds serious flooding along the Po and its tributaries, as well as general famine throughout Italy.[146]

Mediolanum's fate was the most brutal. In 539 CE the Goths sacked the city in punishment for the city's support of the Eastern Roman Empire. They massacred Mediolanum's male population and sold the women and children off to the Burgundians; Procopius claims that in the process more than 300,000 Milanese were killed.[147] While Procopius's tally is probably exaggerated, even at a tenth of the total the sack would have been a demographic disaster for the town, although the town seems to have recovered somewhat by the Lombard period.[148]

Mediolanum's sack meant that Ticinum was for a time the preeminent fortified settlement in the region. Accordingly, Ticinum was able to maintain many of the amenities built by the Romans and the Ostrogoths, including its extensive drain system.[149] When the Lombards under Alboin invaded Italy in 568, Ticinum was a valuable prize, and the Lombards spent three years besieging it. By the time the Lombards arrived, Paul the Deacon, writing in the eighth century, records:

> The city of Ticinum, after withstanding the siege for three years and a few months, surrendered itself to Alboin and to the besieging Lombards. When Alboin entered it from the eastern side of the city through the gate of St. John, his horse fell in the middle of the gate, and, although goaded by kicks and afterwards hit by the whacks of spears, could not be made to stand. Then one of the Lombards said to the king: "'Remember my lord king, what promise you have made. Break so harsh a vow and you will enter the city, for there is a truly Christian people in this city." Alboin had vowed that he would put all the people to the sword because they had been unwilling to surrender. He broke this vow and promised clemency to the people, and then his horse immediately rose, and he entered the city, and he did not inflict harm on anyone but kept his promise. Then all the people, thronging around Alboin in the palace that king Theoderic had built, after so many troubles began to feel relieved, trusting in hope for the future.[150]

The Lombards subsequently made their capital at Ticinum, where they built churches and monasteries, enlarged the palace complex, and stocked their court with scholars like Paul the Deacon; in doing so the Lombard kings set the town up as a rival to Ravenna and Constantinople, as the Carolingians were later to do at Aachen.[151] The Lombard choice of Ticinum as capital was based largely on the infrastructure established there by the Romans and the Ostrogoths, whose use of the town as an imperial base and subsidiary capital also lent the town and its Lombard heirs a useful legitimacy, as also seen in Alboin's use of Theoderic's palace.

Ravenna, under Byzantine exarchs for most of the period between 600 and 750, navigated a careful course between the demands of an often disinterested Eastern Empire and those of the papacy and the Italian aristocracy; in 755 the city passed into the hands of the papacy, a reversal of the two cities' Ostrogothic fortunes.[152] At the end of the eighth century Ravenna's churches and palaces impressed Charlemagne, who used them as a model—and sometimes as a source of marble—for new construction at his court at Aachen. Even Theoderic's equestrian statue in front of the palace was shipped off to Aachen, where it was repurposed for new political uses.[153] The eighth and ninth centuries underwent some urban revival, but regional networks remained rudimentary, and the connectivity of early-medieval northern Italy did not match that of its Roman predecessor.[154]

At Ravenna, Ticinum, and throughout northern Italy, the urban fabric of the Roman era was adapted and repurposed throughout the sub-Roman and early medieval world. Even into the Renaissance, the Roman past both guided urban forms and could itself be manipulated by contemporary political interests to create civic identities. For example, by 1368 CE Verona's Roman-era forum had developed into the Piazza delle Erbe, where the city, then under the rule of the fratricidal Della Scala family, held its fruit and vegetable market.[155] In that year Cansignorio della Scala ornamented a fountain in the center of the piazza with a second-century CE Roman statue, newly refurbished with head, arms, and a bronze streamer bearing a Latin motto proclaiming: "This city is the bearer of justice and the lover of fame."[156] That statue came to symbolize the city itself as "Madonna Verona." On the north end of the piazza, a street followed the old *decumanus maximus*, itself a segment of the via Postumia of 148 BCE, through the Porta Borsari, a first-century CE gate reinscribed in the third century with an inscription of the emperor Gallienus. A road leading from the east end of the Piazza delle Erbe led to Santa Maria Antica, which housed the elaborate Gothic tombs of the Della Scala and which had been rebuilt on the site of a seventh-century Lombard church. Built into the walls of the church was part of a Roman funerary monument (fig. 14). A street on the west led down to the old Roman arena, still used for tournaments in the fourteenth century.

Conclusions

Fernand Braudel, in his history of the Mediterranean in the age of Philip II in the sixteenth century, described a landscape in the northern Italian region of Lombardy that dictated its history, one in which plains experienced growing land reclamation and growing social misery, as wealthy landowners used their resources to build canals and establish vast rice fields that exploited peasant laborers.[157] Braudel describes this as a slow, long-term change, started by twelfth-century monks and continued by sixteenth-century aristocrats, but above all predicted by the geography. Braudel compares the Po Plain to the plains of Spain, Portugal,

Figure 14. Roman funerary monument in Santa Maria Antica, Verona, with Roman inscription. Photograph by author.

Campania, and the Balkans and contrasts them with the forests and mountains of northern Europe.[158] In this model, the plains produced "large estates and serf villages," whereas the forests, more easily and cheaply exploited than the large plains, empowered enterprising farmers and produced freer societies.[159]

In the plains of Roman northern Italy, a different model emerges, again largely as a result of the region's place within the larger Roman world. The plains north and south of the Po River are not drastically different, but Roman preferences and concerns led to the Roman state's treating the Aemilia quite differently from the Transpadana during the Roman Republic. While large estates were a key feature of the Roman-era landscape, so too were small farms, wool merchants, and transalpine networks of enterprising freedmen. Freedmen and freeborn are more equally represented in the *collegia* of northern Italy than in central and southern Italy, and social mobility was a real, if limited, feature of an interconnected urban and rural life. In northern Italy an irrigated and canalized plain did not create a landscape of serfs.

This is not to minimize the importance of the region's geography but rather to argue that such importance stemmed not just from particular geographical features —plains, foothills, coasts, rivers, and mountains—but also from northern Italy's place within a larger world system, namely, a position between Europe, peninsular Italy, and the Mediterranean. Northern Italy was a lynchpin in trade networks between all three, from the Bronze Age through the Roman Empire and beyond, and this intermediate position also helped determine northern Italy's place within the Roman world.

Northern Italy was part of the Roman Empire for seven hundred years. During those years the region's landscape, culture, society, and economy changed dramatically. Roman roads shaped urban networks for centuries. Colonization, immigration, veteran settlement, expulsions, and population transfers remade the human landscape. Latin replaced Italic, Celtic, and Venetic dialects and became the foundation not only of northern Italy's regional languages—such as Venetian, Friulian, Piedmontese, Ligurian, and Lombard—but also of the standard Italian that replaced them in the nineteenth and early twentieth centuries. New gods and sheep were imported, syncretized, and themselves exported.

Nor was change unidirectional. The Transpadani shaped Late Republican politics, while at the same time Vergil and the neoteric poets changed Roman literature. One of northern Italy's inhabitants, Livy, defined Roman history itself.

The Roman state treated the region differently across time, with three distinct phases emerging: (1) a period of invasive but unevenly applied state intervention, from the Roman conquest to the Augustan era, (2) a period of relatively hands-off governance, from the Augustan era to the third century CE, and (3) a return of direct, frequent, and invasive state intervention, in the third through fifth centuries. In the first and third phases, the impact of the Roman state was clear and pronounced, and the effects of the Roman state in the second phase, while largely indirect, were just as pervasive.

The sustained level of those effects across seven hundred years was partially a result of northern Italy's place within a larger imperial system, a shifting and interconnected Roman world in which legions, consumer cities, and administration pulled people and goods across the Europe and the Mediterranean world.

Even when the Roman government was not physically moving people down from the hills to the plains as it was in the Middle Republic, the pull of Rome and the borders nevertheless produced population movements of their own.

The long-term reshaping of northern Italy, however, should not solely be ascribed to the slow and sustained pull of Rome and the militarized borders. Rather, lasting changes also had their origins in the relatively sudden shifts of imperial policy, as in the late first century BCE or in the 270s CE, or in the actions of individuals.

Within the historiography of the Mediterranean, a distinction has been made between a history *of* a region and history *in* a region, with the former being the history of a region as a geographical unit and the latter meaning events happening within that unit.[160] It is this author's view that the two histories are not distinct, that in this case the history *of* northern Italy cannot be separated from history *in* northern Italy. Events dictated by political needs of a particular decade, year, or month, such as the creation of new imperial seats or of new administrative configurations for Italy, had long-term consequences. Individual personalities could and did have a lasting impact, as Ambrose of Milan ably demonstrates. Pliny the Younger's unique political circumstances after the emperor Domitian's assassination altered the urban fabric of Novum Comum, and the renovation of his image in his letters established long-lasting architectural ideals that found expression around Lake Como in the sixteenth century. The history of northern Italy is inextricably tied to its history in the Roman era, and the concept of northern Italy as a unified region, was itself a Roman creation, the product of particular eras, particular politics, and particular fears and ambitions.

Notes

Preface

1. On the history of this debate, see Mattingly 2011.
2. Braudel (1949) 1972 Horden and Purcell 2000.

CHAPTER ONE. **Northern Italy before the Romans**

1. Livy 1.1. Trans. De Sélincourt.
2. De Marinis 1997, 405.
3. An argument might also be made for the Late Neolithic, with the increase in the numbers of alpine rock drawings—some depicting settlements—and monumental stelae (De Saulieu 2013, Arcà 1997).
4. The chronology of the Bronze Age can be daunting, since different dating systems are used for different regions across Eurasia and since, within regions, there are still lingering disputes over the absolute dates of relative chronologies (hence, for example, the "high" and "low" chronologies of Aegean prehistory, which offer two timelines based on two competing dates for the volcanic eruption at Thera). When possible in this chapter, I use both the relative chronology for the Italian Bronze Age (with the "Ancient," "Middle," "Recent," and "Final" Bronze ages), as well as absolute dates derived from radiocarbon dating and dendrochronology, with the caveat that the latter are approximate and are subject to future recalibration. For a discussion of Bronze Age chronologies, see Kristiansen and Larsson 2005, 116–118. Recent overviews of the Bronze Age in northern Italy can be found in Bietti Sestieri 2010 and Nicolis 2013.
5. Bietti Sestieri 2010, 21–25.
6. Menotti 2004, 2; Baioni et al. 2004, 311
7. Pauli 1999, 227.
8. Bietti Sestieri 2010, 25–26; Nicolis 2013, 696.
9. Bietti Sestieri 2010, 47–52; Nicolis 2013, 696.
10. Nicolis 2013, 696; Baioni et al. 2004, 312.
11. Nicolis 2013, 695.
12. See Bernarbò Brea, Cardarelli, and Cremaschi 1997c, 23, on the evolution of the term *marna*, which originally was applied to mineral fertilizer before being applied to the deposits of heavily nitrous, organic dark earth important to Emilian agriculture in the eighteenth and nineteenth centuries. The term *Terramare* became more commonly used to describe the Bronze Age settlements and people of the Po Plain in the 1930s, after just over a century of study of the archaeological remains present in those deposits of earth.

13. Cardarelli 2010, 450.

14. De Marinis 1997, 416; Bernarbò Brea 2009, 11.

15. Nicolis 2013, 695.

16. Cremaschi, Pizzi, and Valsecchi 2006, 89–90; Cremaschi 1997, 111. The average settlement density is 1 per 25 km² (Bernarbò Brea 2009, 11). Cardarelli (2010, 460) puts the population density at fourteen persons per square kilometer, with one inhabitant per hectare of cultivated land.

17. Cremaschi 2009, 36.

18. Cremaschi 2009, 37.

19. Cremaschi, Pizzi, and Valsecchi 90–92.

20. The findings are catalogued in Bernarbò Brea and Cremaschi 2009.

21. De Grossi Mazzorin 2009, 170.

22. Pearce 1998, 744.

23. Bernarbò Brea 2009, 12.

24. Cremaschi, Pizzi, and Valsecchi 2006, 90.

25. Cardarelli 2010, 467.

26. Cremaschi, Pizzi, and Valsecchi 2006, 91–93.

27. Cremaschi, Pizzi, and Valsecchi 2006, 91.

28. On the collapse of the Terramare, see Cardarelli 2010 and Bernarbò Brea, Cardarelli, and Cremaschi 1997b.

29. Cremaschi, Pizzi, and Valsecchi 2006, 91–94.

30. On the possible connection between the two events, see De Marinis 1997. See also Drews 1993 for a survey of the collapse in the Eastern Mediterranean.

31. Pearce 2007, 106–107.

32. Bernarbò Brea 2009, 13; Bietti Sestieri 1997a.

33. De Marinis 1997, 418.

34. Bietti Sestieri 2010, 52.

35. Mihovilić 2012, 411. For an example at Castellazzo in the Friuli, see Montagnari Kokelj 1989, 23–24.

36. Bietti Sestieri 2010, 43–46.

37. Peretto 2010, 102. Calzolari 2007 surveys the basic geography and provides comparison with the Roman period.

38. Mihovilić 2012, 427. It should be noted that the chronological system used for the later Bronze Age and Early Iron Age in Istria is different from those systems used in the rest of northern Italy, central Europe, and Croatia; for a comparison, see Mihovilić 2012, 413.

39. See Kristiansen 2000, 63, on the connection between Urnfield and Villanovan areas. Bietti Sestieri 2012, 249, provides a discussion of the use of the term *Villanovan*, while Pearce 1994, 46–49, surveys proto-Villanovan developments around Milan.

40. Bietti Sestieri 2012, 253–254; see Balista et al. 1996 for the Veneto in particular.

41. The initial excavations at Frattesina, started in 1967 and conducted through the 70s, have been supplemented by studies in the same commune and in the surrounding areas, notably at the Bronze and Early Iron Age settlements at Mariconda, Recenta, Gognano, Michela, Campestrin, and Saline and at the necropoleis at Narde, Fondo Zanotto, and Frassinelle (Peretto 2010).

42. Peretto 2010, 15–18.

43. It is probable that the channel is the same as the Fossa Filistina; cf. Plin. *HN* 3.121 and Calzolari 2004.

44. Towle et al. 2001, 10; Balista, Bonfatti, and Calzolari 2007.

45. Towle et al. 2001, 10.

46. Bietti Sestieri 2012, 259–261; Gonzato 2010. On glass pieces at Frattesina, see Towle et al. 2001.

47. Mycenaean-type pottery at Frattesina, Mycenaean-type pottery in southern Italy, Mycenaean-type pottery in la Marche: Pearce 2007, 103.

48. Braccesi 2001, 48.

49. Angelini 2010; Angelini and Bellintani 2005.

50. Angelini 2010, 141. The identity of southern Italian amber finds has not been conclusively established as succinite.

51. Angelini 2010, 141. The amber from the Palafitte site at Fiavè has been identified as succinite.

52. Angelini 2010, 141–143; Bietti Sestieri 2012, 260; Negroni Catacchio, Massari, and Raposso 2006.

53. Bietti Sestieri 2012, 261.

54. Bietti Sestieri 1997b, 378.

55. Malnati 1996, 181–184.

56. Malnati 1996, 182–183; Sassatelli 2004, 172.

57. Maggiani 2004, 161–163.

58. Fletcher 2007, 67. As Ramsl 2014 notes, some of these north-south connections were indirect rather than direct.

59. Blake 2014 dates the formation of these group identities even earlier, to the Middle Bronze Age.

60. Malnati 1996, 184–187.

61. Lomas 2009, 14.

62. D'Ercole 2011, 438. Braccesi 2004 discusses these Greek connections within a broader chronological context.

63. D'Ercole 2011, 436–437.

64. Briquel 1998.

65. Malnati 1996, 184–187; Capuis 2004, 139; Gambari 263. See Lomas 2009, 13–15 and Boaro 2001, 154–163 on urban development in the Iron Age Veneto.

66. To this very short list might be added Verucchio, in the far southeastern Romagna, and a cluster of smaller sites around Verucchio and Bologna. For surveys of sites with Etruscan materials in the Po Plain, see Sassatelli and Govi 2013 as well as Sassatelli 2008 and 1991.

67. Mandolesi 2009, 27–49. See also Wells 1980, 131.

68. Verucchio: Sassatelli, and Govi 2013, 289–290. Felsina: Sassatelli and Govi 2013, 283–288. Etruscan influence and imports, however, covered a broader area.

69. Livy 5.33.

70. Livy 1.1.

71. The incorporation of the Veneti into Greek mythological traditions was not a unicum in northern Italy. Häussler 2013, 147, points to a passage in Pliny the Elder's *Natural*

History for evidence of a similar tradition about the Lepontii, the Iron Age people living around Mediolanum and the lakes. Pliny (*HN* 3.134) says the Lepontii were considered to have been followers of Hercules who were so slowed down by freezing legs on their Alpine crossing that Hercules left them behind.

72. Sisenna F1, discussed in Cornell 2013, 368. For a full discussion of the Antenor legend, see Braccesi 1984.

73. Polyb. 2.17.4–7: περὶ τὰς ἀνατολὰς τοῦ Πάδου κείμενα Λάοι καὶ Λεβέκιοι, μετὰ δὲ τούτους Ἴνσοβρες κατῴκησαν, ὃ μέγιστον ἔθνος ἦν αὐτῶν· ἑξῆς δὲ τούτοις παρὰ τὸν ποταμὸν Γονομάνοι.τὰ δὲ πρὸς τὸν Ἀδρίαν ἤδη προσήκοντα γένος ἄλλο πάνυ παλαιὸν διακατέσχεν· προσαγορεύονται δ' Οὐένετοι, τοῖς μὲν ἔθεσικαὶ τῷ κόσμῳ βραχεῖ διαφέροντες Κελτῶν, γλώττῃ δ' ἀλλοίᾳ χρώμενοι. περὶ ὧν οἱ τραγῳδιογράφοι πολύν τινα πεποίηνται λόγον καὶ πολλὴν διατέθεινται τερατείαν. ται τερατείαν. τὰ δὲ πέραν τοῦ Πάδου τὰ περὶ

τὸν Ἀπεννῖνον πρῶτοι μὲν Ἄναρες, μετὰ δὲ τού- τους Βοῖοι κατῴκησαν· ἑξῆς δὲ τούτων ὡς πρὸς τὸν Ἀδρίαν Λίγγονες, τὰ δὲ τελευταῖα πρὸς θαλάττῃ Σήνωνες.

74. Polyb. 2.17.10.

75. Gambari and Bondini 2013, 156–160; Ruta Serafini 2001.

76. On the chronological and geographic distribution of Celtic mercenaries in literary sources, see Baray 2014, 18–19. Baray 2014, 27–162, carefully and critically surveys material evidence for Celtic mercenaries around the Mediterranean.

77. On the *dies Alliensis*, marking the Roman defeat at the battle of the Allia, see Livy 6.1.11. The suspension of laws in case of a Gallic invasion is provided for in the Urso Charter: *CIL* II 5439. On the effects of Roman fear of the Gauls, see Williams 2001a, 170–182.

78. See Wells 2014, 313–314, on the distinction the problem in assuming a uniform material culture for "Celts," "Germans," and "Romans." Arslan 1976–8, 451–452, demonstrates a similar difficulty in determining Celticity in Lombardy; see Arslan 2001 for difficulties along the Adriatic coast.

79. Polyb. 2.17, Livy 5.35. On similar narratives in Plutarch, Diodorus Sicilus, and the anonymous *Tractatus de Mulieribus Claris in Bello*, see Péré-Noguès 2014, 146–147.

80. De Marinis 2009, 38.

81. Morandi 2004, 572 (Morandi no. 77); Agostinetti 2004, 82.

82. Häussler 2000, 140.

83. Häussler 2007, 52–54; Curina et al. 2015, 42.

84. On Iron Age periodization and the chronology of La Tène phases and material culture, see Agostinetti et al. 2014, 38–39.

85. Häussler 2007, 53.

86. On the Celts at Marzabotto: Kruta 1999, 220. On Celtic Bononia, see Sassatelli 2005.

87. Agostinetti 2004, 98–102.

88. Vitali 2003, 24–36.

89. Häussler 2007, 53–54.

90. Vitali 2004, 317–318; Häussler 2007, 54. Nor are all characteristically La Tène objects represented in more predominantly "Celtic" areas. For example, torques are rare in

funerary assemblages in the southern Po Plain, even though Livy (36.40) records a Roman triumph over the Boii bringing back 1,471 golden torques (Vitali 2008).

91. Häussler 2007, 53–54.

92. Vitri 2001, 32–33.

93. Vannazzi Lunazzi 2001, 160.

94. Kruta 1999, 206–219.

95. Arnold 2012, 91; see Sheeres et al. 2013 on the mobility of Monte Bibele's population.

96. Curina et al. 2015, 42–45, surveys the population of northern Italy in the third century BCE.

97. Agostinetti 2004, 82–83.

98. Gaggero 2004; Malnati 2004.

CHAPTER TWO. The Roman Conquest

1. On the chronology and nature of the campaigns in Cisalpine Gaul, see Williams 2001b, David 1997, Peyre 1979.

2. Polyb. 2.19, Livy 10.27–29, Dio 21.6, Zonar. 8.1.

3. Polyb. 2.19, App. *Gall.* 11.3.

4. Just. *Epit.* 24.4–8, Livy 38.16–17, Polyb. 4.46, Paus. 10.19.

5. Conspicuous examples can be found in Plut. *Pyrrh.* 26.6, Paus. 1.13.2, Dio 55.70.1, Xen. *Hell.* 7.1.20. A more thorough study of material evidence for mercenary activity by Celtic speakers in the Mediterranean can be found in Baray 2014, who also provides a survey of scholarship going back to Mommsen (10).

6. 282 and 281 BCE battles: Polyb. 2.20, Livy *Per.* 12, Frontin. *Str.* 1.2

7. Polyb. 2.22. The causes of the Telamon campaign have been a source of recent debate, on which see Erdkamp 2009 and Eckstein 2012.

8. A votive deposit of arms and agricultural instruments found at Telamon and dating to the third century may be related to the battle (Michelucci 1985), as might the portrayal of the Seven against Thebes on the pediment relief of a local temple (Von Vacano 1975).

9. Polyb. 2.32–34, Livy *Per.* 20, Zonar. 8.20.

10. Plut. *Marc.* 6–7.

11. The rarity of these *spolia* is celebrated in Prop. 4.10.

12. Plut. *Marc.* 8.2–3; cf. Livy 27.25 on Marcellus's difficulty in fulfilling a vow to dedicate a temple to Honos and Virtus.

13. Plut. *Marc.* 8.6.

14. Plut. *Marc.* 7.5: "καί τούτοις μὲν ἦν εἰρήνη μετρίων τυχοῦσι."

15. Livy 21 passim, esp. 21.25 and 21.55, Polyb. 3.40, Zonar. 8.24.

16. On the return of Cenomani in 197 BCE: Livy 32.29–31, Zonar. 9.16; defeat and treaty with Insubres in 196 BCE: Livy 33.36; campaigns and defeat of the Boii: Livy 35.40, Livy 36.37–38, Oros. 4.20, Zonar. 9.19.

17. Cic. *Brut.* 78. See Ciampoltrini 2004, Gambaro 1999, Harris 1985, 225ff, on the chronology of the campaigns.

18. C. Sempronius Tuditanus, cos. 129, is recorded with victories over the Istri (Pliny *HN* 3.129, *Inscr. Ital.* 13.3.90). The Istrian attack on Tergeste: Caes. *B Gall.* 8.24.

19. For surveys of the history of Cisalpine Gaul in the Republican period, see Williams 2001b, Torelli 1998 (on the Transpadana), David 1997, Ausbüttel 1989, Chevallier 1983, Peyre 1979.

20. Polyb. 2.15.

21. Varro *Rust.* 2.4.11, Polyb. 2.15, Strabo 5.1.12. MacKinnon 2001, 250–256, finds the relative preference, based on faunal remains, for pigs versus sheep, goats, and cattle higher in northern and central Italy than in the south.

22. Strabo 5.1.12. On viticulture in the Roman Cisalpina, see Piccoli 2004, Cracco Ruggini 1998, Tchernia 1986 (particularly on the northern Italian use of barrels), Purcell 1985. On the proverbial prosperity of northern Italy, see also Tact. *Hist.* 2.17.

23. Polyb. 2.17.

24. Livy 5.33. See also Williams 2001a on the theme of envy in Roman portrayals of the Gauls.

25. Livy 5.34. Livy 21.35, where Hannibal points out to his troops the rich Po Plain and the easy living they will have in Italy, follows a similar theme.

26. Livy 5.35, cf. Pliny *HN* 3.116.

27. *Insc. Ital. XIII.2* no.1, Feeney 2007, 103–104; Rüpke 1995, 43, 560–70; Michels 1967, 25. The Roman repulse of a Gallic attack on the Capitoline was also celebrated; in order to commemorate the role of the sacred geese of Juno in warning of the Gallic attempt, on one day each year Juno's geese were paraded around on gold and purple cushion-adorned litters. The guard dogs who failed to bark were remembered less sympathetically; in the ceremony in which the geese were honored, a dog was crucified (Pliny *HN* 29.14, Plut. *De fort. Rom.* 12).

28. Polyb. 2.19 has the Romans fear war with the Senones only when there are reports of movements of transalpine Gauls into Italy in the lead-up to the Sentinum campaign in 295 BCE (cf. Polyb. 2.21 on another influx of Transalpine Gauls, which was leading to war with Rome until the new arrivals began quarreling with their Cisalpine allies). Similarly, before the battle of Telamon in 225 BCE, the Romans send troops north only when they hear that Transalpine Gauls—in this case the Gaesatae—have crossed the Alps south into Italy to aid their Insubrian and Boian neighbors (Polyb. 2.23).

29. Plut. *Mar.* 25. Vercellae has been traditionally identified with modern Vercelli in northwestern Cisalpine Gaul. The location of the battle, however, was disputed by Zennari (1956), who argued that a battle near Vercelli would mean that the Cimbri illogically turned sharply west after crossing the Brenner Pass. Instead, according to Zennari, Vercellae may be interpreted not as a proper name but as a Celtic word referring to a mining area near a river. Such mining areas exist throughout Cisalpine Gaul, and of these the most likely according to Zennari would be near the modern town of Rovigo in the Po Delta. The latter would be even more threatening to the Romans, since this area was near a number of old and important colonies.

30. *ILS* 6087. See also the comments of Woolf 1998, 61, and Williams 2001a, 177, on the Roman fear of a *tumultus Gallicus*. Polyb. 2.35 compares the Celtic attack on Delphi to the Persian invasion of Greece in justifying his attention paid to Roman campaigns against the Celts.

31. In 228 BCE: Plut. *Marc.* 3.3–4, Dio fr. 47,13.3–4, Zon. 8.19, Oros. 4.13.3–4. On this sacrifice, see also Eckstein 2012, 212–217.

32. Oros. 4.13 and Plut. *Marc.* 3, who notes that in his time the Romans performed secret rites there every November in memory of the earlier victims of this practice.

33. Plut. *Quaest. Rom.* 83.

34. On Pompey's 78 BCE siege of M. Iunius Brutus, the father of the tyrannicide, see Plut. *Pomp.* 16 and Badian 1958, 275, while for Antony's siege of Decimus Brutus at Mutina in 43 BCE and the subsequent battle between Antony and the consuls Hirtius and Pansa, see Appian *BC* 3.49–71, Cic. *Fam.* 10.30, Plut. *Ant.* 17 and Plut. *Cic.* 45. Mutina was used as a legionary base even during the Hannibalic war (Livy 21.25, where the three Roman commissioners assigned to establish Placentia fled, and consequently Mutina became the base of the remaining Roman army in the region). Its use as a base in the later Republican period is logical given its central position on the Via Aemilia and its possession of walls.

35. Plut. *Crass.* 9, Livy *Epit.* 69.

36. In 178 BCE Aquileia was used as a base for campaigns against the Istrians (Livy 41.5–6), and Caesar sent the fifteenth legion to Cisalpine Gaul to protect colonies there in 51 BCE (Caes. *B Gall.* 8.24.

37. On recruitment in Cisalpine Gaul, see Brunt 1971, 202, and Chilver 1941, 121. On the population of Roman Cisalpine Gaul during the Republic, see Bandelli 1999, Kron [forthcoming], and De Ligt 2008. The population of Cisalpine Gaul has received scholarly attention disproportionate to other aspects of Cisalpine Gaul because the population numbers are a key part of the ongoing debate over the Augustan census figures.

38. Cf. Livy 23.14 on recruitment during the Hannibalic war; Livy 41.5 records recruitment in Cisalpine Gaul in 178 BCE—in the context of the Istrian wars—of auxiliaries from local settlements and of legionaries from the colonies. Sertorius raised troops there in 90 BCE (Plut. *Sert.* 4.1), and Caesar recruited heavily in Cisalpine Gaul, first for the Gallic wars and then again for the civil wars (*B Gall.* 1.24, 1.54, 2.2, 5.1, 6.1).

39. Arnaud 2004a and Arnaud 2004b.

40. Livy 39.2.

41. Livy 39.2.

42. Pliny *NH* 3.105. *CIL* IX 1455 (= *ILS* 6509); Maggiani 2004; Torelli 2004.

43. Livy 40.53. Gambaro 1999, 44 following Sartori 1965, 14 and Gabba 1987, 47, argues that Flaccus was operating in the territory of the Statellates and suggests that those 3,200 Ligurians moved down into the plains were Statellates.

44. Livy 39.54–55. Livy's statement that when these Gauls left the area around Aquileia they left "Italia" should be understood in its later context, in which Livy was describing an area that had already been incorporated into Italy by Augustus.

45. *CIL* V 8270 = *CIL* I 652a = *CLE* 1859 = *ILS* 8885 = *ILLRP* 335, from Aquileia (= *Insc. Aq.* 28). The inscription is fragmentary.

46. Livy 43.1, which also says the Romans still were not able to fortify the town adequately. That same year they also requested additional colonists, and the Senate sent 1,500 households to the town (Livy 43.17).

47. This is not inconsistent with Cato's description of the Alps as the wall of Italy (*Orig.* 4.10), since Cato does not imply that the Alps were the boundary of Italy but rather that they defended the Italian peninsula—and Gallia Cisalpina—from central Europe.

48. Sena: Livy *Per.* 11.7, Polyb. 2.19. Ariminum: Livy *Per.* 15.4–6; Vell. Pat. 1.14.7. See Bandelli 2001, 17–29 for a fuller discussion of the political context of this expansion.

49. Polyb. 2.21, Cic. *Brut.* 57, Val. Max. 5.4.5.

50. Polyb. 2.35.

51. Polyb. 2.35. Strabo says that the Romans expelled the Boii from their land and that the Boii, having migrated to Pannonia, were annihilated in wars with the Dacians, and yet Strabo may be confusing two similarly named federations (5.1.6), since ancient authors noted the existence of both transalpine and cisalpine federations of Boii, Senones, Cenomani (e.g., Caes. *B. Gall.* 7.75).

52. On population transfer in the Hellenistic period, see Cohen 1983.

53. Cic. *Balb.* 32.

54. Malnati and Manzelli 2015, 45; Desantis 2015a, 76.

55. Calastri and Desantis 2014.

56. Ortalli 2000, 439–443.

57. Livy 39.55; Malnati 2013, 60.

58. Malnati and Catarsi 2013, 63–64, on urban change in republican Parma. On the river-ford sanctuary at Piazza Ghiaia, see Malnati, Catarsi, and Pederelli 2013.

59. Marchesini 2013; Bosi et al. 2011, 1630–1632.

60. Bosi et al. 2011, 1630–1631.

61. Williams (2001b, 96–97) argues that "rather than extirpation, perhaps the willing abandonment of ethnic identities of the Boii and Senones is worth considering as an option to account for their apparent disappearance." He posits that they may have either settled in Roman colonies or reformed as the fora communities along the Via Aemilia.

62. Brixia: Solano 2015; Milan: Ceresa Mori 2015; Grassi 1995.

64. Graffiti in local languages and scripts are collected in Morandi 2004, 515–703.

65. Dyson 1985, 84.

66. Pautasso 1966 remains the standard discussion of coin types. Pautasso 1994 discusses coinage circulating in nearby Alpine areas. The implications of circulation patterns for local identity are discussed by Häussler 2013, 104–108.

67. Cf. Livy 21.55, where Livy describes them as the only Celtic tribe still loyal to Rome (before the battle at the Ticinus River, where Hannibal turns the battle by turning his elephants against the Cenomani on the Roman right), and 21.25, where they aid the besieged Roman force under praetor L. Manlius sent to aid the also besieged Mutina. On the Cenomani's return to an allegiance with Rome, see Livy 32.30, who provides the sole evidence for the political structures of the Cenomani (see also Bonini 1998).

68. Polyb. 2.23.1–3.

69. Livy 23.24, in reference to the defeat of L. Postumius's force in 216. The incident is further discussed by Agostinetti 2004, 91, and Armit 2012, 22–23.

70. See Voisin 1984 on Roman head-hunting. Armit 2012, 25–42, surveys depictions of "Celtic" head-hunting in Greek and Roman sources and surveys the scholarship on the idea of "Celtic head cult," a broad term that has been applied to a variety of religious and military practices in Iron Age Europe and also to artistic representations of "*les têtes coupées*" ("severed heads").

71. Livy 21.29, Polyb. 3.40.

72. On the distribution of horse burials among the Cenomani, Senones, and Veneti, see Vitale 2006. Both Carnic examples come from Kobarid in Slovenia. The first burial, dating to between c. 120–60 BCE and excavated by Marchesetti in 1908 (Božić 2004),

consists of a horse killed and then laid over a cremation burial. In the second, excavated in 2010 at the Bizjakova hiša site, several horses were buried together in a deposit with swords, rings, and harnesses in the late fourth century BCE (Mlinar 2011).

73. On the horse and rider burial of Piovego, excavated in 1989, see Leonardi 2004.

74. Gambacurta and Tirelli 1996.

75. Millo 2013 surveys the importance of the horse and of equestrian status among the Veneti.

76. Ruta Serafini et al. 1992.

77. Lomas 2011, 8–10; Lomas 2009, 14–15.

78. Lomas 2011, 8.

79. Bononia: Livy 37.57, Vell. 1.15. Mutina: Livy 39.55. See also Bandelli 2007, 18–20, on this phase of colonization.

80. For centuriation in general, see Cambi and Terrenato 1994. Research on centuriation in northern Italy owes much to the mid-twentieth-century work of Plinio Fraccaro, whose studies provided templates for future work on both mapping centuriated land and on determining the historical sequence of such centuriation (see Gabba 2001).

81. Chevallier 1983, 43–57; Potter 1987, 121.

82. Prenc 2002; Bosio 1984.

83. Zanda 1998, 52–59.

84. Gran. Lic. 9–10.

85. Pina Polo 2006.

86. Purcell 1990, 16; Calzolari 2004, 23.

87. On these *fora* settlements, see Laurence 1999, 32 (also on their organization and historical development into the imperial period) and Brunt 1971, 568. On the regular spacing of these settlements along the Via Aemilia, the overall sparse settlement away from the road, and the role of markets and *praefetura*, see dall'Aglio 2000.

88. The route, surviving segments, and findings along the Postumia are discussed in Sena Chiesa 1998.

89. Bonomi and Rubino 2007, 85–86.

90. On the phenomenon in Italy as a whole, see Keppie 1983.

91. Keppie 1983, 250.

92. Susini 1976.

93. Keppie 1983, 368.

94. Asc. *Pis.* 3c, Plin. *HN* 3.138.

95. On the process of *attributio*, by which smaller, surrounding communities were incorporated into the territory of a larger town, see Laffi 1966. The evidence for *attributio* comes mostly from the Augustan and Julio-Claudian periods, but given the large territories, especially Brixia, in the early imperial period, the process seems to have begun earlier. Plin. *HN* 3.138 describes Alpine communities as attributed to Italian *municipia* by a *lex Pompeia* under Augustus. The process is attested primarily in the Alpine foothills, such as at Tridentum in Venetia, where the Anauni, Tulliassi, and Sinduni inhabiting Alpine valleys were attributed to the city by the emperor Claudius (*CIL* V 5050 = *ILS* 206), and at Tergeste, where the Carni and Catali were attributed to the Adriatic port (*CIL* V 532 = *ILS* 6680).

96. Genua had already benefited by the actions of Spurius Lucretius in sponsoring the

city's rebuilding after the destruction caused by Mago in 205, and Roman actions afterwards were designed to protect the coast but also not to compromise Genua's position as lead city of the coast (Livy 30.1). Colonies and settlements were founded at a reasonable distance away, the roads did not bypass the city, and *attributio* worked in the city's favor; cf. the boundary dispute between the Genuates and the Langenses Viturii in 117 BCE: *CIL* I^2 584 = *ILLRP* 517). Settlement around Aquileia was controlled, perhaps as much for defensive reasons as to secure the city's economic well-being (Livy 39.54). The regional dominance of both cities was nearly guaranteed by the 148 BCE construction of the Via Postumia, whose termini were at Aquileia and Genua and which was, along with the Via Aemilia and the Po itself, one of the region's three most important arteries. On the development of urban forms in the Transpadane, in particular in Mediolanum, Brixia, Alba Pompeia, and Verona, see Rossignani 2006.

97. Strabo 5.1.11, Purcell 1990, 18.

98. Purcell 1990, 18; Calzolari 2004, 22–24.

99. The difficulties engendered by such projects can be seen in Spain in the *Tabula Contrebiensis*, where the Sosinestani's right to sell land for the construction of a canal to the Salluienses is disputed by the Allavonenses, as are also the Salluienses' right to construct a canal over land other than that which they had bought and, thirdly, the limits of the public and private land of the Sosinestani (Richardson 1983, Birks, Rodger, and Richardson 1984). The legal mess in which the Salluienses, Sosinestani, and Allavonenses found themselves could easily be replicated in Republican northern Italy, as the boundary dispute between the Genoese and the Viturii Langenses in 117 BCE shows (*CIL* I^2 584 = *CIL* V7749 = *ILS* 5946 = *ILLRP* 517). In the case of the Genoese and the Viturii Langenses, it is worth noting that a commission of Roman senators was established to mediate the dispute. As such, it is possible that land redistribution and hydraulic projects might have required further management from Rome sometime after their original completion.

100. Livy *Per.* 46, Cic. Leg. Agr. 2.82, Gran. Lic. 9–10.

101. In Etruria and Umbria, there was armed revolt, and although App. *BC* 1.49 is ambiguous on whether the Etruscans and Umbrians were at war with Rome or just preparing for war, Livy *Epit.* 74 and Oros. 5.18 speak of battles with the Etruscans and Umbrians, and Flor. 2.6.5–6 also indicates war, at least in southern Umbria. On Etruscan and Umbrian concerns over the agrarian laws of Drusus, see App. *BC* 1.36, as well as Harris 1971. On the Social War roles of the Umbrians in particular, see Bradley 2000, 217. The Picentine situation is less ambiguous, and the Picentines were the first Italians in the war to revolt, killing the proconsul Q. Servilius and other Romans at Asculum in Picenum in 91 BCE (Livy *Per.* 72, App. *BC* 1.38, Oros. 5.18, Diod. 37.12–13, Cic. *Font.* 41, Vell. Pat. 2.15).

102. Frontin. *Str.* 1.9.3: Cn. Pompeius, trucidato ab exercitu Mediolani senatu, ne tumultum moveret, si solos evocasset nocentes, mixtos eis, qui extra delictum erant, venire iussit.

103. On the *lex Iulia*: App. *BC* 1.49. On the scope of the *lex Iulia* and a survey of other enfranchisement measures following the Social War, as well as for recent bibliography on these enfranchisement measures, see Bispham 2007.

104. Plut. *Pomp.* 16

105. Plut. *Comp. Dion et Brut.* 5.2. Suet. *Rhet.* 6 mentions a statue of Brutus prominently displayed in Mediolanum; this might be the same statue.

106. Brennen 2000, n368, places the massacre in the context of Pompey's journey to Spain as proconsul in 77 BCE; this scenario seems unlikely in that Pompey's journey through northwestern Italy would more likely follow the coastal Ligurian road. Williams 2001a, 121, supports the first scenario, suggesting that the incident "may refer to soldiers of Pompeius Strabo punishing the Milanese for supporting the Allied cause in the Social War."

107. The extent of the *lex Iulia*'s coverage in the Cispadana has been disputed, with Brunt 1971 arguing that the Cispadane Ligurians were excluded from the *lex Iulia*'s coverage because "these backward hill-dwellers had no interest in political advancement"(169–170), contra Sherwin-White 1973 arguing that Asconius implies that only the Transpadani received special treatment. Ewins 1955 proposes a piecemeal distribution of citizen rights across the Cispadana, with unenfranchised communities, such as unattributed Ligurians, being unimportant and "their agitation for advancement . . . on a negligible scale" (78). Given the demonstrated Roman interest in associating these "hill-dwellers" with communities in the plains, a system of *attributio* might be expected to provide the southern and western Ligurians with citizenship under the *lex Iulia*, but it seems unlikely that, given the demands for legionary recruitment in the post–Social War period, any small Cispadane settlements would be denied in claims of possessing Roman citizenship.

108. Ius dedit Latii, ut possent habere ius quod ceterae Latinae coloniae, id est ut petendo magistratus civitatem Romanam adispiscerentur (Asc. *Pis.* 3C).

109. Pompey Strabo's grant of citizenship to a squadron of Spanish cavalry follows a similar logic of citizenship as a reward for service (*CIL* I 709 = *CIL* VI 37045 = *ILS* 8888 = *ILLRP* 515). Cf. Criniti 1970.

110. The earliest attested magistrates of Cisalpine extraction (not always certain) at Rome are: Cn. Octavius Ruso (possibly Aquileia), quaestor of Marius in 106 BCE; Q. Tittius Mutto (probably Aquileia), *triumvir monetalis* in 90 BCE; C. Poblicius (possibly Verona), *triumvir monetalis* in 80 BCE; Q. Publicius (possibly Verona), praetor in 67 BCE; Tuticanus (probably Verona), father of an equestrian who was present with Caesar at Dyrrachium; C. Hostilius Saserna (possibly Verona), Caesarian legate in Africa, 46 BCE; L. Hostilius Saserna, brother of the above Caesarian legate and *triumvir monetalis* in 48 BCE; P. Hostilius Saserna (possibly Verona), brother of the above two and also Caesarian legate in Africa; C. Helvius Cinna (Brixia), ill-starred tribune of the plebs in 44 BCE; Sepullius Macer (probably Patavium), *triumvir monetalis* in 44 BCE (Alföldy 1999, 261); C. Vibius Varus (possibly Brixia), *triumvir monetalis* in 41 BCE; and P. Alfenus Varus (probably Cremona), legate of Augustus in 41 BCE. On the intersection of Italian identity and the *causa Transpadani*, see chap. 4.

111. Dio 37.9.3, Suet. *Caes.* 8. The actions of Crassus and Caesar were not isolated but rather part of a protracted political struggle after the Social War—but seeming to intensify in the '60s and '50s—over the *causa Transpadani*. For Roman politicians espousing the enfranchisement of the Transpadani, the rewards were a potentially great increase of electoral support; cf. Caesar's sending of Labienus to Cisalpine Gaul to persuade the inhabitants—presumably those south of the Po or those select communities and individuals north of the river already possessing citizenship—to support his candidacy for the consulship (Caes. *B Gall.* 8.52). The potential political support, combined with lingering Roman resentment toward Celts (see Tac. *Ann.* 11.23, where one senator claims that it

is bad enough that the Insubres and Veneti have broken into the Senate), also fueled opposition to the *causa Transpadani*. A letter of Cicero reports rumors that Caesar was ordering the Transpadani to form citizen communities; these rumors were fueled by fears of Caesar's growing political power (*Att.* 5.2.3). The consul M. Claudius Marcellus's 51 BCE beating of a magistrate of Novum Comum, which had been given a citizen colony by Caesar, was a piece of political theater directed at Caesar and the legality of his support for the Transpadani. N.b. Cic. *Att.* 5.11.1, where Cicero claims that the beating was revolting since, although the man being beaten was not really a magistrate—Cicero thus doubts the legality of Caesar's colony—he was nevertheless a Transpadanus and by implication civilized (Marcellus foede in Comensi. Etsi ille magistratum non gesserat, erat tamen Transpadanus). See also Curio's espousal of Transpadane enfranchisement (Cic. *Off.* 3.88). On the *causa Transpadani*, see Mouritsen 1998, 107 and Gruen 1974, 409.

112. Dio 41.36.

113. App. *BC* 5.3, Dio 48.12.5.

114. *CIL* I 205 (= XI 1146).

115. For examination of the possible methodology behind the creation of the Augustan *regiones*, see Laurence 1999, 97. The Augustan concern for northern Italy, largely absent during the exigencies of the triumviral period and its attendant civil wars and land confiscations for veteran settlement, is perhaps reflected in Augustan demonstrations of respect for patrons of the region from opposing political camps. In this category fall Augustus's exemption of Bononia from taking the oath of loyalty before the battle of Actium because the Bononians were long-standing clients of the Antonii (Suet. Aug. 17.2) and his allowing a statue of Brutus to stand in Mediolanum (Plut. *Comp. Dion et Brut.* 5.2). See Suet. *Aug.* 20 on Augustus's use of Mediolanum and Aquileia as bases during the Alpine, Illyrian, and Norican campaigns.

116. There is little indication that Cisalpine Gaul was seen as geographically separate from peninsular Italy in the second century; Cato and Polybius both define Italy as extending to the Alps. Nevertheless, northern Italy's status in the Late Republic as a militarized *provincia* set it apart from central and southern Italy, as did the differing citizen status of the Transpadani in the first half of the first century. The work of high-profile Latin writers born in northern Italy—Livy, Vergil, and Catullus being the most conspicuous examples—certainly helped develop an image of a culturally unified Roman Italy. See also Torelli 1999, 165–183.

117. Cf. Maggi 2006; Maggi 1999.

CHAPTER THREE. **Citizenship and Identity**

1. On the formation of the new states during and following the Napoleon's Italian campaigns, see Godechot 1988 and Broers 2003.

2. A survey of identity studies is provided by Hall 1997 and 2002, with a more critical approach to the subject taken by Hölscher 2011.

3. The terminology used to name those Iron Age polities described in early Greek and Roman sources is notoriously problematic. The label *tribe* is eschewed because, in keeping with the Latin use of *tribus*, it will be used in later chapters to describe Roman voting tribes, and because the term itself is burdened with a significant amount of Victorian

baggage (see Moore 2011). See Williams 2001a and Wells 2014, 308, on Greek and Latin terminology for the Celts and on modern usage of *Gaul* and *Celt*.

4. De Bernardo Stempel 2000, 89–91. Bourdin 2014, 65, provides a list of attestations of these names in ancient authors.

5. Cic. *Balb*. 32: Etenim quaedam foedera exstant, ut Cenomanorum, Insubrium, Helvetiorum, Iapydum, non nullorum item ex Gallia barbarorum, quorum in foederibus exceptum est ne quis eorum a nobis civis recipiatur ("For certain treaties are still extant, as with those of the Cenomani, Insubres, Helvetii, Iapydes, and some of the barbarians from Gaul, in which it is stipulated that none of them should be taken into the citizenship by us"). On the dating of the treaties, see Brunt 1982, 141n24.

6. The Trumplini and Benacenses made a joint dedication to Iulia Augustus, the daughter of the emperor Titus (*CIL* V 4313 = *ILS* 266 = *Inscr. It*. 10–5, 90). The Trumplini and another tribe, possibly the Camuni, made a similar dedication in the Augustan era to Nero Claudius Drusus, the father of the future emperor Claudius (*CIL* V 4310 = *Inscr. It*. 10–05, 87). Both inscriptions were found around Brixia.

7. See also Marzatico 2014, 191, fig. 2.

8. Häussler 2002, 62.

9. Morandi 2004, 572 (no. 77).

10. The standard corpora for Lepontic are Lejeune 1971 and *RIG* vol. 2 (= Lejeune 1988). Updated editions of the Celtic inscriptions in Italy are provided in Morandi 2004.

11. Wallace 2004 provides a concise introduction to the language. The standard corpora are Pellegrini and Prosdocimi 1967 and Lejeune 1974.

12. Pellegrini and Prosdocimi 1967, 13. On the *teuta*, see Pellegrini and Prosdocimi 1967, vol. 2, 173–274; cf. Wallace 2004, 847.

13. Vitale 1998, 262, also discussed by Bourdin 2014, 70–71.

14. Sasatelli 1994a, 59 (illustrated on plate IXa, p. 60); Briquel 1994, 194; D'Ercole 2011, 441; Malnati and Manfredi 1991, 197.

15. D'Ercole 2011.

16. Tomb 9, necropolis of Ca' Cima (Tamassi 2002). The hybrid Celtic-Etruscan nature of the grave goods is not wholly atypical for Atria; his neighbors in Tombs 20 and 39 of the necropolis were buried with torques and fibulas along with their Volterran ceramics. For similar burial assemblages at Ateste, see Bondini 2005, 83.

17. An overview of the inscriptions is provided by Pellegrini and Prosdocimi 1967, 1–24.

18. Häussler 2002, 62.

19. On the shift to bilingual and then entirely Lain inscriptions in the Veneto, see Benelli 2001, 11–12, and Benelli 1999.

20. On these changes in Etruria, see Benelli 1994.

21. Benelli 2001.

22. Bradley 2000, 205–213.

23. Lomas 2008, 122.

24. Agostinetti 2004, 31–34, 84–85; Lomas 2008, 121; Häussler 2002, 62. There is a similar gap in Venetic inscriptions at Patavium in the second century BCE (Lomas 2011, 16–17).

25. Häussler and Pearce 2007, 223–224; Lomas 2008, 121.

26. Lomas 2008, 129.

27. Diod. 37.2.4–5 for Italia; Vell. Pat. 2.16 and Strabo 5.4.2 for Italica.

28. Rutter 2001, nos. 407–428. That some of the coins' inscriptions are in Oscan and not Latin once again points the choice of language as being a cultural or political one.

29. The choice of Italia as a unifying idea among the rebels in the Social War is discussed further by Pobjoy 2000.

30. On the *lex Iulia*: App. *BC* 1.49 (who does not name the law), Gell. *NA* 4. 4.3, Cic. *Balb.* 8.21, and Vell. Pat. 2.16. On the *lex Calpurnia*, see Sisenna fr. 17P (with further discussion in Frasinetti 1972 and Mouritsen 1998). On the *lex Plautia Papiria*, see Cic. *Arch.* 4.7. On the *lex Pompeia*, see Asc *Pis.* 3C (with further discussion in Erwins 1955).

31. While the end result was eventual citizenship, the causes of the war remain controversial. Among notable explanations for the causes of the Social War, Brunt 1965 and Gabba 1954 argue that the Italians wanted a share in Rome's empire. Gabba sees the motivation as primarily economic, arguing that the principal instigators were Italian businessmen, while for Brunt the motivations are more political. Mouritsen 1998 wants to separate the outcome of the war, the enfranchisement of Italy, from the motives of the insurgents and argues against citizenship being the primary motivation for the Italians. Salmon 1982 stresses the material and legal advantages of citizenship and argues that Roman aloofness and the arrogance of its officials pushed Italian communities to abandon their own customs and languages for Roman citizenship. Sherwin-White 1973 argues that no one motive for the war can be pinned down, but rather various sections of the Italian populace had different reasons for wanting citizenship or independence from Rome. For Sherwin-White, the incident at Asculum was unplanned and the embassy asking for citizenship an attempt to allot blame for the incident to the obstinacy of the Romans. For further discussion of the history of this topic, see Seston 1978 and Pobjoy 2000.

32. Häussler 2002, 64–65.

33. Morandi 2004, 588–590. For the Latin part see *CIL* I 3403a and *Supp. It.* 19 Vercelli 1. The Celtic translation is taken from Morandi. The stone was found on the bank of the Sesia in 1960 and accordingly has no useful archaeological context for dating. Morandi dates the inscription to a little before the middle of the first century BCE.

34. Dio 37.9.3. Plut. *Caes.* 9.

35. App. *BC* 2.26, trans. H. White. Cf. Cic. *Att.* 5.11.2 (who is laconic about the events but expresses his disapproval at Marcellus's actions, saying that even if the man was not a magistrate—i.e., that Caesar's actions in founding a new colony were not legal—the action was in itself shameful and also bothersome to Pompey) and Plut. *Caes.* 29.

36. Cic. *Att.* 5.2.3.

37. Alföldy 1999, 261.

38. Alföldy 1999, 300–314. The attribution of Cinna to Brixia is made on the basis of Gell. 19.13.5, with its reference to the *Genumana* (= Cenomani), and on the appearance of Helvii in Brixian inscriptions (Gregori 1999, 96); see also Andemahr 1994.

39. Catullus's father: Suet. *Iul.* 73; Catullus in Bithynia: Catull. 10, 28, 56.

40. Catull. 35, 68.

41. Catull. 100, 113.

42. On Catullus's family villa at Sirmio see Catull. 31, and on the relationship between

the so-called Grotto di Catullo (Wiseman 1990) and the Valerii Catulli, see Wiseman 1987 and 1993. While the Valerii continued to be active in the area well into the early imperial period, and while the *gens Valeria* certainly held property in and around Sirmio, there is no convincing reason to connect the imperial-era structure and property of the Grotto di Catullo with the poet Catullus. Tivoli: Catull. 44.

43 Cic. *Leg.* 5.

44. Catull. 39.10–19.

45. Contra Dench 2005, 340, who suggests that "Catullus is perhaps once again gently digging at a distinctive aspect of contemporary pride, pride in, precisely, being so newly and so narrowly 'Italian.'"

46. Catull. 84.

47. Cic. *Brut.* 169–170.

48. On the connection between the spread of citizenship and the spread of Italian self-identification, see Giardina 1994.

49. Williams 2001, 124.

50. Sall. *Cat.* 49.2; Cic. *Off.* 3.88.

51. Cic. *Att.* 5.2, Caes. *BC* 3.87. On the evolution of the *IIIIviri*, see Bispham 2007, 247.

52. *CIL* III 14429 (= *AE* 1902, 0126). In contrast, there are at least sixty-three attestations of forms of the word *Transpadanus* in Latin literature and inscriptions.

53. Strabo 5.4.

54. Cf. Galsterer 1994.

55. Such group identification without a significant ethnic component is almost without parallel in Italy. Of the Augustan *regiones* of Italy, all except Aemilia (VIII) and Transpadana (XI) are based on ethnic constructions. The choice of Aemilia for the southeastern Po Valley possibly reflects, in addition to the great importance of the via Aemilia for the region, the expulsion of many inhabitants during and following the Roman conquest (cf. Polyb. 2.27 and 2.35, Peyre 1979). With the expulsion of many of the Boii and Senones, the region lost much of its pre-Roman ethnic identity, and the defining feature of the Republican-period region was the new military trunk road. On the use of ethnic markers for the other *regiones*, see Laurence 1999 and Nicolet 1991, as well as Farney 2007 on aristocratic manipulation of these ethnic markers. In the rest of the empire such non-ethnically based geographic identities are similarly rare. Exceptions are the *Alpes Cottiae*, which draw their name from the Augustan-era dynast Cottius and his family (Plin. *HN* 3.136–8); the *Alpes Maritimae*, clearly named after the geographical features; the *Alpes Poeninae* or *Alpes Graiae*, which Livy says were named after a local deity (21.38); the brief province of Mesopotamia; and *Africa proconsularis*, used in place of any references to Carthaginian rule. The lack of ethnic markers to describe the western Alps can perhaps be attributed to general lack of Roman attention paid these areas and their inhabitants. In contrast, the Norici and Raeti are commemorated in named provinces whose importance to the Danube and Rhine borders merited more Roman attention.

56. Caesar's enfranchisement of the Transpadani by means of the *lex Roscia*: Dio 41.36. The triumvirs' incorporation of Cisalpine Gaul into Italy: App. *BC* 5.3, Dio 48.12.5.

57. Plin. *HN* 3.123, 130, 138; 10.77; 16.66; 17.49, 201; 18.66, 127, 182, 205; 19.16; 37.44. Tacitus at *Hist.* 2.32 lists important Transpadane cities at Mediolanum, Novaria, Eporedia, and Vercellae, all of which fall within *regio* XI.

58. *Res Gestae* 16; *CIL* III 5212 (= *AE* 2002, 105: "*cives Romani [e]x Italia et aliis provincis in Raetia consistentes*"); Tac. *Ann.* 13.4.

59. On the *ius Italicum*, see Dio 50.15.1–8, and Plin. *HN* 3.25 and 3.139.

60. *Ep.* 9.23.

61. Syme 1999, 73–74. Cf. Farney 2007, 233.

62. *CIL* VII 704 (= *RIB* 1686).

63. *AE* 1953, 188.

64. A short list of Greek and Latin inscriptions listing region of origin is provided below:

Place of Origin (regio, if in Italy)	*Site and Province of Inscription*	*References*
Augusta Taurinorum, Italy (XI)	Bolcske, Pannonia	*AE* 2003, 1436 and 1437
Brixia, Italy (XI)	Vindolanda, Britain	*RIB* 1686
Mediolanum, Italy (XI)	Lepcis Magna, Tripolitana	*AE* 1953, 188
Tigullis, Liguria, Italy (IX)	Sala, Mauretania Tingetana	*AE* 1992, 1944
Liguria, Italy (IX)	Ephesus, Asia	*CIL* III 6085 = *CIL* III 7135–6
Florentia, Italy (VII)	Taurunum, Pannonia	AE 1964, 256
Priverno, Italy (I)	Amorium, Asia	*CIL* III 353
Italy, town unspecified	Rome	*CIL* VI 1636
Italy, town unspecified	Kotiaion, Phrygia	*CIG* 3823 = *IGR* 4.539
Arles, Gallia Narbonensis	Bolcske, Pannonia	*AE* 2003, 1426
Hispania	Tyana, Cappadocia	*AE* 1991, 1555
Saldae, Mauretania Sitifensis	Alauna, Britannia	*RIB* 812
Girba, Africa	Lavinium, Campania, Italia	*AE* 1998, 282 + *AE* 2000, 242
Sufibus, Africa	Bolcske, Pannonia	*AE* 2003, 1432
Thalenis, Africa	Stockstadt, Germania Superior	*CIL* XIII 11783
Africa	Fanum Martis, Lugudunesnsis	*CIL* XIII 1347
Philoppopolis, Thrace	Lugdunum, Lugudunensis	*CIL* XIII 01856 = *CLE* 841
Britannia	Bostra, Arabia	*IGLS* 13.1, 9188

65. *AE* 1956, 233.

66. Tac. *Ann.* 3.55. simul novi homines e municipiis et coloniis atque etiam provinciis in senatum crebro adsumpti domesticam parsimoniam intulerunt, et quamquam fortuna vel industria plerique pecuniosam ad senectam pervenirent, mansit tamen prior animus. sed praecipuus adstricti moris auctor Vespasianus fuit, antiquo ipse cultu victuque.

67. On Tacitus's self-presentation, see Sailor 2008.

68. *Ep.* 1.14.6, on Serrana Procula, from Patavium. The first-century BCE senator Asinius Pollio had disparagingly referred to his fellow historian Livy's *patavinitas*. Whether *patavinitas* referred to a lack of Latinitas or urbanitas (Latte 1940), a style of writing history (Syme 1939, 485–486), or traces of a Patavian dialect (Whatmough 1939; Levene 2010, 276) is an old debate.

69. *Ep.* 1.14.4. Patria est ei Brixia, ex illa nostra Italia quae multum adhuc verecundiae frugalitatis, atque etiam rusticitatis antiquae, retinet ac servat.

70. For introduction to issues of Italian identity and the Augustan Age, see Purcell 2005, Dench 2005; Rowe 2002, 103–104.

71. Suet. *Claud.* 25.2 (on passage through Italian towns). *CIL* X 1401 = *ILS* 6043 (the *SC Hosidianum*, 45 CE).

72. *CIL* X 1401 = *ILS* 6043. Patterson 2003, 97, suggests that the prohibition of wagons and carts through Italian towns may have been symbolic as well, since it might "stop people riding through Italian towns as though they were conquered or provincial centres."

73. Plin. *Ep.* 6.19. See Patterson 2003 and Woolf 1990 for a discussion of the relationship between imperial attention to the concept of the *totius Italiae aeternitas* and imperial legislation and alimentary schemes, respectively.

74. On the notion of imperial policy in general, see Millar 1977, and on imperial policy toward Italy in particular, see Patterson 2003.

75. On the articulation and presentation of imperial virtues, see Noreña 2009 and Ando 2000. For a contrary view, see Lendon 2006, and for Italian municipal comparanda, see Forbis 1996.

76. Suet. *Vesp.* 1.

77. Suet. *Vesp.* 1. Cf. Levick 1999, 6.

78. Suetonius Paullinus's speech at Tac. *Hist.* 2.32 also suggests that Italy beyond the Po might be viewed as separate from Italy, for he says that although the enemy has control of Italy beyond the Po his army still has the resources of Italy and Rome at their command and the Po River as their front.

79. On the imperial transition to a system relying largely on the transfer of documents, see Nicolet 1991.

80. Even burial plots in Brixia could be huge; one measured 200 by 160 feet (*CIL* V 4787 = *Inscr. It.* 10–5, 809 = *ILS* 8355). On the process of *attributio*, by which surrounding territory and communities were incorporated into the political body of a larger urban center, see Laffi 1966. The process is attested in northern Italy's alpine foothills, such as at Tergeste, where the Carni and Catali were attributed (*CIL* V 532 = *ILS* 6680); Tridentum, where the Anauni, Tulliassi, and Sinduni inhabiting Alpine valleys were attributed to the city and had their Roman citizenship confirmed by the emperor Claudius (*CIL* V 5050 = *ILS* 206); and most probably Brixia as well (*CIL* V 4313 = *ILS* 266 = *Inscr. It.* 10–5, 90, a dedication by the Benacenses and Trumplini at Brixia). The *Benacenses*, the inhabitants of the west shore of Lake Garda (where their other dedications—*CIL* V 4867, *CIL* V 4868, *CIL* V 4869—are located), are not recorded as having their own *municipium* or local magistrates, and they are almost certainly the responsibility of the magistrates at Brixia. On the *attributio* of communities to Brixia, see Todisco 1999, 146, and Laffi 1966, 53–54. The Camunni to the north of Brixia appear to have a separate municipal government, although there are still very strong connections between the two communities. On the relationship of Brixia and the Camunni, see Gregori 2008, as well as *CIL* V 4964, *CIL* V 4957 = *ILS* 6713, *CIL* V 7817 (the *Tropaeum Augusti* at La Turbie), and *CIL* XI 42 from Ravenna (where the commemorated is described as belonging to the "*nat(ione) Camunn(us)*"). Plin. *HN* 3.138 describes Alpine communities conquered by Augustus as attributed to *municipia* by a *lex Pompeia*.

81. Tac. *Hist.* 1.66 (Vienne), 2.21 (Placentia).

82. Anti-Nucerian graffiti at Pompeii: *CIL* IV 1293, 1329, Smallwood 48.

83. Electoral advertisements: *AE* 1990, 176a; *CIL* IV 3865, 3874, and 3875. Gladiatorial announcements: *CIL* IV 3882 *CIL* 04, 04299, 9972, 9973. The violence between Nuceria and Pompeii in 59 CE was serious enough to require imperial intervention (Tac. *Ann.* 14.17). Pompeian market-day calendars: *CIL* IV 5380, 8863.

84. Lendon 1997, 76. See also the celebration of the *concordia* between Concordia and Aquileia (*AE* 2001: 1007a).

85. *CIL* V 4443. This *IIIIvir* belongs to the Poblilia tribe and is therefore Veronese.

86. *CIL* V 4485, *CIL* V 4416, *CIL* V 4418, and *CIL* V 4392.

87. For Brixia the evidence is a Tiberian period-building inscription that refers to the town as a *colonia* (*CIL* V 4307 = *Inscr. It.* 10–5, 85 = *ILS* 114). Other inscriptions refer to Brixia as a *colonia augusta*: *Inscr. It.* 10–5, 817 (= *AE* 2001, 1067); *Inscr. It.* 10–5, 83. *CIL* V 4466 (= *Inscr. It.* 10–5, 255) from Brixia is the epitaph to a decurion of a *colonia*, which is almost certainly Brixia. Tacitus refers to Verona as a *colonia* (*Hist.* 3.8), and the third-century inscription on the Porta Borsari in Verona names the town as a *Colonia Augusta Verona nova Gallieniana* (*CIL* V 3329 = *ILS* 544). The date at which Verona received the title of *colonia* is thus more problematic, especially with Catull. 17, which addresses the town "O Colonia." On the date of Verona's acquisition of the title, see Sartori 1964 and Sartori 1960, who sees two phases of the colony, one in which the town received the honorary title of *colonia* sometime between the Augustan age and the 69 CE civil wars, and another in which it received a newer title from Gallienus, when he was rebuilding its walls two centuries later. On the title and Catullus 17, see Cenerini 1989.

88. *CIL* V 3329 = *ILS* 544.

89. On the nomenclature of towns in the context of the imperial system, see Thomas 2007; Boatwright 2003; Lendon 1997, 136; Price 1985; Bowersock 1985.

90. Sartori, Passi Pitcher, and Natta 1996, 125–127. Bedriacum seems to have benefited, however, from its nearness to Cremona and that city's concentration of well-connected elites. On Bedriacum as a subsidiary settlement of Cremona, see Arslan 1996.

91. Zanker 1990, 329. Veronese elites who had contributed to the cost of the theater's renovation had their names inscribed on the portico columns, which would associate these elites not just with the theater but also with the general appearance of the town (*CIL* V 3441). On the arena and theater in Verona, see Tosi 1994. For a survey of structures across northern Italy, see Chevallier 1983; for Brixia see, Frova 1994 and Mirabella Roberti 1964.

92. Chevallier 1983.

93. On the relationship between the emperor and civic competition as expressed through monumental building, see Thomas 2007, who rightly stresses the role of the emperor and the Senate as the source of validation in competition for provincial preeminence.

94. The Capitolium of Brixia has been the subject of thorough recent studies, collected in Rossi 2002.

95. Alföldy 1984. For their inscriptions see *AE* 1992, 739a–c.

96. On the placement and proliferation of imperial statue bases see Højte 2005 and Alföldy 1984, and on the impact of the Augustan period on that proliferation, see Alföldy 1991. Perhaps just as important as visual reminders of the imperial position are the mile markers placed along important roads (those from around Brixia, Mantua, Cremona, Verona, and Bedriacum are included in Basso 1986).

97. Gradel 2002; see also the reply of Fishwick 1987–2005, 3.3, 211.

98. The exact distinctions between the sevirs, the augustales, and the *seviri augustales* have been much contested, and it is not certain whether the difference is one of terminology or whether the titles describe significantly different offices. Sevirs were an older, six-man municipal organization that did not necessarily have religious obligations. The augustales seem certainly to have been involved in the imperial cult, and it is possible that the *seviri augustales* may either have been both sevirs and augustales or an indication that in these locations the augustales were organized in the model of these older sevirs. In northern Italy at least, the sevirs and augustales do not seem to be separate offices. Chronological and regional variation is probably to be expected. At Ostia, the augustales had their own *ordo* (*ILS* 6141, 6164). Abramenko 1993 sees development over time, with sevirs occurring more frequently in the first century CE and gradually superseded in terminology by the augustales. The augustales are traditionally seen as positions suited for freedmen, as in the depiction of Trimalchio in the *Satyricon*. Nevertheless, in northern Italy a large proportion, perhaps as much as a third, was freeborn. On the insignia and iconography of the sevirs and augustales, see Schäfer 1989, and for the augustales and sevirs in general, see Fishwick 1987–2005 and Duthoy 1976.

99. *CIL* V 4416 (= *Inscr. It.* 10–5, 209), from Brixia. While his service in both towns signals a friendly social connection between the towns, the inscription also suggests friendly competition, with a sevir at Brixia showing himself—and by extension his town—so worthy that even Verona acknowledged him.

100. *CIL* XI 3614 = 4347.

101. Abramenko 1993; Gregori 1999, 156; and Mollo 1997 on the proportion of freeborn sevirs in Brixia. For Verona and Brixia, see Breuer 1996, 64. George 2005, 65, sees this discrepancy as "a peculiar feature of urban northern Italy" and the result of a population of a newly enfranchised classes that "shared the marginalization of successful freedmen," but there is no indication that the sevirate was seen in northern Italy as an office for the marginalized. On the tension between elites and elite freedmen in commemoration and office-holding, see Mouritsen 1997 and 2005.

CHAPTER FOUR. **Governing Northern Italy**

1. The most comprehensive work on northern Italy in the imperial period remains Chevallier 1983, but see also Chilver 1941. Patterson 2006b focuses on central and southern Italy, but the comparison is made with northern Italy.

2. Eck 1979, 25. The position in the republican period at least was seen as politically useful. Plutarch (*Caes.* 5) says that Caesar, as curator of the via Appia, used large sums of his own money to restore the road, while in Cic. *Att.* 1.1, one man's previous work as a curator for the via Flaminia is seen as helping his campaign for the consulship. On the chronological distribution of the *curatores* and their political context, see Laurence 1999, 37.

3. Laurence 1999, 46.

4. *Curatores viarum* are attested for the Aemilia: L. Funisulanus Vettonianus, cos. 78 CE, commemorated in Aemilia at Forum Popili (*CIL* XI 571) and at Andautonia in Pannonia (*CIL* III 4013 = *ILS* 1005); C. Iulius Cornutus Tertullus, a friend of Pliny (Plin. *Epist.* 5.14); a senator commemorated at Rome (*CIL* VI 1428 = 31651); and Ser. Calpurnius Dex-

ter, another senator commemorated at Rome (*CIL* VI 1368 = *ILS* 1175). No *curatores* are attested for the two other major roads in Aemilia, the Annia and the Popilia, but as these were state-built named roads, they would have been the responsibility of the imperial *curatores*, at least according to the definition provided by Siculus Flaccus's *de Condicionibus Agrorum* in the early second century CE. According to Flaccus (146) public roads were built by the state, bore the names of their builders, were maintained by the *curatores* and contractors working for them, and were supplemented by taxes that could be collected from adjoining landowners.

5. Liv. 7.16; Eck 1979, 114–124.

6. Dio 55.25.6; Eck 1979, 113, 125–145.

7. The *vicesima quinta venalium mancipiorum*: Dio 55.31; Eck 1979, 113n13. The *centesima rerum venalium*: Tac. *Ann.* 1.78. Eck 1979, n12.

8. Tac. *Ann.* 1.78.

9. On the mechanics of the collection of taxes in Roman Italy, see Corbier 1991 and Brunt 1990.

10. Suet. *Cal.* 16.3, Dio 59.9.6.

11. *BMC Imp.* 3.21 nos. 119–211 ("*VEHICULATIONE ITALIAE REMISSA*").

12. The *lex Caecilia* of 60 BCE had eliminated *portoria* (customs duties) for Italy, but Caesar had reinstituted duties on foreign goods (Dio 37.51.3, Cic. *Att.* 2.16.1, Suet. *Iul.* 43). For the *portorium* at Aquileia in the Republic: Cic. *Font.* 2; in the imperial period, see *AE* 1934 234 and *CIL* V 820. Tergeste: *CIL* V 706 and De Laet 1949, 179–180, on *CIL* V 792 and *ILS* 1851. Pola: *CIL* V 8139. Tricesimum: *CIL* V 1801. Altinum: *CIL* V 2136, Glemona: *CIL* V 8650. Iulium Carnicum: *CIL* V 1864. Ploricum: *AE* 1923, 46. For the collection of *portoria* in Italy, see Brunt 1990, 430–431, and De Laet 1949. For probable contractors associated with the collection of the *portoria* within northern Italy, see *CIL* V 5090 (dedication of a freedman assigned to *statio Maeinsis*, Venetia), and *CIL* V 7852 (epitaph of a man assigned to *statio Pedonensis*, Liguria). There was also a station for collection of the *portoria* at Ostia: *CIL* XIV 4708. De Laet 1949 remains the standard work on the collection of the *portoria* throughout the empire; this work does not include the later discovered 62 CE customs dossier from Ephesus (*SEG* XXXIX 1189 = *AE* 1989, 681).

13. Augustus excused Italy from contributing crown gold for his triumphs (*Res Gestae* 21.3), and Hadrian canceled debts owed to the state by the inhabitants of Rome and Italy (*SHA* Hadr. 7.6)

14. It is possible that the *vicesima quinta venalium mancipiorum* was also remitted, as it is not attested after the first century CE.

15. Ulp. *D.* 15.50.1.

16. On the functions and dating of the *curatores*, see Jacques 1984 and 1983, Eck 1979, 190–228, and Burton 1979.

17. Attested pre-Severan *curatores* in Italy:

Aecae (*regio* II)—1 (*CIL* IX 1619 = *ILS* 5502)
Aesernia (IV)—1 (*CIL* IX 2860 = *ILS* 5178)
Ancona (V)—2 (*CIL* X 6006 = *ILS* 1066; *CIL* IX 5899 = *ILS* 441)
Ariminum (VIII)—2 (*CIL* VIII 7030 = *ILS* 1119; *CIL* VI 1449 = *ILS* 1107)
Asculum Picenum (V)—1 (*CIL* XIV 3900 = *ILS* 1182)

Bovillae (I)—2 (*AE* 1927, 115; *CIL* XIV 2409 + 2410 = *ILS* 6189 + 6190)
Caere (VII)—1 (*CIL* XI 3614, 4347 = *ILS* 5918a)
Comum (XI)—1 (*CIL* V 4368 = *Inscr. It.* 10–5 157 = *ILS* 6725)
Faventia (VIII)—1 (*CIL* VI 1450 = *ILS* 2935)
Lanuvium (I)—1 (*CIL* XIV 2124)
Lavinium (I)—1 (*CIL* XIV 2070 = *ILS* 6183)
Mantua (I)—1 (*CIL* V 5036 = *ILS* 5016)
Marruvium (IV)—1 (*CIL* VI 1336, 31634, 41177 = *ILS* 1151)
Matilica (VI)—1 (*CIL* XI 5646 = *ILS* 2081)
Nola (I)—1 (*CIL* VIII 7030 = *ILS* 1119)
Otesia (VIII)—1 (*CIL* V 5126 = *ILS* 2722 = *AE* 2004, 344)
Puteoli (I)—4 (*CIL* X 1814; *AE* 1920, 4; *CIL* X 1791; *CIL* II 4121 = *ILS* 1145)
Saturnia (VII)—2 (*AE* 1962, 153)
Suessa Aurunca (I)—1 (*CIL* X 4750)
Tarracina (I)—2 (*CIL* X 6006 = *ILS* 1066; *CIL* XIV 3900 = *ILS* 1182)
Teanum Sidicinum (I)—1 (*CIL* II 4114 = *ILS* 1140)
Trebula Mutuesca (IV)—1 (*AE* 1972, 153)
Velitrae (I)—1 (*CIL* II 4212 = *ILS* 1145)
Total = 31

Attested pre-Severan *curatores* in the provinces:

Aquae Sextiae, Gallia Narbonensis—1 (*CIL* XII 3212 + 3213)
Avennio, Gallia Narbonensis—1 (*CIL* XII 3274 + 3275 = *ILS* 6980)
Cabellio, Gallia Narbonensis—1 (*CIL* XII 3274 + 3275 = *ILS* 6980)
Catina, Sicily—1 (*CIL* X 7024 = *AE* 1960, 202)
Ephesus, Asia—1 (*AE* 1932, 50)
Forum Iulii, Gallia Narbonensis—1 (*CIL* XII 3274 + 3275 = *ILS* 6980)
Narbo, Gallia Narbonensis—1 (*CIL* X 6006 = *ILS* 1066)
Smyrna, Asia—1 (Philostr. *VS* 1.19)
Syria—1 (*CIL* X 6006 = *ILS* 1066)
Trapezoplis, Asia—1 (*OGIS* 492)
Total = 10

18. *CIL* V 4368 (= *ILS* 6725).

19. See also *CIL* V 5126 (= *ILS* 2722), the commemoration of a *curator rei publicae Otesinorum*, commemorated at Bergomum. One important exception is L. Burbuleius Optatus Ligarianus, a *curator rei publicae* at Tarracina, Ancona, and Narbo (*CIL* X 6006 = *ILS* 1066). Boatwright 2003, 74, has suggested that Ligarianus either was from or owned land at Minturnae, which explains his position at nearby Tarracina. All three were port cities.

20. On patterns of *curator* officeholding in Asia, see Dmitriev 2005, 189. On the western provinces, see Jacques 1983.

21. Beneventum: *CIL* IX 1419. Venusia: *CIL* IX 1160 = *ILS* 6485. C. Ennius Firmus, the *curator* at Beneventum, also held a number of local magistracies and can safely be assumed to be a local man, while the *curator* at Venusia was from a neighboring town

(Boatwright 2003, 73). The flexibility of the title *curator* can also be seen in the emperor Titus's selection of *curatores* by lot from among ex-consuls for disaster relief in Campania following the eruption of Vesuvius (Suet. *Tit.* 8.3–4).

22. Ariminum: *CIL* VIII 7030 = *ILS* 1119 (from Cirta, Numidia); Otesia: *CIL* V 5126 = *ILS* 2722 (from Bergomum); Faventia: *CIL* VI 1450 = *ILS* 2935 (Rome). Large regions and multiple cities might also be under the temporary care of a *curator*; under Trajan or Hadrian, a P. Oppius Marcellinus was *curator civitatium complurimum* (*CIL* IX 1006 = *ILS* 6484).

23. *CIL* VIII 7030 = *ILS* 1119 (from Cirta, Numidia).

24. SHA *Marc.* 14.6 is vague about the defenses made by Marcus. An inscription from Thibilis in Numidia mentions a *praetentura Italiae et Alpium*—a garrison or frontier zone of Italy and the Alps—in the *cursus* of Q. Antistius Adventus. Although it is generally agreed that the *praetentura* was temporary and created in response to the incursion of the Marcomanni, its nature and exact dating has been disputed; cf. Fitz 1966. Also potentially connected to these defenses is the office of *legatus pro praetore Italiae Transpadanae*, held in its one attested instance by L. Vitrasius Flamininus (*CIL* X 3870 = *CIL* X 4414; from Capua).

25. SHA *Marc.* 11: Curatores multis civitatibus, quo latius senatorias tenderet dignitates, a senatu dedit.

26. Both senators and *equites* (members of the equestrian order) are attested as *curatores rei publicae*. *Curatores* of certain senatorial rank form about 60% of the total *curatores* for Italy (Sartori 1989, 6).

27. *CIL* V 5126 = *ILS* 2722 = *AE* 2004, 344 (from Bergomum). Pliny lists Otesia among the *municipia* of *regio* VIII (*HN* 3.15), but its modern location is uncertain.

28. Plin. *Ep.* 7.22.2: *ornamentum regionis meae seu dignitate seu moribus*.

29. App. *BC* 1.38.

30. Dio 79.2; SHA *Hadr.* 22, *Ant. Pius* 2–3, *Marc.* 11. A similar interchangeability of imperial representatives can be found in the jurisdiction of the praetorian prefect, who seems to have had some jurisdiction in Italy outside the hundredth-mile marker from Rome—within which was the urban prefect's jurisdiction—according to an inscription from Saepinum on flock harassment (*CIL* IX 2438 = *AE* 1983, 331). Yet even within Saepinum inscription, the praetorian prefects' jurisdiction is vague, and the prefects are consulted only after an imperial freedman's authority is found to be insufficient in persuading municipal decurions.

31. *FIRA* I 295 + 297.

32. Aemilia and Etruria: *AE* 1920, 45; Aemilia and Liguria: *CIL* VI 332; Aemilia, Etruria, and Tuscia: *CIL* VIII 597. Questions of if, why, and how the jurisdictions of the *iuridici* changed have been vexed by the lack of much evidence for their duties outside a few brief references in the *Historia Augusta* and in the titles preserved in inscriptions (on the relevant evidence and references for *iuridici* in Italy, see Eck 1979, 247–66). While Corbier 1973 argued for fairly rigid and standard jurisdictions based on regions, Simhauser 1973, 240, and Eck 1979, 24, favor more fluid, makeshift assignments, a position that seems to be supported by the fact that *iuridici* are attested for regions where they had already held some office or owned land, which suggests that the assignments were at least sometimes custom-made for individual officeholders.

33. SHA. *Ant. Pius* 2.11: *electus est ad eam partem Italiae regendam, in qua plurimum possidebat, ut Hadrianus viri talis et honori consuleret et quieti.*

34. *CIL* VIII 7030 = *ILS* 1119.

35. *CIL* VI 41127 = *AE* 1995, 231.

36. On the details, purpose, and distribution of the alimentary lists, see Woolf 1990, Patterson 1987, Duncan-Jones 1964, and Lo Cascio 1978. In northern Italy, by far the best evidence comes from the Veleia tablet (*CIL* XI 1147 = *ILS* 6675 = *AE* 2005, 528–532); for text and commentary on Veleia's *tabula alimentaria*, see Criniti 1991.

37. *Epit. de Caes.* 12.4; Woolf 1990, 198–199.

38. Woolf 1990.

39. Exceptions are a scheme established by Hadrian at Antinoöpolis in Egypt (*SB* 7602) and a proposed alimentary scheme at Athens (*IG* II^2 2776).

40. *CIL* V 5262, Plin. *Ep.* 7.18.

41. Dio 52.22.6.

42. Plin. *Pan.* 28 (cf. Dio 68.5.4).

43. On the legal privileges and substantial tax exemptions enjoyed by the citizens of Antinoöpolis, see Zahrnt 1988.

44. *CIL* IX 1160 = *ILS* 6485 (Aeclanum, *regio* II): *curatori operum publ(icorum) Venusiae dato ab divo Hadriani. CIL* XII 3212 (Nemausus, Gallia Narbonensis): *curat[o]ri Aquensi c[oloniae]dato ab Imp(eratore) T[rai(ano). CIL* V 4368 = *Inscr. It.*10–05, 157 = *ILS* 6725 (Brixia): *curat(ori) rei p(ublicae) Bergom(atium) dat(o) ab Imp(eratore) Hadriano. AE* 1969/70, 155 (Luceria, *regio* II): *c]ur(atori) [rei publicae d]ato ab Imp(eratore)*. The phrase *dato ab imperatore* is also used of the *curatores* of minor roads: *CIL* IX 2655 (Aesernia, *regio* IV: *curator(i) viae Cubulter(inae) dato a divo Hadria[ano]* and *curatori viae Allifanae dato ab Imp(eratore) Anton[ino Pio]*. This suggests that occasional construction or restoration work on minor roads could also be seen as a sign of imperial benefaction, as were probably the occasional appointment of *curatores kalendari*, for whom the same phrase is used; the curator of *CIL* IX 1160 was also *curat(ori) Kal(endari) Nolanorum dato ab Imp(eratore) Antonino Aug(usto) Pio.*

45. Into the first part of this policy also fall Domitian's abortive edict on vines (Suet. *Dom.* 7.2, 14.2), which privileged Italy, and Trajan's edict that senators must have a third of their wealth investing in Italian land (Plin. *Ep.* 6.19). On Domitian's edict, see also Stat. *Silv.* 4.3.11–12; Piccoli 2004, 118–119; Purcell 1985, 9; and Tchernia 1986.

46. On the relative size of Cisalpine cities, see de Ligt 2008.

47. C. Galerius, the augur and *duovir—duoviri* were high-ranking magistrates in Roman municipalities—commemorated at Ariminum (tribal affiliation *Aniensis*), must, by his tribal affiliation (*Lemonia*), be a citizen of Bononia; it is possible that he held his duovirate in both towns (*CIL* XI 413). *CIL* XI 6793a also records a citizen of Bononia commemorated in Ariminum. *AE* 1973, 237, an epitaph from Mutina, commemorates a decurion of Bononia. One *vestiarius* from Bononia held a sevirate at Cremona (*CIL* XI 6839 = *AE* 1896, 113). Although town charters are not preserved for either Bononia or Ariminum, it is possible that magistracies in neighboring towns had residency prerequisites. The Republican period charter from Tarentum specifies that potential decurions of Tarentum own a house with at least 1,500 roof tiles in the city of Tarentum or its territory (*CIL* I^2 590 = *ILS* 6086).

48. LDDD at Bononia: *CIL* XI 694 (dedication to Isis); *CIL* XI 696 = *ILS* 4313 (dedication to I.O.M.D.). LDDD at Ariminum: *CIL* XI 377 (commemoration of a *iuridicus*); *CIL* XI 378 = *ILS* 1381 (commemoration of a governor of Pannonia under Antoninus Pius); *CIL* XI 385 (commemoration of a *primus pilus* centurion); *CIL* XI 386 = *ILS* 6659 (commemoration of a *primus pilus* centurion); *CIL* XI 387 = *ILS* 6660; *CIL* XI 392 (commemoration of local *duumvir*); *CIL* XI 393 = *ILS* 2739 (commemoration); *CIL* XI 405 (commemoration of a woman); *CIL* XI 411 (commemoration of *augur* and *duumvir*); *CIL* XI 417 = *ILS* 6661 (commemoration of *duumvir*); *CIL* XI 418 (commemoration of augur and *duumvir*); *CIL* XI 420 (commemoration of sevir); *CIL* XI 422 (commemoration of local decurion). The discrepancy in numbers between Ariminum and Bononia probably does not reflect differing corpus sizes—for both cities the surviving number is just over five hundred—but rather differing compositions of inscription types, with fewer honorific inscriptions for Bononia, where funerary inscriptions greatly predominate. For the use of LDDD in funerary inscriptions in imperial Italy, see Milano and Pistarino 2008.

49. The *vici* at Ariminum: *CIL* XI 377; *CIL* XI 379 = *ILS* 6664 (a *vicus Dianensis*); *CIL* XI 404 (possibly a *vicus Fortunae*); *CIL* XI 417 = *ILS* 6661 (a *vicus Velabri*); *CIL* XI 418; *CIL* XI 419 = *AE* 1997, 53 (a *vicus Cermali*); *CIL* XI 421 = *ILS* 6662 (a *vicus Aventini*). The two of the *vici* at Ariminum also share names with *vici* at Psidian Antioch, an Augustan colony, which suggests that the organization of Ariminum into *vici* took place during the Augustan period (Chilver 1941, 18; cf. Keppie 1983, 91, and Mansuelli 1941, 47. That division into *vici* at Ariminum seems to have continued through the second century CE. Elsewhere in Italy divisions of cities into *vici* are attested at Rome (on the division by Augustus, see Suet. *Aug.* 30 and Plin. *HN* 3.66, as well as Lott 2004. For individual *vici*, see Aul. Gell. 18.4; Suet. *Aug* 57; *CIL* VI 975; *CIL* VI 9185, *CIL* VI 2225; *CIL* VI 2226), Pompeii, Ostia (*ILS* 5395), Volcei (*CIL* X 415), Spoletum (*CIL* XI 4815), Puteoli (*CIL* X 1631 = *ILS* 6322 = *AE* 2000, 342; *ILS* 6323 = *AE* 1890, 65 = *AE* 1977, 200), Pisaurum in Umbria (*CIL* XI 6367; *CIL* XI 6359; *CIL* XI 6362 = *ILS* 7364; *CIL* XI 6378), Fanum Fortunae (*CIL* XI 6237 = *ILS* 6653), and Castrum Novum in Etruria (*CIL* XI 3585. Divisions into *curiae* are found in Italy at Lanuvium (*CIL* XIV 2114 = *ILS* 6201; *CIL* XIV 2120 = *ILS* 6199 = *AE* 2005, 309; *CIL* XIV 2126 = *ILS* 6202), Tarentum (*FIRA*[2] 1.168), and Savaria (*CIL* III 4150). Cf. Nicolet 1988.

50. *CIL* VIII 7030 = *ILS* 1119 (from Cirta, Numidia).

51. Suet. *Nero* 7 mentions the speech but not the fire, and Tac. *Ann.* 12.58.3 does not go into detail about the extent of the fire. Work on the Flaminia by Augustus: *Res Gestae* 20.5; *CIL* XI 365 = *ILS* 84 (building inscription on the Arch of Augustus at Ariminum). Restoration of the Via Aemilia by Augustus: *CIL* XI 8103 = *ILS* 9371 = *AE* 1903, 164 (Bononia); *AE* 2000, 584 (near Parma); AE 1952, 56 (Ariminum). *CIL* XI 366 (= *ILS* 133) records that *C(aius) Caesar August(i) f(ilius) co(n)s(ul) vias omnes Arimini stern(it)*: C. Caesar, consul and son of Augustus, paved all the roads of Ariminum.

52. Ariminum: *CIL* XI 368 (building inscription of Domitian); *CIL* XI 371 = Horster 2001, 329–330, cf. *CIL* XI 375 = Horster 2001, 329.

53. Tac. *Hist.* 3.34 records that Cremona received aid both from other Italian towns and from Vespasian, whose troops had just sacked it. See Suet. *Tit.* 8 for Titus's aid to the Campanian cities after Vesuvius's eruption and to Rome after a fire.

54. Suet. *Claud.* 25.3.

55. *AE* 1984, 508.

56. The *Fasti Praenestini*, dating from the Augustan period and set up by M. Verrius Flaccus in the forum at Praeneste near Rome (*Inscr. It.* 13–2, 17, Suet. *Gram.* 17), shows the frequency of public holidays commemorating Augustus and the deified Caesar. The *feriale Duranum*, a cohort's festival calendar preserved on an early third-century papyrus, also shows a high frequency of festival days dedicated to the imperial family; the calendar even proscribes specific sacrifices to be made for deified members of the imperial family (*P. Dura* 54).

57. Claudius's edict on Jewish rights also came with a proviso that the edict be displayed for at least thirty days (Joseph. *AJ* 19.91).

58. *CIL* XI 368; cf. Horster 2001, 328–329.

59. *CIL* IX 2438.

60. Tac. *Ann.* 3.33, Dio 59.15.

61. On Faventia in general, see Guarnieri 2000; for Caesena, see Grazia Maioli 2000.

62. *CIL* XI 556 = *ILS* 5687. Antononius: *CIL* VIII 7030 = *ILS* 1119

63. SHA *Pert.* 2.

64. *AE* 1991, 694 = *AE* 2002, 477 (building inscription). Caesena (deLigt 2008, 169) seems to have been—on the basis of similar descriptions by Strabo—about the same size as Faventia. The imperially sponsored work on the Balneum Aurelianum at Caesena dates from the reign of Aurelian in the third century (*CIL* XI 556 = *ILS* 5687)

65. Plin. *Ep.* 5.4, 5.13. The Vicetian representatives in Rome had hired the hapless Tuscilius Nominatus to speak on their behalf, but Nominatus did not show up in court; Vicetian connections apparently had their limits.

66. *CIL* XI 565.

67. On Greek and Roman funerary imprecations, particularly on the rather threatening corpus from Asia Minor, there is a vast bibliography, for which see Chaniotis 2004.

68. Viroconium: *RIB* 292 = *CLE* 806 = *AE* 1959, 158 = *AE* 1995, 997. Mogontiacum: *CIL* XIII: 6961. Carnuntum: *CIL* III 11214, *AE* 1929, 204; Scardona: *CIL* III 2817 = *ILS* 02467 = *AE* 2002, 87. Rome: *AE* 1966, 33 (cf. *AE* 1969/70, 196); *AE* 1916, 51.

69. Troesmis: *CIL* III 6203.

70. *AE* 1999, 647. The relevant portion of the inscription reads DECUR NUCERIAE APL, with Susini 1958 providing a restoration of *decur(io) Nuceriae Ap(u)l(ae)* and a suggestion that *Nuceria* here stands for *Luceria*, on the basis of the restoration of *Apulae*, on the attestation of another veteran of the IIII Macedonica and on the not uncommon substitution of Nuceria for Luceria. Todisco 1999 cites Suetonius's reference to Vitellius's domus at Nuceria (Suet. *Vit.* 2.2) and Tacitus's citation of Vitellius's domus at Luceria (Tac. *Hist.* 3.86.1); Todisco also proffers a second century *curator rei publicae Nucerinorum Apulorum et Spoletinorum* (*AE* 1952, 220). It should be added that the attribution of Pomponius Severus to the IIII Macedonica is probable but not certain, given the heavy damage to the top half of the stone; the V Macedonica is possible but not likely, "on the grounds of space available" (Keppie 2000, 324). There is a Nuceria Camellaria in Umbria, near Perusia, and a decurionate there would be more reasonable, given the general range of intercity officeholding in imperial Italy (mostly within the same or neighboring regiones), yet this site would require another interpretation of the APL abbreviation.

71. *CIL* XI 352. The inscription notably bears a funerary imprecation, with the stipulation that anyone disturbing the tomb pay a fine to the municipal treasury of Ravenna;

this underlines the choice available to local inhabitants, with two Caesenans choosing two different means of enforcing the inviolability of their burial places. Other connections between inhabitants of Ravenna and towns along the Via Aemilia can be seen at Mutina (*CIL* XI 863 = *ILS* 665 = *AE* 2003, 661), Faventia (*CIL* XI 61, a *verna*), Bononia (*CIL* XI 21, veteran of *legio VII Claudia Pia Fidelis*), Ferrara (*ILS* 9223 = *AE* 1898, 144), Cremona (*CIL* XI 347, a *decurio Cremonae* commemorated at Ravenna). It is important to note that Ravenna was anomalous for northern Italy, and veterans drawn through Ravenna into northern Italy are clustered around the eastern end of the Po Valley.

CHAPTER FIVE. **Novum Comum**

1. Luraschi 2013, 8–9.

2. Strabo 5.1.6 records that Gaius Strabo, otherwise unattested and possessing a praenomen not normally used by the Scipiones, established three thousand colonists at Como in 77 BCE, but the episode—even if Gaius Scipio is to be identified with L. Cornelius Scipio Asiaticus Aemilianus, the son of the M. Aemilius Lepidus who led a short-lived revolt in northern Etruria and Cisalpine Gaul in 77—finds little verification at Como (Luraschi 2013, 18–20). Strabo also mistakes Strabo's grant of Latin colonial status for colonization. On Caesar's colony of 59, there is ample documentation for its foundation and its contested status: App. *BC* 2.26, Suet. *Caes*. 28.3, Strabo 5.1.6, Plut. Caes. 20.2, Cic. *Att*. 5.11.2. See also Bargnesi 2013 on the territory of Como.

3. Maggi 2013, 138–139; Luraschi 2013, 20–23, 30; Sacchi 2013, 151–152. Novum Comum's walls are mentioned by Catullus 35, which suggests that construction was finished by 56 BCE.

4. On euergetism in the Roman Empire, Veyne 1976 remains the standard treatment. Among more recent works, Zuiderhoek 2011 and 2007 stress the relationship between euergetism and elite vulnerability in the Greek east, while Lomas and Cornell 2003 survey the history of euergetism in Italy.

5. Sacchi 2013, 153–155. A fragmentary, late first-century inscription from Como (Pais 747 = Sartori 1994b, no. P00]) commemorates the construction, restoration, or ornamentation of a [nym]phaeum. The temple to Rome and Augustus (or to Rome and the Augusti) is mentioned in Pais 745 [= Sartori 1994b no. P006]. Castelletti and Nobile 1985, tav. Ix provides a map of finds up to 1984; this is updated by Uboldi 1993.

6. Plin. *Ep*. 5.11. On Fabatus's other Italian estates, see Plin. *Ep*. 6.30 (a decaying villa in Campania) and 8.20 (a villa in Ameria in Umbria).

7. Cilo: *CIL* V 5279 = Sartori 1994b, P010; Secundus: Pais 745 = Sartori 1993 P06.

8. Pliny discusses the speech with which he dedicated his new library in *Ep*. 1.8. The dedication of the baths is recorded in the Great Comum inscription (*CIL* V 5263).

9. Plin. *Ep*. 5.7. On Calvisius Rufus, see Birley 2000, 46–47.

10. Saturninus is probably to be identified with a Pompeius Saturninus, but not the orator Pompeius Saturninus of letters 1.8, 1.16, 5.21, 7.7, 7.8, 7.15, and 9.38 because, in 1.16.1, Pliny specifies "*amabam Pompeium Saturninum, hunc dico nostrum*" and because Comum's Pompeius Saturninus died in *Ep*. 5.7, whereas the orator is most definitely alive in books 7 and 9 (Birley 2000, 81; Syme 1968, 143).

11. *CIL* V 5263 and Plin. *Ep*. 4.13 and 7.18. At nearby Novaria, Gaius Valerius Pansa spent 200,000 sesterces on the renovation of baths in the early second century CE (*CIL* V 6513).

12. The possible size of Pliny's fortune is discussed by Duncan-Jones 1982, 32.

13. Sacchi 2013, 157. On the piazza Cacciatori delle Alpi temple, see Sacchi 2006 and Jorio 2004.

14. Sena Chiesa 1993; the two urban necropoleis are those to the city's south (Camerlata, Rebbio, and S. Carpoforo) and west (Borgovico).

15. Lomas 2003, 31–34.

16. Morandi 2004, 588–590, *CIL* I 3403a, and *Supp. It.* 19 Vercelli 1.

17. Fagan 1999, 41–43, 105–109; see Just. *Epit.* 44.2.6 for a possible point of introduction in the early second century BCE.

18. Grumentum (in Lucania): *ILLRP* 606 (= *ILS* 5665); Praeneste: *ILLRP* 659 (*ILS* 5667).

19. Fagan 1999, 42. Pliny *HN* XXXVI 121.

20. For the sanctuary at Lagole, excavated between 1949 and 1956, the most recent publication is Foglari and Gambacurta 2001.

21. *CIL* V 6513.

22. On the construction of bathhouses in northern Italy, see Häussler 2013, 237–238; Chevallier 1983; Fagan 1999. Bergomum: *CIL* V 5136; Novaria: *CIL* V 6513, *CIL* V 6522; Placentia: *CIL* XI 1222 (= *ILS* 1554); Mediolanum: *AE* 1974, 347 (= Sartori 1994a, 54); Asola (near Mantua): *AE* 1972, 202; Brixia: *CIL* V 4412; Verona (*CIL* V 3342 = *ILS* 1148). At Aquileia, a large inscribed epistyle records a possible restoration or construction of a bath (*CIL* V 880 = *IAquil* 505).

23. Brusin 1928, 283; Fagan 1999, no. 168/169; while the baths mentioned are in Altinum, the inscription was found between Aquileia and Grado. The first lines of the inscription are missing, leaving the donor anonymous. Whether either of the two baths mentioned, in use from the Augustan period until the end of the second century if not later, is the same as those excavated between 1995 and 1997 on the via Eliodoro is unclear. The via Eliodoro baths may have been private or public, and the inscription may postdate the main period of activity for the via Eliodoro baths (Cipriano 2010, 159–160, 165).

24. The phrase *in perpetuam* is not preserved in the inscription, but the formula is a common one and can safely be restored; see Cenerini 1987–88, 200n5.

25. *CIL* XI 720 (*ILS* 5674). There are two rasuras (erasures) in the inscription, both in the nomenclature and titulature of the second imperial benefactor. Cenerini 1987–88 suggests Nero as the most probable candidate based on the speech that Nero gave to the Senate on behalf of a fire-ravaged Bononia (Suet. *Ner.* 7.2, Tac. *Ann.* 12.58.2). Fagan 1999, 233, argues for Caligula on the grounds that the *rasura* is not lengthy enough to include Nero's typical titulature for 53–54 CE.

26. Cic. *Fam.* 12.5.2, Suet. *Aug.* 17.2. See Woolf 1990 on the distribution of these schemes.

27. *Epitome de Caesaribus* 12.4. Duncan-Jones 1964, 126–128; the alimentary schemes recorded in *ILS* 977 (from Atina in Latium) and *CIL* XI 1602 represent the earliest dateable examples. There are a handful of inscriptions from outside Italy; these are collected by Patterson 1990n116.

28. *CIL* XI 1147 = *ILS* 6675.

29. Ostia: *CIL* XIV 4450. Terracina: *CIL* X 6328.

30. Plin. *Ep.* 1.8, Plin. *Ep.* 7.18, *CIL* V 5263.

31. Plin. *Ep.* 7.18.

32. Duncan-Jones 1964, 267, gives a population figure of 17,500 free colonists in the late first century BCE. De Ligt 2008 and Kron (forthcoming) discuss high and low estimates for the regional population.

33. It was however larger than the earlier private foundation at Atina and the imperial scheme at Ligures Baebiani (Duncan-Jones 1982, 27).

34. Plin. *Ep.* 7.18.5: Sed oportet privatis utilitatibus publicas, mortalibus aeternas anteferre.

35. On *Aeternitas* in imperial issues, see Noreña 2011b, 174–177, 335–342, and Balbuza 2010. On its relation to other virtues related to generosity and prosperity, see Forbis 1996, 93.

36. Plin. *Ep.* 3.21.6: Tametsi quid homini potest dari maius, quam gloria et laus et aeternitas?

37. Plin. *Ep.* 4.13.3–5, 9. Trans. B. Radice.

38. Pliny says neither how much will be spent on hiring teachers nor how many will be hired, and so the number of pupils benefiting from this benefaction is difficult to estimate. A letter from the Antoninus Pius (Digest 27.1.6.1–2.) to the province of Asia stipulates that in small towns up to three rhetors and three *grammatici* are to be exempt from liturgies, as compared to five each for large cities.

39. (= Agusta-Boularot 1994 no. 21). Agusta-Boularot dates the inscription to the late first or second century; hence the temptation to ascribe Septicianus's position to Pliny and his fellow townsmen's fund is exceptionally tempting.

40. Within the Transpadana Septicii are represented at: *CIL* V 5285 (Comum), *AE* 1995, 665 (Mediolanum), *CIL* V 6785 (Eporedia), *CIL* V 7059 = *ILS* 8545 (Augusta Taurinorum), *AE* 1986, 264 (Vercellae).

41. *CIL* V 3433.

42. Dix 1996, 87. The absence of the baths from the *Letters*—they are mentioned in the Great Comum inscription—suggest a later date. On the confluence of libraries, politics, and eurgetism in the ancient world, see König, Oikonomopoulou, and Woolf 2013.

43. Mirabella Roberti 1974 suggests the viale Lecco baths as the possible site of the library, but Pliny's baths and library seem to be separate benefactions.

44. Plin. *Ep.* 1.8.

45. The speech is one of only two that Pliny says he is preparing for publication. The other is a *laudatio* for Spurinna's son and a somber contrast with the optimistic discussion of the *alimenta* and the future of Comum's children in the library speech.

46. Chevallier 1983, 135–137.

47. Pliny to Maximus: *Ep.* 6.34

48. Although the greatest number of Septicii are attested in Rome, the second largest concentration comes from the Transpadana, with attestations at Vercellae, Eporedia, Mediolanum, and Comum.

49. Gibson and Morello 2012, 19–20 and app. 3, on the dating of book 1 and for bibliography on the dating of individual books of the *Letters*.

50. A funerary inscription from Comum commemorates freedman L. Atilius Philetus from Mediolanum (*CIL* V 5277), and another commemorates L. Romatius Trophimus, who served as a sevir both at Comum and Mediolanum (*CIL* V 5303); on Mediolanenses

holding offices elsewhere in the Transpadana, see Garnsey 1976, 20–22. On the economic connections, see Luraschi 1984.

51. Inscriptions mentioning Pliny from outside the Transpadana: *CIL* XI 5272 (Hispellum in Umbria).

52. *CIL* V 5262 (= *ILS* 2927). Eck 1997, 99. The definitive text of the inscription is provided by Mommsen in *CIL* V.

53. On this history of the inscription and its possible placement, see Alföldy 1999, 221–244; Eck 2001.

54. Alföldy 1999, 222; Mommsen in *CIL* V 5262.

55. Eck 2001, 232–235, on the location of the monument and also the unusual use of the nominative case for Pliny. Henderson 2002, 163, presents the inscription as Pliny's will placed above his baths at Comum. There is no secure evidence for such an assertion.

56. Gibson and Morello 2012, 270.

57. Pliny as scholar dominates the *Letters*; his activities while hunting (Plin. *Ep.*1.6 and 9.36) are but one example.

58. On the chronology of Pliny's career, see Sherwin-White 1966 and Gibson and Morello 2012, 266–269.

59. Gibson and Morello 2012, 271; Eck 1997. Since the inscription does not list anyone responsible for setting up the inscription, and since Pliny's own name is placed in the nominative, the author of the inscription's text must be Pliny (Eck 1997, 99).

60. On Pliny's emphasis on Trajan's consulships and the start of his own consulship, see Noreña 2011b, 36–37. A written copy of the *Panegyricus* was circulated to his friends after it was delivered (Plin. *Ep.* 3.13. and 3.18), exactly as had been done with his library speech (Plin. *Ep.* 1.8).

61. See Noreña 2007 and Woolf 2015 on Pliny's self-portrait in book 10 and connections with the first nine books.

62. On Pliny's innovations, see Noreña 2011b, 11, and Henderson 2002.

63. Sena Chiesa 1993, 201.

64. Fortunati Zuccala 1993, 185. The exact boundaries between the territories of the three municipia is difficult to determine and remains controversial.

65. Vavassori 1993, 263–264, 267–269.

66. *CIL* V 5295, from Como.

67. *CIL* V 5911 (= *ILS* 7527).

68. Luraschi 2013, 24. Forty percent of male remains from the excavations showed signs of injuries associated with heavy use of the back and arms, in a manner consistent with contact sports or the use of a puntàl in maneuvering a gondola.

69. The development of the villa landscape in Roman imperial Italy is not regionally uniform. In central Italy, the number of villas peaked in the first century CE (Marzano 2007, 241–245) and declined in the third and fourth centuries. In northern Italy as in Sicily, the third and fourth centuries saw a resurgence, particularly of large monumental villas. Nevertheless, the villa landscape of northern Italy has its origins in the first century BCE through first century CE. For a well-documented example of the development of a northern Italian villa rustica, albeit one with a hypocaust and extensive interior decoration, see the description of the villa at Isera (in the Trentino-Alto Adige) in Ciotola and Maurina 2011. The villa was in use from the late Augustan era to the second half of the

first century. For an aristocratic maritime villa, see the large Roman villa at the end of the Sirmione peninsula on Lake Garda, in use from the Augustan era to the fourth century (Roffia 1994, 126–131).

70. Plin. *Ep.* 9.7.

71. Gibson and Morello 2012, 200–201.

72. Plin. *Ep.* 9.36 and 40.

73. See esp. De la Ruffiniere du Prey 1994.

74. De la Ruffiniere du Prey 1994, 5–6.

75. Models of cultural change in the Roman Empire have been much discussed in recent decades. For a short history of the debate, see Mattingly 2011, 38–42.

76. Tac. *Agr.* 21.

CHAPTER SIX. **The Tanaro Valley and Italian Networks**

1. The routes and ports by which silk entered the Roman world remain problematic (Parker 2008, 156–157). On the development of Italian sericulture, see Monnas 2008, 4–12. See Bender Jørgensen on silk production predating the Roman empire.

2. Monnas 2008, 6–7.

3. Monnas 2008, 17.

4. Liu 2013, 128–129. White fleeces: Pliny *HN* 8.190–193. Ligurian coarse wool: Strabo 5.1.12.

5. Mutina: Strabo 5.1.12, Colum. 7.2.3. Pollentia: Mart. 14.157, Pliny *HN* 8.191. Altinum: Mart. 14.155. Parma: Mart. 14.155.

6. Chapter 25 (cf. Rees 2004, Corcoran 1995, 205–233, Reynolds 1981). As Liu (2009, 74n81) observes, a full third of the surviving chapters of the price edict cover textiles.

7. Pliny *NH* 19.9.

8. Strabo 5.1.7, Mart. 14.143.

9. Mart. 14.152.

10. Mart. 14.153. Of Martial's thirty-seven epigrams on textiles in book 14, sixteen refer to clothes and fabrics from specific places, and five of those refer to places in northern Italy.

11. Mart. 14.127, 129.

12. Liu 2009, 29–31, 75–77.

13. Liu 2009, 358–377, provides a catalogue and commentary on inscriptions mentioning *collegia centonarii*.

14. Gleba 2012, 219–220.

15. Gleba 2002, 32–33; Lipkin 2012, 103.

16. Gleba 2012, 220.

17. Gleba 2012, 222.

18. Columella *Rust.* 2.12.5, Pliny *NH* 19.7.

19. Gleba 2002, 19, 25.

20. Bazzanella 2012, 205–209.

21. Gleba 2008.

22. Vicari 1994.

23. Jongman 2000.

24. On the "brand-naming" of textiles, see Horden and Purcell 2000, 354–357.

25. Sebesta 1994, 72.

26. Mart. *Ep*. 14.155, Pliny *HN* 8.190–193, Columella *Rust*. 7.2–4. A hooded cloak from Canusium in Apulia is valued at 4,000 *denarii* in the Edict on Prices (*BE* 9.4).

27. Sebesta 1994.

28. Columella *Rust*. 7.4–5.

29. Horden and Purcell 2000, 355–356, on the general underrepresentation of ancient textiles.

30. Corti 2012a, 217–218, on Modense weights; Bergamini 2009 on weight designs across the lower Po.

31. See Bernabò Brea, Bianchi, and Lincetto 2003 on the dimensions, distributions, and forms of Middle Bronze Age Terramara loom weights.

32. Churchin 2004, 157.

33. Vindolanda: *RIB* 2445.6.

34. Dyson 1992, 136.

35. Corti 2012a, 219.

36. Cremaschi 2009.

37. Corti 2012b.

38. Verboven 2011, 190, highlights important differences between medieval guilds and ancient *collegia*. See Liu 2013, 136–139, on possible parallels between the guilds and *collegia*.

39. Liu 2013, 128, collects inscriptions mentioning *collegia* of textile workers and dealers; for the *collegia centonariorum*, see Liu 2009.

40. For a history of scholarship on the Roman *collegia*, see Perry 2006.

41. Patterson 1994, 233–234.

42. Tran 2006, 97, 409–459.

43. *AE* 1946, 210.

44. *CIL* V 6123 (= Sartori 1994a, 91), *CIL* V 5943 (= Sartori 1994a, 93).

45. *CIL* V 5925 (= *ILS* 7578), *CIL* V 5926, *CIL* V 5928 (= *ILS* 7580), *CIL* V 5929 (= *ILS* 7579).

46. Brixellum: *CIL* XI 1031 (= *ILS* 7290). Aquileia: *IAquil* 678a+b.

47. AE 1915, 58 (the inscription dates to 117–136 CE).

48. SHA *Pert*. 3–4. Liu 2009, 66–69, discusses the terminology and uses for felt in relation to the larger category of *centones*. Cf. SHA *Pert*. 13.4 on Pertinax's running of an unnamed business at Vada Sabatia (Vado Ligure) after he became emperor.

49. Liu 2013, 129; Strabo 5.1.7.

50. SHA *Pert*. 8.1–3.

51. Dio 74.3.1–2 says that his father kept a cloth shop, which is reasonable given the Tanaro Valley's wool industry.

52. SHA *Pert*. 1–2. *PIR* H 73. See Donati 2002, Devijver 1988, and Alföldy 1974b on Pertinax's career.

53. Dio 74.8–11.

54. Passerini 1939, 173; Šašel 1972. Freis 1967 and Mench 1968 both put estimates at the percentage of Italians in the urban cohorts between 85%–90%. Busch 2007 provides updated estimates for the total military presence in Rome.

55. Tac. *Ann*. 4.5.

56. Šašel 1972, 474; 89% of the men on the list are Italian.

57. *CIL* VI 2649 (= *ILS* 2035).

58. Dio 75.2.

59. *CIL* II.7 355 (= *EAOR* VII 31).

60. *Inscriptions of Roman Tripolitania* 606 (= *AE* 1953, 188).

61. *CIL III* 12925 (= *ILS* 5119).

62. *CIL* XI 862 (= *ILS* 7559 = *EAOR* 2.14). The altar is dated to the first or second century CE.

CHAPTER SEVEN. Aquileia and Imperial Networks

1. Herodian 8.5.7–9.

2. Herodian 8.6.3–4.

3. Livy 37.46–47.

4. Livy 39.55, 40.34.

5. Livy 40.34.

6. Livy 43.1.

7. Calderini (1930, 336) provides estimates of Aquileia's population during the Principate, which range from 100,000 to 800,000. Even the lower estimate represents a huge increase in population from the initial colonial foundation of 3,000 settlers and their families. In comparison, Delia 1988 puts the maximum population of Alexandria, the Mediterranean's most important port city, at 500,000–600,000 during the Principate, with a number near Diodorus's 300,000+ probably closer to reality.

8. "πόλις μεγάλη": Strabo 5.1.8. Conventi 2004; Bertacchi 1965 put Aquileia's walls at 355 x 1154 m, an increase more than the 1080 m length provided by Brusin 1934. Verona: Conventi 2004, 113–116; Richmond and Holford 1935; Conforti Calcagni 1999, 17.

9. Alföldy 1999, 261, 286. See also Broughton 1968, 206, and Crawford 1974, n241. A Cnaeus Octavius Muso, a quaestor of Marius in 106 BCE, might also have an Aquileian origin. See Alföldy 1999, 285–286, for the identification of this Muso (Sall. *Iug.* 104), with the Cn. Octavius listed as a member of Pompey Strabo's *consilium* in the decree of *CIL* VI 37045 (= *ILS* 8888 = *ILLRP* 515).

10. Aquileia is referred to as a *munipium* in *CIL* V 968, a tablet commemorating a gift made to the city by a citizen of Interamna (= *ILLRP* 541 = *IAquil* 51). The change to *municipium* is also marked by the transition from colonial *duoviri* to municipal *quattuorviri* in the first century BCE; the earliest attested *quattuorviri* are on inscriptions *CIL* V 966 (= *IAquil* 36), *CIL* V 8288 (= *IAquil* 37), both dated the middle of the first century BCE, while the last—and indeed only—mention of *duoviri* at Aquileia is in *CIL* V 971, dating to the early first century BCE (= *IAquil* 33). For the Velina tribe at Aquileia, see Forni 1989.

11. Cic. *Font.* 2.

12. Livy records the stationing of troops or ships at Aquileia throughout the campaigns against the Istrians (41.1, 41.5, 41.10, 43.1), and the city probably served as a base again during the campaign of Tuditanus in 129, as the Aquileian findspot of the Elogium of Tuditanus suggests (in two fragments, see *CIL* I^2 652 = *ILLRP* 335 = *Inscr. It.* XIII 3n90, *Inscr. It.* X 4n31; for possible restorations see Lettich 2003, Fontana 1997, and Bandelli 1989). Vedaldi Iasbez 1989 proposes that the Aurelius Cotta of *CIL* V 863 (= *CIL* I^2 739) is C. Aurelius Cotta, cos. 75 BCE, and that this Cotta was also present at Aquileia.

13. Caes. *BG* 1.10, Suet. *Aug.* 20. Suet. *Tib.* 7 also indicates the presence of Julia and Tiberius at Aquileia around 11–10 BCE. Augustus and Herod: Joseph. *AJ* 16.91.

14. For the fleet detachment at Aquileia, see *IAquil* 2816 and *CIL* V 960, as well as Panciera 1977. For the praetorians at Aquileia, see Keppie 2000, 115–116.

15. Bertacchi 2003, 16.

16. Dio 54.20 and *CIL* III 2973 (= *ILS* 899) for the campaigns of P. Silius; Suet. *Aug.* 20, 25, *Tib.* 16.

17. Herod. 8.2.3–4. Trans. Echols.

18. Picolli 2004. Pliny is able to name a number of Adriatic vintages growing in popularity at the end of the first century BCE (*HN* 14.67), one of which, the *vinum punicum*, Livia cited as the reason for her longevity.

19. Herodian 8.3.

20. Panciera 1972, 92, who also notes the dedication of a *vestiarius Aquiliensis* in Bogliuno in Istria (*CIL* V 324). See also *IAquil* 678a+b, the funerary *cippi* (markers) of the cemetery of the *vestiarii*.

21. *Purpurarii*: *AE* 1956, 74a, *CIL* V 1044 (= *IAquil* 724), *IAquil* 723; *fabri*: *CIL* V 1030, *AE* 1992, 709, *IAquil* 703, *IAquil* 704, *IAquil* 709; *lintiones*: *CIL* V 1041 (= *IAquil* 706); *negotiatores*: *CIL V* 1047 (= *IAquil* 717), *AE* 1991, 786, *AE* 2003, 678, *IAquil* 713, and *Insc. Aq.* 715, *IAquil* 718.

22. The Gavii at Aquileia: (a) liberti: *IAquil* 599, *IAquil* 1149, *CIL* V 793 (= *IAquil* 274), *CIL* V 1032 (= *IAquil* 1147), *CIL* V 1227 (= *IAquil* 1145), *CIL* V 1230 (= *IAquil* 1148), and *CIL* V 1232 (= *IAquil* 1150), (b) unspecified: *CIL* V 8973 (= *IAquil* 612), *IAquil* 113, *IAquil* 667, and *CIL* V 1008 (= *IAquil* 617). For the Veronese Gavii, see Alföldy 1999, 159–193, and Chilver 1941, 90.

23. For Aquileia, see *CIL* V 819 = *IAquil* 340, *IAquil* 289, and *IAquil* 516. In Brixia, where documentation on the sevirate in northern Italy is the fullest, about 7% of attested sevirs hold the sevirate in another town, while at Forum Iulii, closer to Aquileia, the proportion is 25%. In order to create a sufficiently large sample size, the category of *seviri* here includes those described as *seviri* and *seviri augustales*, although it should be noted that the precise distinction among *seviri*, augustales, and *seviri augustales* remains somewhat unclear, despite extensive study (Hope 2001, 30).

24. Pola: *CIL* V 71 (= *Inscr. It.* 10–1, 296); Forum Iulii: *CIL* V 1758, *CIL* V 1768 (= *Sup. It.* 16: 6 = *AE* 1998, 572).

25. Altinum: *AE* 1981, 406; Aquileia: *IAquil* 289; Ateste: *CIL* V 2525; Opitergium: *CIL* V 1977; Patavium: *CIL* V 2875; Forum Cornelii: *CIL* V 1884 (the inscription is from Concordia).

26. *Praeceptores*: *IAquil* 722; *rhetorici*: *IAquil* 2435, *CIL* V 1028 (= *IAquil* 726).

27. Concordia: Vedaldi Iasbez 1994, 306.

28. Plin. *Ep.* 4.13.

29. While about a third of inscriptions recording doctors come from Aquileia, their concentration in Aquileia is no doubt exaggerated by the large number of inscriptions found there. Aquileia has nearly five times the inscriptions as the next largest sources of inscriptions—Mediolanum, Brixia, and Verona—and nearly ten times as many as nearby Concordia and Tergeste. Altinum: *CIL* V 2183; Vicetia: *CIL* V 3156.

30. Chevallier 1983, 128. Indeed, the existence of *familia gladiatoria Transpadana* (attested at Concordia and Aquileia: *CIL* V 8659, *IAquil* 487), as well as the commemoration of gladiators outside their hometown (such as the Aquileian citizen, from Bellunum, buried at Salona in Illyricum: *CIL* III 12925), suggests that the games in northern Italy drew from a regional pool of trained gladiators and that the support structure of supplies and men for the games was broadly based. Animals for the games would have had to be supplied from outside the region; one of Pliny's correspondents at Verona was unable to get the African panthers he had bought for his games in time because of travel delays caused by weather (*Ep.* 6.34).

31. Strabo 4.6.12.

32. *CIL* III 4788. Both Horace (*Carm.* 1.16.9) and Ovid mention Norican iron (*Met.* 14.712).

33. For the Baltic amber trade, see Plin. *HN* 37.11, Giovannini 2002. The amber road, passing through Carnuntum, Savaria, and Celeia, later fell within the provincial borders of Pannonia.

34. Giovannini 2002, 159; Bergonzi 1997.

35. Calvi 2005.

36. *CIL* III 4843 (= *ILS* 2015); see also Alföldy 1974a, 76.

37. Piccottini 1976.

38. Verzár-Bass 1996 sees the confluence of northern Italian and Balkan/Macedonian artistic traditions in these later monuments.

39. Tchernia 2016, 86. For the distribution of lamps, see di Filippo Balestrazzi 1996.

40. Mócsy 1974, 130.

41. At least some of this trade seems to have been in swords and other metal military equipment, made from provincial ores but manufactured at Aquileia (Buora 1996).

42. The Liburni and the Veneti, for example, shared similar onomastic patterns (Wilkes 1992, 71).

43. Harl 1996 attributes the migration of Dalmatian miners to promises of good pay, free board, and "perhaps a tacit understanding that miners could cart off unreported production"(80–81).

44. Bolla 1996.

45. Strabo 5.1.8.

46. Zaccaria 1996.

47. For the prosopography of the Barbii, see Šašel 1966. For their role in trade, see Tchernia 2016, 61–62.

48. For third-century examples, see *IAquil* 952 and Lettich 2003, no. 452, both sarcophagi.

49. *CIL* V 864.

50. *IAquil* 676, the funerary monument for the *collegium sac(rum) Mart(is)*, whose members included the freedwoman Barbia Amanda and the *medicus* Aulus Barbius Zmaragdus. *IAquil* 96 records the third-century dedication of L. Barbius Montaus, a *primus pilus* centurion.

51. Altinum: *AE* 2001, 1035, *CIL* V 2209; Ateste: *CIL* V 2712, *Sup. It.* 15, 143; Atria: *I.Adria* 16; Bellunum: *AE* 2002, 545; Concordia: *CIL* V 1916; Forum Iulii: *AE* 1998, 575;

Opitergium: *CIL* V 1985; Pola: *Inscr. It.* 10–1, 230, Tergeste: *CIL* V 577–579, *Inscr. It.* 10–4, 1–4; Vicetia: *CIL* V 3127; Ravenna: *CIL* XI 80, 165.

52. Brixia: *CIL* V 4546 (= *Inscr. It.* 10–5, 345); Cremona: *CIL* V 4104.

53. Puteoli: *CIL* X 1654, 2162.

54. A Ti. Barbius is commemorated in the inscription (*CIL* III 4815) on the sixteenth-century cast of the Magdelensburg youth, but although the inscription may be a copy of an ancient one, it is still a modern addition whose veracity cannot be verified. For Dalmatia, see Zaccaria 1985.

55. *CIL* III 4156, a late-first-century CE dedication to Isis. An augustalis at Savaria is also attested at Aquileia (*CIL* V 1011 = *IAquil* 838).

56. For Grado, see Vedaldi Iasbez 1994, 333–334, and Rebecchi 1980.

57. Slane 2002, 328.

58. Calvi 2005.

59. Duncan-Jones 2002, 32.

60. Maselli Scotti 2002b, Fontana 2010, Fontana 1997, and Chevallier 1990, 74–76. The dedication to Anubis Augustus (*CIL* V 8210) is otherwise unparalleled.

61. Blake 2014, 41. LHIIIC = twelfth–eleventh centuries BCE.

62. On the diffusion of Aquileian glassware, see Facchini 2005. Aquileian origins are cited in the epitaph of a praetorian interred at Fundi in northern Campania (*CIL* X 6229) and in the charming verse epitaph of L. Tettienus Vitalis from Augusta Taurinorum (*CIL* V 7047 = *AE* 1999, 783 = *AE* 2000, 639 = *AE* 2002, 563 = *AE* 2003, 699, 775a).

63. The epitaph of C. Birrius from Placentia: *AE* 1935, 9 (= *AE* 1964, 212). The epitaph of L. Cantio from Hasta: *CIL* V 7563.

64. Roncaglia 2015.

65. Surviving rosters with Aquileians: *CIL* VI 2375 (= *CIL* VI 2404 = *CIL* VI 32515 = *AE* 1999, 421), *CIL* VI 2378 (= *CIL* VI 32519 = *CIL* VI 32911), *CIL* VI 2379 (= *CIL* VI32520 = *AE* 1968, 26 = *AE* 1999, 421), *CIL* VI 2380 (= *CIL* VI 2381 = *CIL* VI 32522), *CIL* VI 2382 (= *CIL* VI 32638 = *AE* 1964, 120a), and possibly *CIL* VI 3886 (= *CIL* VI 32531). The epitaph of the praetorian Q. Caedius also gives an Aquileian origin (*CIL* VI 37214).

66. Alföldy 1999, 1984, 1982.

67. Brusin 1934; Bertacchi 2003. For the *macellum*, see Maselli Scotti, Mandruzzato, and Tiussi 2006.

68. *CIL* V 875 = *ILS* 1374 = *IAquil* 495a–b.

69. SHA *Marc.*13–14, SHA *Verus* 10.

CHAPTER EIGHT. **Late Antique Transformations**

1. Northern Italy was the primary battleground in 69 CE, with two decisive battles fought on the road between Cremona and Bedriacum, the first fought in March, between Otho and Vitellius's subordinates Caecina and Valens (Tac. *Hist.* 2.23–45) and the second in October, between the Vitellians and Vespasian's subordinate Antonius (3.15–33). The main victim of the war was Cremona, which was thoroughly sacked by Flavian troops after the second battle of Cremona (3.32–34), although Placentia too lost its amphitheater to fire during a siege by Caecina (2.21), and atrocities were committed in western Liguria, particularly at Albintimilium, by Othonian troops in preparation for the Vitellian inva-

sion (2.12–13 and Tac. *Agr.* 7, which counts Tacitus's mother-in-law as among the victims around Albintimilium). Also lost were many north Italians in the legions; certainly a portion of the dead after the second battle of Cremona had family members who were close enough to provide them with burial (Tac. *Hist.* 2.45).

2. Most immediate was an unwillingness on the part of Italian buyers to purchase slaves from Cremona; later, a proclamation by Vespasian's subordinate Antonius forbid the keeping of any captives from Cremona. Funds for rebuilding the town's buildings came as benefactions from other Italian towns (Tac. *Hist.* 2.34), generosity possibly spurred by the presence of Italians from other towns present in Cremona during the siege who had come to the town for an annual fair (2.30).

3. On the destruction of Opitergium and the siege of Aquileia, see Lucian *Alex.* 48 and Amm. Marc. 29.6, as well as Fitz 1966. At Opitergium (modern Ozerzo), damage to the city seems to have been exaggerated by Lucian, and the town continued to function and indeed survived further sackings by Visigoths and Huns in the fifh century (Stella Busana 1994, 28). The *praetentura Italiae et Alpium*, for which the evidence is the *cursus honorum* preserved in an honorific inscription of Q. Antistius Adventus Postumius Aquilinus at Thibilis in Numidia (*ILS* 8977), seems to have been one of the unspecified measures taken by Marcus Aurelius and Lucius Verus for the defense of Italy and Illyricum (SHA *Marc.* 14); there is no evidence that the *praetentura* outlasted the wars with the Marcomanni. This is not to suggest that the invasion was not psychologically traumatic, particularly since invasions of Italy by foreign troops had not been seen since the end of the second century BCE; cf. Zaccaria 2002 on the use at this time of apotropaic religious iconography particularly tied with foreign invasions. It should also be noted that the dating of this invasion has been disputed, with the dates 167 and 170 CE most often cited, although other dates have been proffered (cf. Fitz 1966 for 169 CE). The reasons cited for the 167 campaign are the presence of the *praetentura* in 168 or 169 (according to its place in Aquilinus's *cursus*), which would have prevented an invasion; the discussion of *tantus timor* at Rome in 167 or 168 (SHA *Marc.* 12), suggesting that the larger invasion occurred at that time; and the lack of mention of Marcus Aurelius as being at the *limes* during the larger invasion, as he would have probably been in 170. For 170, the most commonly cited reasons are the mention only of Marcus and not of Lucius Verus—who died in 169—during the campaign, and Lucian's story of the charlatan Alexander advising Marcus to throw two lions into the Danube to stop the invasion—the lions quickly swam to the other side and were clubbed by the Marcomanni—which suggests a later date following Roman campaigns on the Danube. On the basis of the references to Marcus alone in reference to the campaign, as well as the lack of later mentions of the *praetentura*—suggesting that it was either out of service by the time of the larger invasion or proven ineffective by that invasion and then discontinued—I prefer the 170 date.

4. On Maximinus at Aquileia: Herodian 7–8 and SHA *Max.* 21–22.

5. On Philip the Arab at Verona: Aur. Vict. *Caes.* 28.10, Zosimus 1.22, Eutropius 9.3, Zonaras 12.19. The location of the battle is not entirely certain; a fragment of John of Antioch places the battle at Beroea in Macedonia instead of Verona (*FHG* 4.597–598).

6. The chronology of this period of the third century is not altogether certain, owning to the relative paucity and unreliability of the sources. The major literary sources are Aurelius Victor's *De Caesaribus*, published around 361 CE; the world history of the

twelfth-century Byzantine chronicler Zonaras; the first book of the history of Zosimus, written at the end of the fifth and beginning of the sixth century; in the *Historia Augusta* the unfortunately unreliable lives of Gallienus, Claudius II Gothicus, and Aurelian; Eutropius's abridged Roman history, written in the second half of the fourth century; and Jordanes's sixth-century *Getica*.

7. On the 254 invasion: Zon. 12.22, Dexippus, *FHG* 3.682, Oros. 7.22. On the 259 invasion: Zos. 1.37, Eutrop. 9.8, Aur. Vict. *Caes*. 33.

8. The defeat and invasion of the Juthungi are recorded on a votive inscription, found in 1992, set up by M. Simplicinius Genialis, the general who defeated them (*AE* 1993, 1231).

9. *AE* 1993, 1231, ln. 10.

10. *AE* 1993, 1231, ln. 11.

11. Aur. Vict. *Caes*. 33.18, Eutrop. 9.11, SHA *Gall*. 14.

12. SHA *Aur*. 18.3, 21.1, Zos. 1.49, *Epit. Caes*. 35.2, Dexippus, *FHG* 3.685–686. Cf. *CIL* XI 6308 and 6309, two inscriptions from Fano, related to Aurelian's victory there.

13. SHA *Claud*. 12.2, Zon. 12.26, Zos. 1.46, Eutrop. 9.11. The effects and symptoms of the epidemic at Carthage are described by the contemporary Cyprian (*de mortalitate*). Jord. *Get*. 104 says the epidemic hit Alexandria and Egypt particularly hard. Cf. Eutrop. 9.5, Oros. 7.21.5, SHA *Gall*. 5.2ff, Euseb. *HE* 7.22, Zos. 1.26.3, Zon. 12.21. In northern Italy this combination of plague and wars put a halt to normal life. In later third-century Aemilia there were few new buildings, while older ones were poorly maintained, converted from luxury homes to service buildings or abandoned entirely (Ortalli 1992 At Tridentum, building outside the walls ceased, and buildings on the west side of the city show signs of destruction (Ciurletti 2003).

14. Ticinum: SHA *Claud*. 5, Aur. Vict. *Caes*. 33, *Epit*. 34. Mediolanum: Zos. 1.40.1.

15. Throughout the provinces in the late 250s and 260s other mints—such as those at Colonia Agrippina, Siscia, and Smyrna—were established close to combat zones (de Blois 1976, 93).

16. Verona, begun under Gallienus: *CIL* V 3329 (= *ILS* 544), the building inscription on the Porta Borsari. After the construction of these walls, extramural buildings in Verona were abandoned (Cavalieri-Manasse and Bruno 2003, 51). Rome, begun under Aurelian: SHA *Aurel*. 21 and 39, Aur. Vict. *Caes*. 35.7, Oros. 7.23, Eutrop. 9.15.

17. de Blois 1976, 28.

18. The transition of the town's name from *Ticinum*, as the town appears in Roman period literary and epigraphic sources, to the modern *Pavia*, from the medieval *Papia*, has been the source of debate (the name *Papia* is first clearly attested for Ticinum in the seventh century). Celtic, Ligurian, Roman, and Byzantine origins for the name *Papia* have been suggested. For a summary of theories and scholarship, see Gabba 2000, who proposes that the name derived from an informal name of the city during the Roman period as *urbs Pupia* or simply *Papia*, itself derived from the name of a Papius presumably involved with the organization of the city following its enfranchisement in 49 BCE. The voting tribe of the town in the imperial period was Papiria (cf. *CIL* V 6411, 6419, 6427, 6431, among others), as it was at Bellunum (Belluno).

19. Conventi 2004, 58, 96, 111, 182.

20. *Sup. It*. 9, 24. Although this inscription belongs to a late second- or third-century sarcophagus, *collegia nautarum* are attested throughout northern Italy before Late Antiquity,

and there is no reason to assume that Ticinum's *collegium* postdated these others significantly. *Collegia nautarum* are attested at Brixia (*Inscr. It.* 10–5, 1070 *CIL* V 4990 = *Inscr. It.* 10–5, 1065), Comum (*CIL* V 5295), Mediolanum (*CIL* V 5911 = *ILS* 7527; *AE* 1932, 73), Mantua (ILS 7265), Atria (*CIL* V 2315), and Arilica on Lake Garda (*CIL* V 4016 = *ILS* 8373; *CIL* V 4017 = *ILS* 8372). Venetia and Transpadana—there are no attestations from Liguria or Aemilia—account for around a third of all attestations of *collegia nautarum* throughout the empire.

21. Augusta Taurinorum: *CIL* V 6991 (= *ILS* 6751). Verona: *CIL* V 3469; the commemorator, L. Sollius Secundio, had the monument constructed while he was still alive, so the identification of himself as Ticinensis is self-made. *Sup. It.* 9, 19 (Ticinum) shows dual officeholding at Novaria and Ticinum.

22. On senators and *equites* from Ticinum, see Alföldy 1999, 323–325. Ticinenses in the Praetorian Guard and Urban cohorts: *CIL* VI 33038, *CIL* VI 2924, *CIL* VI 32520, *CIL* VI 221 = *ILS* 2160, AE 1984, 104, *AE* 1984, 29. Legionaries and veterans are attested at Iader in Dalmatia (*CIL* III 2913), Colonia Claudia Ara Agrippinensium (*CIL* XIII 8287) and Bonna (*CIL* XIII 8058) in Germany, at Carnuntum (*CIL* III 11209, *AE* 1973, 423) and Ebersdorf (*CIL* III 459) in Pannonia, and at Velitrae in Latium (*CIL* X 6578).

23. As with the setup of a mint at Mediolanum in 259 CE, which was part of a broader policy change of establishing more mints closer to the armies, the transfer of the mint to Ticinum was one of several changes Aurelian made to the configuration of imperial minting operations. Aurelian added new mints and reorganized existing operations; he had the mints at Colonia Agrippina and Treviri transferred to Lugdunum. These changes to the mints were accompanied by a revamping of the monetary system (Crawford 1984, 251; Watson 2004, 130; Harl 1996, 146).

24. Aurelian had temporarily closed the mint at Rome in 271 CE following a violent urban revolt there that prominently featured mint workers displeased at imperial attempts to reform the mint; the revolt was suppressed only with difficulty and in a pitched battle on the Caelian hill near the mint (Zos. 1.49, Eutrop. 9.14, *Epit.* 35.4, SHA *Aurel.* 38.2–4, and Aur. Vict. *Caes.* 35.6, who says that the revolt's leader, Felicissimus, urged the moneyers to file off their coins' mint marks in protest). The *Historia Augusta* claims that 7,000 soldiers died in the battle on the Caelian, but this seems exaggerated.

25. Auson. *Ordo nob. urb.* 7 (Mediolanum).

26. Sid. Apoll. *Carm.* 20.41.

27. *RIC* VI, p. 299.

28. *RIC* VII, p. 87.

29. Crawford 1984, 252.

30. *P. Gen. Lat.* 1, a list of legionary duties dating from the end of the first century CE, records a legionary being sent out for duty at the mint (the specific assignment is dated to the first year of Domitian's reign). Likewise, a cohort at Lugdunum in the first century was probably connected with guarding the imperial mint there (Tac. *Ann.* 3.41). It is reasonable to assume that late-third-century mints, in more unsettled times, had larger groups of soldiers assigned to them. On the production of gold and silver coinage at Ticinum, see *RIC* V–VII, Chiaravalle 1987, and Crawford 1984.

31. See *RIC* VI, p. 105, on early fourth-century mint organization. On job titles in the mint at Rome, see *CIL* VI 42, 43, 44, 239, 741 (115 CE); *CIL* VI 1145 (Constantinian).

32. Chiaravalle 1987, 6–7. *RIC* VI, p. 266. The *officinae* at Ticinum are marked as *P*, *Q*, *S*, and *T* on the mint marks, in addition to the *T* indicating Ticinum.

33. *CIL* VI 43 = *ILS* 1643.

34. C. Valerius Sabinus at Ticinum: *CIL* V 6421 = *AE* 1973, 242. Cf. Watson 2004, 127–128, on Sabinus as Felicissimus's probable successor.

35. Zos. 1.49, Eutrop. 9.14, *Epit.* 35.4, SHA *Aurel.* 38.2–4, and Aur. Vict. *Caes.* 35.6.

36. *RIC* VII, p. 358–359.

37. Crawford 1984, 252.

38. *Exc. Val.* 6.

39. *Not. Dign. Occ.* 42.

40. The practice seems to have continued throughout the fourth century. In the 370s, defeated Goths and Taifali were settled along the via Aemilia at Mutina, Parma, and Reggio Aemilia, where they were given unoccupied land to work (Amm. Marc. 31.9). The presence of these barbarian settlements is also attested by surviving place names (Christie 2006, 309), which Paul the Deacon (*HL* 2.26) attributes to men brought in by the Lombard king Alboin in the sixth century.

41. Hendy 2008, 383.

42. *Not. Dign. Occ.* 11. Augusta Vindelicensis = Augusta Vindelicorum (Augsburg).

43. *Not. Dign. Occ.* 6.

44. See Christie 2006, 308, on the conjunction of arms factories, barbarian settlement, road maintenance, the *annona*, and the billeting of troops. Although the evidence from the Notitia Dignitatum belongs to the early fifth century, there is scattered evidence of arms workshops earlier. In the mid third century *CIL* XIII 6763 = *ILS* 1188, a dedication to Iuppiter Optimus Maximus from Mogontiacum (Mainz) mentions arms-making in Mediolanum, and *CIL* V 1883 = *ILS* 1939 from second century Concordia mentions a *decuria armementaria*, or group of arms manufacturers. Both Mediolanum and Concordia were in areas that supplied the high imperial *limes*, and the appearance of arms workshops here is not surprising (on Concordia's history of arms manufacture, see Lettich 1982). The difference with the later period, at least on the limited evidence available, seems to be the number of *fabricae* and their degree of specialization. Ward-Perkins 2005, 103, aptly notes the implications of their quantity, specialization, and dispersal: "The sheer number of these *fabricae* is impressive; but considerable administrative coordination must also have been required to collect, transport, and distribute their finished products. Somehow an archer facing the barbarians across the Rhine had to be united with his bow from Pavia and his arrows from Concordia, as well as his socks from Milan or Aquileia."

45. Glas and Hartmann 2008, 668.

46. Rebecchi 1993.

47. The procurement of raw materials, since it presented opportunities for embezzlement, was regulated by the government (*Cod. Theod.* 10.22.2), as was the output of *fabricae* (cf. *Cod. Theod.* 10.22.1).

48. *Cod. Theod.* 10.22.7.

49. Christie 2006 gives the range of scholarly estimates of the workforce of individual *fabricae* as between 200 and 500. A passage of Ammianus, which describes the crowd of people (*multitudo*) employed by the *fabrica* at Adrianople as being *ampla*, suggests that

fabricae were of varying sizes, since Ammianus specifies the size of the workshop in that particular place (*illic*) to his readers (*Amm. Marc.* 31.6.2).

50. *Cod. Theod.* 10.22.6.

51. *Cod. Theod.* 10.22.4, 10.22.6.

52. On the function and organization of the late imperial *gynaecea*, see Wild 1976. Complementing the woolen factories were the *linyfia*—state *fabricae* for the production of linen cloth, for which there are only two attested, one at Vienne in Gaul and the other in Italy at Ravenna—and *bafii*, imperial dyeing workshops, of which one of the nine attested is in Italy, at Cissa in Istria (*Not. Dign. Occ.* 11). The status of the workers in the *gynaecea* was very low, and an edict of 336 CE orders a son of Constantine's rival Licinius, once he has been apprehended, to be bound in chains and sent to serve in the woolen workshop in Carthage (*Cod. Theod.* 4.6.1).

53. *Not. Dign. Occ.* 11.

54. On wool production in the Tanarus Valley, see Mart. *Ep.* 14. 157 (on Pollentian wool), Strabo 5.1.12 (wool production in Liguria in general), Columella *Rust.* 7.2 (on Pollentian dark wool), and Pliny *HN* 8.73 (again on Pollentian dark wool). Supplementing the sheep-rearing was wool-carding and -combing at Brixia (*CIL* V 4501 = *Inscr. It.* 10–5, 294) and Brixellum (*CIL* XI 1031; *Inscr. It.* 10–5, 875). Continuities of production is likely, based on parallels with other wool-producing towns in northern Italy, since Altinum and Parma, famous for their white wool under the early empire (Mart. *Ep.* 14.155), both have prices for wool listed in Diocletian's Edict on Prices.

55. *Sup. It.* 9, 51 (Ticinum); On the dating of the inscription and the relevance of court connections, see Clemente 1984, 261, and Gabba and Tibiletti 1960. Judging by the name *Valeria*, which becomes very common after Diocletian, and the letter forms (which should be used with zealous caution in dating inscriptions), the inscription could be as late as the mid fifth century, but is probably not earlier than the very end of the third.

56. For travel patterns of northern Italians in general in Late Antiquity, see Handley 2001, 72–74.

57. Ticinum was a stopping point for emperors even in the early imperial period. Augustus met Drusus's funeral cortege there (Tac. *Ann.* 1.32, Val. Max. 5.5.3) in 9 BCE, and Vitellius dined there in 69, when a riot broke out between his legionaries and auxiliaries (Tac. *Hist.* 2.68). In 355 Constantius II was on the road between Ticinum and Laumellum —at a point that Ammianus says is marked by two columns—when he heard about the loss of Colonia Claudia Ara Agrippinensium (Amm. Marc. 15.15.18).

58. *Cod. Theod.* 7.8.1–16.

59. *Cod. Theod.* 7.8.4.

60. *Cod. Theod.* 7.8.8.

61. The 312 CE war between Maxentius and Constantine should be seen in the context of the civil wars following the retirements of Diocletian and Maximian in 305 and the death of the successor *Augustus* Constantius early in 306. These wars made their way to northern Italy in 306, when the *Augustus* Severus moved south from his seat at Mediolanum to suppress Maxentius's revolt at Rome; Severus's army deserted him, and he fled north to Ravenna, where he surrendered early in 307 (Euseb. *Vit. Const.* 27.3, Zos. 2.10, Lactant. *De mort. pers.* 26–27). More serious for northern Italy was the war between Maxentius and Constantine in 312, when Constantine crossed the Cottain Alps to march against Maxen-

tius, in control of Rome and most of Italy. Constantine's army first took Segusio and then was received by Augusta Taurinorum, Mediolanum, and Brixia. After a closely fought but successful siege of a Maxentian army in Verona (depicted prominently on the Arch of Constantine at Rome), Constantine accepted the surrenders of Aquileia, Mutina, and Ravenna before moving on to Rome and the battle of the Milvian Bridge (*Pan. Lat.* 9.5–11, Zos. 2.15, Euseb. *Hist. Eccl.* 9.9.3, Euseb. *Vit. Const.* 37.2, Aur. Vict. *Caes.* 40.16, Eutrop. 10.4). Both wars in northern Italy lasted less than a year, and the war between Maxentius and Constantine in the region was limited to the spring and summer of 312.

62. Amm. Marc. 15.2.7, Julian. *Ep. ad. Ath.* 272–274.

63. Zos. 5.31. Among those officials killed were the praetorian prefects of Gaul and Italy and the *magister officiorum*.

64. Zos. 5.26, 45.

65. Jord. *Get.* 42, Leo *Epist.* 159. Physical signs of destruction stemming from the Huns' sack are few, although the event does seem to have inaugurated a period of decline, particularly in the northern areas of the city (Verzár-Bass 2003Aquileia's bishop had, presumably with other inhabitants, escaped the Huns by fleeing to Grado, a defensible island whose population in this period rose as that of inland towns fell (Calderini 1930, 87).

66. Mainardis 2008, 23. On the urban and political history of Iulium Carnicum, see Mainardis 2008, 36–43.

67. *CIL* V 1862 (= *ILS* 5885).

68. For other cases of the formula *res publica* + the genitive plural, Mainardis 2008, 129–130, brings *CIL* X 199, *CIL* XIV 3586, *CIL* VI 1408, *Inscr. It.* IV 89, and *AE* 1926, 79, in as comparanda. The use of *res publica* + genitive plural of the ethnonym to stand in for the municipal name (hence *Iuliensi Karni* for *Iulium Carnicum*) is part of the archaizing trend in Late Antiquity of resurrecting earlier ethnonyms, in the case, the somewhat antiquated *Karni*. In Britain the largely third-century use of *res publica* + genitive plural of the ethnonym superseded the earlier second-century use of *civitas* + genitive plural of the enthnonym (Prag 2008, 71).

69. *CIL* V 8002 (= *ILS* 208); see also Osgood 2011, 187.

70. *CIL* V 1864.

71. Christie 2006, 325. Šašel and Petru 1971 provide a collection of references to the *Claustra Alpium Iuliarum* in ancient authors.

72. Ciglenećki 2015, 395, 402.

73. Ciglenećki 2015, 402.

74. Colussa 2010, 59, 93–94.

75. Mainardis 2008, 46–48.

76. Colussa 2010, 61–62. In the Gothic era, the town had a public granary (Cassiod. *Var.* 12.26). The town's increased importance in the sixth and seventh centuries is amply attested by the rich burials of the Collina di San Mauro necropolis, first discovered in 1886 and more thoroughly excavated between 1994 and 1998 (Ahumada Silva 2010, 9, 21).

77. Christie 2006, 326–327; Ciglenećki 2015, 386, 402.

78. Preceding Maximian's establishment of his court at Mediolanum, both Diocletian and Maximian had an important conference, complete with the Roman Senate, at the city in the winter of 290/91 CE (*Pan. Lat.* 3.11). On Mediolanum as imperial capital, see Krautheimer 1983.

79. For Ticinum as subordinate to Mediolanum's regional hegemon, see Clemente 1984, 262.

80. Krautheimer 1983, 69–70. An octagonal tower from the late third-century walls still survives in the complex of the modern archaeological museum.

81. Dey 2015, 73–75, 86–87.

82. Ordo Urbium Nobilium 7 (Mediolanum).

Et Mediolani mira omnia, copia rerum,
innumerae cultaeque domus, facunda virorum
ingenia et mores laeti, tum duplice muro
amplificata loci species populique voluptas,
circus, et inclusi moles cuneata theatri, templa
Palatinaeque arces opulensque moneta
et regio Herculei celebris sub honore lavacri;
cunctaque marmoreis ornata peristyla signis
moeniaque in valli formam circumdata limbo.
Omnia quae magnis operum velut aemula formis
excellunt nec iuncta premit vicinia Romae.

83. See Tiussi, Verzár, and Villa 2013 on the urban form of Late Antique Aquileia and, in the same volume, Rubinich 2013 (on the fourth-century palace) and Mian and Villa 2013 (on the palace).

84. Christie 2006, 419, on the Desenzano, Toscolano Maderno, and Sirmione villas.

85. There is no indication that these new landowners were given land at the expense of others, and the fairly even distribution of *praefecti Sarmartarum* across the Po Plain and a general trend toward settlement in smaller towns suggest that the government made efforts to settle these families on unclaimed or unworked land.

86. Christie 2006, 419, on surveys of the Piedmont, the Aquileian hinterland, and the area between the Adda and Adige Rivers.

87. McLynn 1994, 5.

88. On Ambrose's election, see Williams 1995, 104–127.

89. See Humphries 1999, 45, on evidence for the earliest churches in northern Italy.

90. See Lizzi-Testa 1989 on ecclesiastic hierarchies in the region in general.

91. Humphries 1999, 148, explains the early dominance of Mediolanum's see, even before Ambrose, by suggesting that "the bishop of Milan, living in a city regularly occupied by the court, proved to be a useful intermediary between the emperor and other ecclesiastics, thus giving him a certain prestige outside the city."

92. Ambrose *De Off.* 2.150–151.

93. Lanzani 1984, 355, 366.

94. Paulinus *Vita Ambrosii* 14, 29, 32–33. On the Arian controversy and the dispute between Ambrose and Valentinian, see Williams 1995, and McLynn 1994.

95. During the Arian controversy with Valentinian, Ambrose made at least one attempt to flee to Ticinum (McLynn 1994, 46), suggesting that he thought he had reliable supporters in the town.

96. The chronology of Theodosius's death and the exhumation of Saints Nazarius and Celsus is difficult to determine. Paulinus *Vita Ambrosii* 32 says that the exhumation was

done *quo in tempore* of Theodosius's death. Ambrose's miraculous discovery of two saints, Vitalis and Agricola, at Bononia two years earlier suggests that the ceremonies surrounding the finding of saints' relics were useful in spreading regional influence.

97. Ennodius *Vita Epiphanii* 41–42.
98. McLynn 1994, 285.
99. St. Tecla: Krautheimer 1983, 75–77.
100. McLynn 1994, 232.
101. Krautheimer 1983, 79.
102. Ambrose *Epistula* 77. 2. Trans. Liebeschuetz.
103. Ambrose *Epistula* 77. 7. Trans. Liebeschuetz.
104. McLynn 1994, 229.
105. On Damasus's programmatic use of martyrs, see Lønstrup Dal Santo 2015.
106. On the Testamentum Porcelli, see Champlin 1987.
107. *Inscr. It.* 10–14, 21. Augustus also seems to have enlarged the town's territory: a monumental inscription from the mid second century CE (*CIL* V 532 = *ILS* 6680) records that the Carni and Catali had been attributed to Tergeste.
108. Morselli 2007, 138–139.
109. Temple of Magna Mater: Morselli 2007, 139.
110. Maselli Scotti and Ventura 2001, 207.
111. Borzacconi and Morselli 2007, 150, who also notes that while the repurposing of urban spaces to funerary usage was concentrated in Late Antiquity and particularly the third century, it also occurred in parts of the Tergeste, such as the *domus* of the via Donata, as early as the late first and early second centuries.
112. *CIL* V 8205. Humphries 1999, 209.
113. Morselli 2007.
114. Traviglia and Morselli 2007, 153; Humphries 1999, 203.
115. Humphries 1999, 85–86.
116. Traviglia and Morselli 2007, 156.
117. On Ravenna's portrayal as a capital for cowardly and ineffective fifth-century emperors, see Gillett 2001, 136–137.
118. See esp. Gillett 2001.
119. Gillett 2001, 162.
120. Augenti 2012, 51.
121. Bratož 2003, 512–521.
122. Deliyannis 2010, 63–70.
123. Procop. *Goth.* 5.1.16–20.
124. Procop. *Goth.* 5.1.24.
125. Procop. *Goth.* 5.1.26, *Anon. Val.* 55.
126. *Anon. Val.* 60–71. At Ticinum work was done in this period on an amphitheater, walls, baths, granaries, and drains, and Theodoric had a palace built here (Agnellus, *Liber pontificalis ecclesiae Ravennatis [LPR]* 94). This work was accompanied by church-building and the first intramural churches at Ticinum; previously churches had been constructed outside the city walls around cemeteries (Christie 2006, 107). Looking beyond Theoderic, Brogiolo 2010 argues for the importance of "barbarian" immigrants in the urban evolution of the fifth century.

127. Theoderic's emulation—and lack thereof—of Roman imperial trappings also illustrates the complicated, classicizing, and fluid nature of ethnic identity in Ostrogothic Italy (Amory 1997, 13–14).

128. Deliyannis 2010, 110.

129. Deliyannis 2010, 114; Bjornlie 2016, 56–57.

130. Moorhead 1992, 143.

131. Augenti 2005; Deliyannis 2010, 120–121.

132. Deliyannis 2010, 115.

133. On the alteration, see Urbano 2005.

134. *Anon. Val.* 71.

135. *CIL* XI 10.

136. On the mausoleum, see Deliyannis 2010, 124–136.

137. Moorhead 1992, 143.

138. Gillett 2001, 141.

139. Bjornlie 2016, 56–57. Gillett 2001, 155. Bjornlie points to Theoderic's remembrance in the medieval period as Dietrich von Bern (Theoderic of Verona) as an indication of the close connection between Verona and Theoderic.

140. Gillett 2003, 207, *Anon. Val.*14.81–87.

141. Bjornlie 2016, 15, *Anon. Val.*14.87.

142. Procop. *Goth.* 9.3–6.

143. For the survival strategies of Italian towns during these wars, see Kouroumali 2013.

144. Mercando 2003 on Aquae Statiellae and Segusio, and Cavalieri Manasse and Bruno 2003 on Verona.

145. Christie 2006, 500–504 on the sixth-century plagues in Italy.

146. *HL* 2.24 (floods), 2.26 (famine).

147. Procop. *Goth.* 2.21.39. Procopius at *Goth.* 2.5.38 ranks Mediolanum as the second most populous city in Italy, after Rome.

148. See Bjornlie 2013, 29–30, on "the most brutal spectacle of the entire war" and on Cassiodorus's role in it.

149. Tomaselli 1976 describes the organization and construction of these drains, which were built of two-level (at least on the main lines) brick-vaulted channels, which carried water from the river Ticino. Ward-Perkins 1984, 134, cites the drains' descriptions by Liutprand of Cremona, a native of Ticinum; i.e., the drains were described on one unusual occasion as blocked with human remains and on another as flowing with molten gold (Liutprand, *Antapodasis* 1.35, 3.3).

150. *HL* 2.27:

> At vero Ticinensis civitas post tres annos et aliquot menses obsidionem perferens, tandem se Alboin et Langobardis obsidentibus tradidit. In quam cum Alboin per portam quae dicitur Sancti Iohannis ab orientali urbis parte introiret, equus eius in portae medio concidens, quamvis calcaribus stimulatus, quamvis hinc inde hastarum verberibus caesus, non poterat elevari. Tunc unus ex eisdem Langobardis taliter regem adlocutus est dicens: "Memento, domine rex, quale votum vovisti. Frange tam durum votum, et ingredieris urbem. Vere etenim christianus est pop-

> ulus in hac civitate." Siquidem Alboin voverat quod universum populum, quia se tradere noluisset, gladio extingueret. Qui postquam tale votum disrumpens civibus indulgentiam promisit, mox eius equus consurgens, ipse civitatem ingressus, nulli laesionem inferens, in sua promissione permansit. Tunc ad eum omnis populus in palatium, quod quondam rex Theudericus construxerat, concurrens, post tantas miserias animum de spe iam fidus coepit [ad] futura relevare.

There are several possibilities for interpreting this passage: first, the incident was genuine and the Lombard decision to spare the city was based on such an interpretation of an omen; second, the incident was real but staged, and the reasons behind Alboin's decision were more practical in that the city and its inhabitants were more useful to the Lombards intact; and third, the incident was fabricated after the fact to explain the city's survival of the siege.

151. On Lombard Ticinum, see Brogiolo 2000 and Bullough 1966.

152. Deliyannis 2010, 278–283.

153. Arnold 2014, 108.

154. Balzaretti 1996, 228.

155. On the della Scala (also called the *Scaliger* or *Scaligeri*) family, see Rossini 1975.

156. Randolph 2002, 51, who quotes the Latin couplet on the banner: "Est iusti latrix urbs haec et laudis amatrix."

157. Braudel 1972, 72–75.

158. Braudel 1972, 75–77.

159. Braudel 1972, 77.

160. See Horden and Purcell 2000, 2 and 541–542, on this distinction.

Bibliography

Abramenko, A. 1993. *Die munizipale Mittelschicht im kaiserzeitlichen Italien: Zu einem neuen Verständnis von Sevirat und Augustalität*. Frankfurt: Lang.

Agostinetti, P. P. 2004. Vol. 1 of Agostinetti and Morandi 2004, *Celti d'Italia*. Rome: Spazio Tre.

Agostinetti, P. P., and A. Morandi. 2004. *Celti d'Italia*. Rome: Spazio Tre.

Agostinetti, P. P., V. Blandino, V. Esposito, E. Giannini, J. Kaurin, R. Knobloch, C. Montalvo Puente, and C. Tavolini, 2014. "Contributo alla cronologia della tarda età di la Tène nella Cisalpina centrale." In Barral et al., *Les Celtes*, 37–62.

Agusta-Boularot, S. 1994. "Les références épigraphiques aux Grammatici et Γραμματικοὶ de l'Empire romain (Ier s. av. J.-C., IVe s. ap. J.-C.)." *Mélanges de l'École française de Rome. Antiquité* 106: 653–746.

Ahumada Silva, I., ed. 2010. *La collina di San Mauro a Cividale del Friuli: Dalla necropoli longobarda alla chiesetta bassomedievale*. Borgo San Lorenzo: All'Insegna del Giglio.

Alföldy, G. 1999. *Städte, Eliten und Gesellschaft in der Gallia Cisalpina: Epigraphisch-historische Untersuchungen*. Stuttgart: Franz Steiner.

Alföldy, G. 1991. "Augustus und die Inschriften: Tradition und Innovation." *Gymnasium* 98: 289–324.

Alföldy, G. 1984. *Römische Statuen in Venetia et Histria: Epigraphische Quellen*. Heidelberg: Winter.

Alföldy, G. 1982. "Senatoren aus Norditalien: Regiones IX, X, und XI." *Epigrafia e ordine Senatorio: Atti del Colloquio Internazionale AIEGL (Roma 1981)*: 309–368.

Alföldy, G. 1974a. *Noricum*. London: Routledge.

Alföldy, G. 1974b. "P. Helvius Pertinax und M. Valerius Maximianus." *Situla* 14–15: 199–215.

Amory, P. 1997. *People and Identity in Ostrogothic Italy, 489–554*. Cambridge: Cambridge University Press.

Andemahr, A. M. 1994. *Totus in Praediis: Senatorischer Grundbesitz in Italien in der Frühen und Hohen Kaiserzeit*. Bonn: Rudolf Habelt.

Ando, C. 2000. *Imperial Ideology and Provincial Loyalty in the Roman Empire*. Berkeley: University of California Press.

Angelini, I. 2010. "Indagini archeometriche degli ornamenti in ambra provenienti dalla necropoli di Narde." In Colonna and Salzani, *La fragilità dell'urna*, 135–145.

Angelini, I., and P. Bellintani. 2005. "Archaeological ambers from northern Italy and FTIR-DRIFT study of provenance with comparison with the geological amber database." *Archaeometry* 47: 441–454.

Arcà, A. 1997. "Settlements in topographic engravings of Copper Age in Valcamonica and Mt. Bego rock art." *Proceedings of the XIII International Congress of Prehistoric and Protohistoric Sciences—Forlì 1996*: 9–16.

Armit, I. 2012. *Headhunting and the Body in Iron Age Europe*. Cambridge: Cambridge University Press.

Arnaud, P. 2004a. "L'integrazione delle popolazioni indigene negli ordinamenti giuridico-amministravi romani." In De Marinis and Spadea, *I Liguri*, 459–460.

Arnaud, P. 2004b. "Modelli insediativi in area celto-ligure." In De Marinis and Spadea, *I Liguri*, 473–375.

Arnold, B. 2012. "Gender, temporalities, and periodization in Early Iron Age west-central Europe." *Social Science History* 36: 84–112.

Arnold, J. 2014. *Theoderic and the Roman Imperial Restoration*. Cambridge: Cambridge University Press.

Arslan, E. A. 2001. "I Celti nell'Alto Ariatico alla luce dei dati archaeologici." *Antichità Altoadriatiche* 48: 325–334.

Arslan, E. A. 1996. "Le monete e la circolazione monetaria." In Passi Pitcher, *Bedriacum*, 101–118.

Arslan, E. A. 1976–78. "Celti e Romani in Transpadana." *Études Celtiques* 15: 441– 481.

Augenti, A. 2012. "Classe: Archaeologies of a Lost City." In *Vrbes extinctae: Archaeologies of Abandoned Classical Towns*, edited by N. Christie and A. Augenti, 45–75. Aldershot, UK: Ashgate.

Augenti, A. 2005. "Archeologia e topografia a Ravenna: Il Palazzo di Teoderico e la Moneta Aurea." *Archaeologia Medievale* 31: 7–34.

Ausbüttel, F. M. 1989. "Die Eingliederung Oberitaliens in das römische Reich." *Prometheus* 15: 165.

Baioni, M., B. Grassi, C. Mangani, and N. Martinelli. 2014. "Pile-dwelling villages of northern Italy: Research and finds." In *Archaeology of Lake Settlements, IV–II Mill. BC: Chronology of Cultures, Environment, and Palaeoclimatic Rhythms*, edited by A. N. Mazurkevic, 311–316. St. Petersburg: Gosudarstvennyĭ Ėrmitazh.

Balbuza, K. 2010. "Aeternitas—An Element of Emperor Trajan's Self-Representation (an Outline of the Problem)." In *Res Historica: Terra, mare et homines*. Vol. 2, *Studies in Memory of Professor Tadeusz Łoposzko*, edited by H. Kowalski, 27–32. Lublin: Wydawn. Uniw. Marii Curie-Skłodowskiej.

Balista, C., P. Bellintani, A. M. Bietti Sestieri, G. Gambacurta, and A. Ruta Serafini. 1996. "Il Veneto." In Bietti Sestieri and Kruta, *The Iron Age in Europe*, 9–21.

Balista, C., L. Bonfatti, and M. Calzolari 2007. "Il paesaggio naturale e antropico delle Valli tra Spina e Comacchio e le sue trasformazioni dall'Età etrusco all'Alto Medioevo." In Berti, *Genti nel delta di Spina a Comacchio*, 19–31.

Balzaretti, R. 1996. "Cities, emporia, and monasteries: Local economies in the Po valley c. AD 700–875." In *Towns in Transition: Urban Evolution in Late Antiquity and the Early Middle Ages*, edited by N. Christie and S. Loseby, 213–234. Aldershot, UK: Ashgate.

Bandelli, G. 2007. "Considerazioni storiche sull'urbanizzazione cisalpina di età repubblicana (283–89 a.C.)." In Brecciaroli Taborelli, *Forme e tempi dell'urbanizzazione nella Cisalpina*, 15–28.

Bandelli, G. 2001. "Roma e l'Adriatico fra III e II secolo." In *Strutture Portuali e Rotte Marittime nell'Adriatico di Età Romana*, edited by C. Zaccaria, 17–41. Trieste: Centro di antichita altoadriatiche.

Bandelli, G. 1999. "La popolazione della Cisalpina dalle invasioni galliche alla guerra Sociale." In *Demografia, sistemi agrari, regimi alimentari nel mondo antico: Atti del convegno internazionale di studi (Parma, 17–19 ottobre 1997)*, edited by D. Vera, 189–215. Bari: Edipuglia.

Bandelli, G. 1989. "Contributo all'interpretazione del cosiddetto elogium di C. Sempronius Tuditanus." *Antichità Altoadriatiche* 35: 111–135.

Baray, L. 2014. *Les mercenaires celtes et la culture de La Tène: Critères archéologiques et positions sociologiques*. Dijon: EUD—Éditions Universitaires.

Bargnesi, R. 2013. "Aspetti dell'organizzazione del territorio in età romana." In Rumi, *Storia di Como*, 183–195.

Barral, P., J.-P. Guillaumet, M.-J. Roulière-Lambert, M. Saracino, and D. Vitali, eds. 2014. *Les Celtes et le Nord d'Italie Premier et Second Âges du fer*. Dijon: Revue archéologique de l'Est Basso, P. 1986. *I miliari della Venetia romana*. Padua: Società archeologica veneta.

Bazzanella, M. 2012. "Italy: Neolithic and Bronze Age." In *Textiles and Textile Production in Europe from Prehistory to AD 400*, edited by M. Gleba and U. Mannering, 202–213. Oxford: Oxbow Books.

Bender Jørgensen, L. 2013. "The question of prehistoric silks in Europe." *Antiquity* 87: 581–588.

Benelli, E. 2001. "The Romanization of Italy through the Epigraphic Record." In *Italy and the West: Comparative Issues in Romanization*, edited by S. Keay and N. Terranato, 7–16. Oxford: Oxbow Books.

Benelli, E. 1999. "La romanizzazione attraverso l'epigrafia: Il Veneto e il modello etrusco." In *Protostoria e storia del Venetorum Angulus: Atti del XX Convegno di studi etruschi ed italici, Portogruaro, Quarto d'Altino, Este, Adria (16–19 ottobre 1996)*, edited by O. Paoletti, 651–664. Pisa: Istituti editoriali e poligrafici internazionali.

Benelli, E. 1994. *Le iscrizioni bilingui etrusco-latine*. Florence: Olschki.

Bergamini, M., ed. 1991. *Gli Etruschi maestri di idraulica*. Perugia: Electa.

Bergamini, S. 2009. "Le figurazione impresse sui pesi da telaio romani del basso Po: Note e ipotesi per uno studio." *Quaderni della Bassa Modenese* 55: 5–40.

Bergonzi, G. 1997. "L'ambra della terramare nel contesto italiano ed europeo." In Bernarbò Brea, Cardarelli, and Cremaschi, *Le Terramare*, 602–609.

Bernarbò Brea, M. 2009. "Le terramare nell'età del Bronzo." In Bernarbò Brea and Cremaschi, *Acqua e civiltà nelle Terramare*, 5–18.

Bernarbò Brea, M., and M. Cremaschi, eds. 2009. *Acqua e civiltà nelle Terramare: La Vasca votiva di Noceto*. Milan: Skira.

Bernarbò Brea, M., A. Cardarelli, and M. Cremaschi, eds. 1997a. *La Terramare: La più antica civiltà padana*. Milan: Electa.

Bernarbò Brea, M., A. Cardarelli, and M. Cremaschi. 1997b. "Il crollo del sistema Terramaricolo." In Bernarbò Brea, Cardarelli, and Cremaschi, *Le Terramare*, 745–753.

Bernarbò Brea, M., A. Cardarelli, and M. Cremaschi. 1997c. "Cinque secoli di vita nella grande Pianura." In Bernarbò Brea, Cardarelli, and Cremaschi, *Le Terramare*, 23–29.

Bernarbò Brea, M., A. Cardarelli, and M. Cremaschi. 1997d. "Le terramare nel tempo." In Bernarbò Brea, Cardarelli, and Cremaschi, *Le Terramare*, 295–378.

Bernabò Brea, M., P. Bianchi, and S. Lincetto. 2003. "La produzione tessile nell'età del Bronzo. Fusaiole e pesi da telaio nelle terramare emiliane: Esempi di studio dai villaggi di S. Rosa di Poviglio (RE) e Forno del Gallo a Beneceto (PR)." In *Textiles: Intrecci e tessuti dalla Preistoria Europea, Cat. Mostra a Riva del Garda 2003, Provincia Autonoma di Trento*, edited by M. Bazzanella, A. Mayr, L. Moser, and A. Rast Eicher, 111–120. Trento: Provincia autonoma, Servizio beni culturali, Ufficio beni archeologici.

Berrendonner, C., M. Cébeillac-Gervasoni, and L. Lamoine, eds. 2008. *Le quotidien municipal dans l'occident Romain*. Clermont-Ferrand: Presses universitaires Blaise-Pascal.

Bertacchi, A. 1965. "Aquileia: Le più antiche fase urbanistiche." *Notizie degli Scavi*, suppl.: 1–11.

Bertacchi, L. 2003. *Nuova Pianta Archeologica di Aquileia*. Udine: Edizioni del Confine.

Berti, F., ed. 2007. *Genti nel delta di Spina a Comacchio: Uomini, territorio, e culto dall'antichità all'alto medioevo*. Ferrara: Corbo.

Bietti Sestieri, A. M. 2012. "Il Villanoviano: Un problema archeologico di storia mediterranea." In *Le origini degli Etruschi: Storia, archeologia, antropologia*, edited by V. Bellelli, 249–277. Rome: L'Erma di Bretschneider.

Bietti Sestieri, A. M. 2010. *L'Italia nell'età del bronzo e del ferro: Dalle palafitte a Romolo (2200–700 a.C.)*. Rome: Carocci.

Bietti Sestieri, A. M. 1997a. "Il territorio padano dopo le terramare." In Bernarbò Brea, Cardarelli, and Cremaschi, *Le Terramare*, 757–772.

Bietti Sestieri, A. M. 1997b. "Italy in Europe in the Early Iron Age." *Proceedings of the Prehistoric Society* 63: 371–402.

Bietti Sestieri, A. M., and Vencenslas Kruta, eds. 1996. *The Iron Age in Europe*. Forlì: ATBACO.

Birks, P., A. Rodger, and J. S. Richardson. 1984. "Further aspects of the Tabula Contrebiensis." *Journal of Roman Studies* 74: 45–73.

Birley, A. 2000. *Onomasticon to the Younger Pliny: Letters and Panegyric*. Munich: Saur.

Birley, A. 1987. *Marcus Aurelius: A Biography*. 2nd ed. London: Routledge.

Bispham, E. 2007. *From Asculum to Actium: The Municipalization of Italy from the Social War to Augustus*. Oxford: Oxford University Press.

Bjornlie, M. S. 2016. "Governmental Administration." In *A Companion to Ostrogothic Italy*, edited by J. Arnold, S. Bjornlie, and K. Sessa, 47–72. Leiden: Brill.

Bjornlie, M. S. 2013. *Politics and Tradition between Rome, Ravenna, and Constantinople: A Study of Cassiodorus and the* Variae. Cambridge: Cambridge University Press.

Blake, E. 2014. *Social Networks and Regional Identity in Bronze Age Italy*. Cambridge: Cambridge University Press.

Boaro, S. 2001. "Dinamiche insediative e confini nel Veneto dell'età del ferro: Este, Padova, e Vicenza." *Padusa* 37: 153–197.

Boatwright, M. 2003. *Hadrian and the Cities of the Roman Empire*. Princeton: Princeton University Press.

Bolla, M. 1996. "Il ruolo dell'area altoadriatica nella diffusione dei recipienti di bronzo (I sec. a.C.–I sec. d.C.)." In Buora, *Lungo la via dell'ambra*,185–203.

Bondini, A. 2005. "Le necropoli di Este tra IV e II secolo a.C.: I corredi dello scavo 2001/2002 in via Versori (ex fondo Capodalgio)." *Ocnus* 13: 45–88.

Bonini, A. 1998. "I Cenomani." In Sena Chiesa, *Tesori della Postumia*, 91–96.

Bonomi, S., and M. A. Rubino. 2007. "Adria fra Etruschi e Romani." In Brecciaroli Taborelli, *Forme e tempi dell'urbanizzazione nella Cisalpina*, 85–90.

Borzacconi, A., and C. Morselli. 2007. "La destinazione funeraria e la perdita di identità dell'area." In Morselli, *Trieste antica*, 146–151.

Bosi, G., M. Bandini Mazzanti, A. Florenzano, I. Massamba N'siala, A. Pederzoli, R. Rinaldi, P. Torri, and A. Maria Mercuri. 2011. "Seeds/fruits, pollen and parasite remains as evidence of site function: Ppiazza Garibaldi—Parma (N Italy) in Roman and mediaeval times." *Journal of Archaeological Science* 38: 1621–1633.

Bosio, L. 1984. "Capure la terra: La centurazione romana del Veneto." In *Misurare le terra: Centuriazione e coloni nel mondo romano. Iil caso Veneto*, edited by R. Bussi and V. Vandelli, 15–21. Modena: Panini.

Bourdin, S. 2014. "Problèmes d'identités ethniques en Cisalpine: Sociétés multi-ethniques ou itendités multiples?" In Barral et al., *Les Celtes*, 63–73.

Bowersock, G. W. 1985. "Hadrian and Metropolis." In *Bonner Historia Augusta Colloquium 1982–83*, 75–88. Bonn: Habelt.

Božič, D. 2004. "The funaion of the bronze D-shapedring from the Late Republican horse burial in Kobarid, Soča valley (SI)." *Instrumentum* 20: 6–8.

Braccesi, L. 2004. "The Greeks on the Venetian Lagoon." In *Greek Identity in the Western Mediterranean*, edited by K. Lomas. 349–362. Leiden: Brill.

Braccesi, L. 2001. *Hellenikòs kolpos: Supplemento a Grecità adriatica*. Rome: L'Erma di Bretschneider.

Braccesi, L. 1984. *La leggenda di Antenore: Da Troia a Padova*. Venice: Marsilio.

Bradley, G. 2000. *Ancient Umbria: State, Culture, and Identity in Central Italy from the Iron Age to the Augustan Era*. Oxford: Oxford University Press.

Bratož, R. 2003. "Aquileia tra Teodosio e i Longobardi (379–568)." *Antichità Altoadriatiche* 59: 477–527.

Braudel, F. (1949; 1966) 1972. *The Mediterranean and the Mediterranean World in the Age of Philip II* [*La Méditerranée et le Monde Méditerranéen à l'Epoque de Philippe II*]. London: Collins.

Brecciaroli Taborelli, L., ed. 2007. *Forme e tempi dell'urbanizzazione nella Cisalpina: Atti delle giornate di studio (Torino, 4–6 maggio 2006)*. Florence: All'Insegna del Giglio.

Breuer, S. 1996. *Stand und Status: Munizipale Oberschichten in Brixia und Verona*. Bonn: Habelt.

Briquel, D. 1998. "Aspetti politici." In *Spina e il delta Padano*, edited by F. Rebecchi, 41–65. Rome: L' Erma di Bretschneider.

Briquel, D. 1994. *Iscrizioni e graffiti della città etrusca di Marzabotto*. Bologna: Bologna University Press.

Broers, M. 2003. "The myth and reality of Italian regionalism: A historical geography of Napoleonic Italy, 1801–1814." *American Historical Review* 108: 688–709.

Brogiolo, G. P. 2010. "Immigration and Urban Transformation in the Capitals of the West in the 5th Century." In *Le trasformazioni del V secolo: L'Italia, i barbari, l'Occidente romano*, edited by P. Delogu and S. Gasparri, 215–236. Turnhout: Brepols.

Brogiolo, G. P. 2000. "Capitali e residenze regie nell'Italia longobarda." In *Sedes Regiae (ann. 400–800)*, edited by G. Ripoll and J. M. Gurt, 135–162. Barcelona: Reial Acadèmia de Bones Lletres.

Broughton, T. R. S. 1968. *The Magistrates of the Roman Republic*. Cleveland: American Philological Association.

Brunt, P. A. 1990. *Roman Imperial Themes*. Oxford: Oxford University Press.

Brunt, P. A. 1982. "The legal issue in Cicero, pro Balbo." *Classical Quarterly* 32: 136–147.

Brunt, P. A. 1971. *Italian Manpower, 225 B.C.–A.D. 14*. Oxford: Oxford University Press.

Brunt, P. A. 1965. "Italian aims at the time of the Social War." *Journal of Roman Studies* 55: 90–109.

Brusin, G. 1934. *Gli scavi di Aquileia: Un quadriennio di attività dell'Associazione Nazionale per Aquileia (1929–1932)*. Udine: La Panarie.

Brusin, G. 1928. "Grado: Nuove epigrafi romane e cristiane." *Notizie degli Scavi di Antichità*, 282–284.

Buora, M., ed. 1996. *Lungo la via dell'ambra: Apporti altoadriatici alla romanizzazione dei territori del Medio Danubio (I sec. a.C.–I sec. d.C.). Atti del convegno di studio (Udine-Aquileia 16–17 settembre 1994)*. Udine: Arti grafiche friulane.

Buora, M., ed. 2002. *Roma sul Danubio: Da Aquileia a Carnuntum lungo la via dell'ambra*. Rome: L'Erma di Bretschneider.

Burton, G. P. 1979. "The *Curator Rei Publicae:* Towards a reappraisal." *Chiron* 9: 465–487.

Busch, A. 2007. "Militia in urbe: The Military Presence in Rome." In *The Impact of the Roman Army (200 B–AD 476): Economic, Social, Political, Religious, and Cultural Aspects. Proceedings of the Sixth Workshop of the International Network Impact of Empire (Roman Empire, 200 B.C.–A.D. 476), Capri, March 29–April 2, 2005*, edited by L. de Blois and O. Hekster, 314–341. Leiden: Brill.

Calastri, C., and P. Desantis. 2014. "Nuovi dati sulla Felsina etrusca: Lo scavo di viale Aldini 200 a Bologna." In *Il santuario etrusco di Villa Cassarini a Bologna*, edited by S. Romagnoli, 115–134. Bologna: Bononia University Press.

Calderini, A. 1930. *Aquileia romana: Ricerche di storia e di epigrafia*. Milan: Società editrice Vita e Pensiero.

Calvetti, A. 1999. *Romagna Celtica*. Ravenna: Longo.

Calvi, M. C. 2005. *Le ambre romane di Aquileia*. Aquileia: Associazione nazionale per Aquileia.

Calzolari, M. 2007. "Il Delta padano in Età romana: Idrografia, viabilià, insediamenti." In Berti, *Genti nel delta di Spina a Comacchio*, 153–172.

Calzolari, M. 2004. *Il Po in età romana: Geografia, storia e immagine di un grande fiume europeo*. Reggio Emilia: Diabasis.

Calzolari, M. 2001. "I pesi fittili di età romana." In *Pondera: Pesi e Misure nell'Antichità*, edited by C. Corti and N. Giordani, 327–330. Campogalliano: Museo della bilancia.

Cambi F., and N. Terrenato. 1994. *Introduzione all'archeologia dei paesaggi*. Rome: Nuova Italia Scientifica.

Camerin, N. 1999. "L'Italia antica: Italia settentrionale." In *Carri da guerra e principi etruschi: Catalogo della Mostra: Viterbo, Palazzo dei Papi, 24 maggio 1997–31 gennaio 1998, edited by* A. Emiliozzi, *33–44. Rome: L'Erma di Bretschneider.*

Camporeale, L. 2004. "The Etruscans in Europe." In Camporeale, *The Etruscans outside Etruria*, 102–129.

Camporeale, L., ed. 2004. *The Etruscans outside Etruria*. Los Angeles: J. Paul Getty Museum.

Cantino Wataghin, G. 2000. "Christianisaition et organisation ecclesiastique des campagnes: l'Italie du Nord aux Ive–VIIe siecles." In *Towns and Their Territories between Late Antiquity and the Early Middle Ages*, edited by G. P. Brogiolo, N. Gauthier, and N. Christie, 209–234. Leiden: Brill.

Capuis, L. 2004. "The Etruscans in Veneto." In Camporeale, *The Etruscans outside Etruria*, 130–145.

Cardarelli, A. 2010. "The collapse of the Terramare culture and growth of new economic and social systems during the Bronze Age in Italy." *Scienze di Antichità: Storia, archeologia, antropologia* 15: 449–520.

Càssola, P., and S. Vitri. 1997. "Gli insediamenti arginati della pianura friuliana nell'età del Bronzo." In Bernarbò Brea, Cardarelli, and Cremaschi, *Le Terramare*, 257–262.

Castelleti, L. 1993. "L'evoluzione dell'ambiente e del paesaggio vegetale negli ultimi millenni." In *Carta Archeologica della Lombardia*. Vol. 3, *Como: La città murata e la convalle*, edited by M. Uboldi, 111–114. Modena: Panini.

Castelletti, L., and I. Nobile. 1985. "Como." In *Archeologia urbana in Lombardia: Valutazione dei depositi archeologici e inventario dei vincoli*, edited by R. Bussi and A. Molinari. 99–104. Modena: Panini.

Cattaneo, C. 2005. "Analisi antropologiche e patologiche dei resti scheletrici." In *Extra Moenia 2: Gli scavi di Via Benzi: i reperti*, edited by D. Caporusso, 351–370. Como: New Press.

Cavalieri-Manasse, G., and B. Bruno. 2003. "Edilizia abitativa a Verona." In Ortalli, *Abitare in città*, 47–64.

Cavallo, G. 1983. "La cultura a Ravenna tra corte e chiesa." In *Le Sedi di Cultura nell'Emilia Romagna: L'Alta Medioevo*, edited by O. Capitani, 29–51. Bologna: Federazione delle casse di risparmio e delle banche del Monte dell'Emilia e Romagna.

Cencig, D., and G. Franceschin. 2012. *Idrografia e viabilità nel territorio centro orientale die Aquileia Romana: Conferme, nuove osservazioni, aggiunte e correzioni*. Mariano del Friuli: Edizioni della laguna.

Cenerini, F. 2008, "Donne e società nei municipi della Cisalpina romana: qualche spunto di riflessione su Bononia." In *Est enim flos Italiae . . . Vita economica e sociale nella Cisalpina romana: Atti delle Giornate di studi in onore di Eio Buchi (Verona 30 novembre–1 dicembre 2006)*, 141–145. Verona: QuiEdit.

Cenerini, F. 1989. "O colonia quae cupis ponte ludere longo (Catullus 17): Cultura e politica." Athenaeum 67: 41–55.

Cenerini, F. 1987–88. "Evergetismo ed epigrafia: lavationem in perpetuom." *Rivista storica dell'antichità* 17–18 (1987–88): 199–220.

Ceresa Mori, A. 2015. "Milano nel III secolo a.C." In Malnati and Manzelli, *Roma e le genti del Po*, 91.

Ceresa Mori, A.,ed. 2004. *L'anfiteatro di Milano e il suo quartiere. Percorso storico-archeologico nel suburbio sudoccidentale*. Milan: Skira.

Champlin, E. 1987. "The testamentum of the piglet." *Phoenix* 41: 174–183.

Chaniotis, A. 2004. "Under the Watchful Eyes of the Gods: Divine Justice in Hellenistic and Roman Asia Minor. In *The Greco-Roman East: Politics, Culture, Society*, edited by S. Colvin, 1–43. Cambridge: Cambridge University Press.

Chevallier, R. 1990. *Aquilée et la romanisation de l'Europe*. Tours: Université de Tours.

Chevallier, R. 1983. *La Romanisa tion de la Celtique du Pô*. Rome: École française de Rome.

Chiaravalle, M. 1987. *Le monete di Ticinum nella Collezione di Franco Rolla: Catalogo delle Civiche Raccolte Numismatiche di Milano*. Milan: Comune di Milano.

Chilver, G. E. F. 1941. *Cisalpine Gaul: Social and Economic History from 49 B.C. to the Death of Trajan*. Oxford: Clarendon Press.

Christie, N. 2010. *The Fall of the Western Roman Empire: An Archaeological and Historical Perspective*. London: Bloomsbury Academic.

Christie, N. 2008. "From the Danube to the Po: Late Roman Defence in Pannonia and Italy." In *The Transition to Late Antiquity, on the Danube and Beyond. Proceedings of the British Academy*. Vol. 141, edited by A. Poulter, 547–577. Oxford: Oxford University Press.

Christie, N. 2006. *From Constantine to Charlemagne: An Archaeology of Italy, AD300–800*. Aldershot, UK: Ashgate.

Christie, N. 1995. *The Lombards: The Ancient Langobards*. Chichester: Wiley-Blackwell.

Christie, N. 1991. "The Alps as a frontier, AD 168–774." *Journal of Roman Archaeology* 4: 410–430.

Churchin, L. 2004. *The Romanization of Central Spain: Complexity, Diversity and Change in a Provincial Hinterland*. London: Routledge.

Ciampoltrini, G. 2004. "Lucca colonia latina: I Liguri della valle del Serchio tra deportazione e Integrazione." In De Marinis and Spadea, *I Liguri*, 454–455.

Ciglenećki, S. 2015. "Late Roman Army, Claustra Alpium Iuliarum and the Fortifications in the South-Eastern Alps / Poznorimska Vojska, Claustra Alpium Iuliarum in Utrjena Krajina v Jugovshodnih Alpah." In *Evidence of the Roman Army in Slovenia / Sledovi Rimske Vojske Na Slovenskem*, edited by J. Istenič, B. Laharnar, and J. Horvat, 385–430. Ljubljana: Narodni muzej Slovenije.

Ciotola, A., and B. Maurina. 2011. "Scavi 1973–1996: Sequenza stratigrafica, periodizzazione e descrizione delle strutture rivenute." In *La villa romana di Isera: Ricerche e scavi (1973–2004)*, edited by M. De Vos and B. Maurina, 65–111. Rovereto: Edizioni Osiride.

Cipriano, S. 2010. "L'edificio termale di Altino." *Quaderni di Archeologia del Veneto* 25: 159–167.

Ciurletti, G. 2003. "Il caso Tridentum." In Ortalli, *Abitare in città*, 37–45.

Clemente, G. 1984. "Ticinum: Da Diocleziono alla caduta dell'impero d'Occidente." In *Storia di Pavia*, 1: 255–268. Milan: Banca del Monte di Lombardia.

Cocchi Genick, D. 2004. "Le ceramiche nel ruolo di indicatori cronologici e regionali." In *L'età del bronzo recente in Italia*, edited by D. Cocchi Genick, 22–52. Viareggio: M. Baroni.

Cohen, G. 1983. "Colonization and Population Transfer in the Hellenistic World." In *Egypt and the Hellenistic World. Proceedings of the International Colloquium Leuven, 24–26 May 1982*, edited by Edmond Van 't Dack, 63–74. Leuven: Katholieke Universiteit Leuven.

Colonna, C., and L. Salzani, eds. 2010. *La fragilità dell'urna: I recenti scavi a Narde, Necropoli di Frattesina (XII–IX sec. a.C.)*. Rovigo: Museo dei Grandi Fiumi.

Colonna, G. 1998. "Etruschi sulla via delle Alpi Occidentali." In *Archeologia in Piemonte*. Vol. 1, *La Preistoria*, edited by L. Mercando and M. V. Gambari, 261–266. Turin: U. Allemandi.

Colonna, G. 1993. "Doni di Etruschi e di altri barbari occidentali nei santuari panellenici." In *I Grandi santuari della Grecia e l'occidente*, edited by A. Mastrocinque, 43–76. Trento: Dipartimento di scienze filologiche e storiche.

Colussa, S. 2010. *Cividale del Friuli: L'impianto urbano di Forum Iulii in epoca romana; carta archeologica*. Galatina: Congedo.

Conforti Calcagni, A. 1999. *Le mura di Verona: La città e le sue difese, dalla fondazione romana All'unità d'Italia*. Caselle di Sommacampagna (VR): Cierre Edizion.

Conventi, M. 2004. *Città romane di fondazione*. Rome: L'Erma di Bretschneider.

Corbier, M. 1991. "City, Territory, and Taxation." In *City and Country in the Ancient World*, edited by J. Rich, 211–239. London: Routledge.

Corbier, M. 1973. "Les circonscriptions judiciaires de l'Italie, de Marc-Aurèle à Aurélien." *Mélanges de l'École française de Rome* 85: 609–690.

Corcoran, S. 2000. *The Empire of the Tetrarchs: Imperial Pronouncements and Government, AD 284–324*. Oxford: Clarendon Press.

Cornell, T. 2013. *The Fragments of the Roman Historians*. Oxford: Clarendon Press.

Corti, C. 2012a. "L'economia della lana a Mutina." In *La lana nella Cisalpina romana: Economia e società. Studi in onore di Stefania PesaventoMattioli: Atti del Convegno, Padova-Verona, 18–20 maggio 2011*, edited by M. S. Busana and P. Basso, 213–229. Padua: Padova University Press.

Corti, C. 2012b. "Il culto di Ercole e l'economia della lana a Mutina." In *Pagani e cristiani: Forme ed attestazioni di religiosità del mondo antico nell'Emilia centrale* 11: 19–40.

Cracco Ruggini, L. 1998. "Roma e il vino nord-italico." In *La mémoire perdue: Recherches sur L'administration romaine*, 345–364. Rome: École française de Rome.

Crawford, M. H. 1984. "La zecca di Ticinum." In *Storia di Pavia*, 1:249–269. Milan: Banca del Monte di Lombardia.

Crawford, M. H. 1974. *Roman Republican Coinage*. Cambridge: Cambridge University Press.

Cremaschi, M., M. Marchetti, and C. Ravazzi. 1994. "Geomorphological Evidence for Land Surfaces Cleared from Forest in the Central Po Plain (Northern Italy) during the Roman Period." In *Evaluation of Land Surfaces Cleared from Forest in the Mediterranean Region during the Time of the Roman Empire*, edited by B. Frenzel, 119–132. Stuttgart: Gustav Fischer Verlag.

Cremaschi, M., C. Pizzi, and V. Valsecchi. 2006. "Water management and land use in the terramare and a possible climatic co-factor in their abandonment: The case study of the terramara of Poviglio Santa Rosa (northern Italy)." *Quaternary International* 151: 87–98.

Cremaschi, M. 2009. "Foreste, terre coltivate e acque: L'originalita del progetto terramaricolo." In Bernarbò Brea, and Cremaschi, *Acqua e civiltà nelle Terramare*, 34–42.

Cremaschi, M. 1997. "Terramare e paesaggio padano." In Bernarbò Brea, Cardarelli, and Cremaschi, *Le Terramare*, 107–125.

Criniti, N. 1991. *La tabula alimentaria di Veleia*. Parma: Deputazione di storia patria per le province parmensi.

Criniti, N. 1970. *L'epigrafe di Asculum di Gn. Pompeo Strabone*. Milan: Università Cattolica del Sacro Cuore.

Curina, R., L. Malnati, V. Manzelli, F. Rossi, G. Spagnolo Garzoli, and M. Tirelli. 2015. "La Cisalpina tra III e I secolo a.C. alla luce dell'archeologia." In Malnati and Manzelli, *Roma e le genti del Po*, 42–54.

Dall'Aglio, P. L. 2000. "Geografia fisica e popolamento di età romana." In Marini Calvani, *Aemilia*, 51–56. Venice: Marsilio.

David, J.-M. 1997. *The Roman Conquest of Italy*. Oxford: Blackwell.

De Bernardo Stempel, P. 2000. "Ptolemy's Celtic Italy and Ireland: A linguistic analysis." In *Ptolemy: Towards a Linguistic Atlas of the Earliest Celtic Place-names of Europe*, edited by D. N. Parsons and P. Sims-Williams, 83–112. Aberystwyth: CMCS.

De Blois, L. 1976. *The Policy of the Emperor Gallienus*. Leiden: Brill.

Defente, V. 2003. *Les Celtes en Italie du Nord*. Rome: École française de Rome.

De Grozzi Mazzorin, J. 2009. "Fauna ed economia animale." In Bernarbò Brea and Cremaschi, *Acqua e civiltà nelle Terramare*, 170–174.

De Grozzi Mazzorin, J. 2013. "Considerazioni sullo sfruttamentoanimale in ambito Terramaricolo." In *Economia e ambiente nell'Italia padana dell'età del bronzo: Le indagini bioarchelogiche*, edited by J. De Grozzi Mazzorin, A. Curci, and G. Giacobini, 155–160. Bari: Edipuglia.

De Laet, S. 1949. *Portorium: Étude sur l'organisation douanière chez les Romains surtout a l'époque du Haut-empire*. New York: Arno Press.

De la Ruffinière du Prey, P. 1994. *The Villas of Pliny: From Antiquity to Posterity*. Chicago: University of Chicago Press.

Delia, D. 1988. "The population of Roman Alexandria." *Transactions of the American Philological Association* 1988: 275–292.

De Ligt, L. 2008. "The Population of Cisalpine Gaul in the Time of Augustus." In *People, Land, and Politics: Demographic Developments and the Transformation of Roman Italy 300 BC–AD 14*, edited by L. de Ligt and S. Northwood, 139–183. Leiden: Brill.

Deliyannis, D. 2010. *Ravenna in Late Antiquity*. Cambridge: Cambridge University Press.

De Maria, S. 1991. "Bologna (Bononia) and the Reno Valley." In *Roman Landscapes: Archaeological Survey in the Mediterranean Region*, edited by G. Barker and J. Lloyd, 96–105. London: British School at Rome.

De Marinis, R. C. 2009. "La culture de Golasecca. Une histoire de plusieurs siècles." In *Golasecca: Du commerce et des hommes à l'âge du fer (VIIIe-Ve siècle av. J.C.): Musée d'Archéologie nationale, château de Saint-Germain-en-Laye, 27 novembre 2009–26 avril 2010*, edited by C. Lorre and V. Cicolani, 38–44. Paris: Éditions de la Réunion des musées nationaux.

De Marinis, R. C. 2001. "I Celti e la Lombardia." In *Antichità Altoadriatiche* 48: 203–226.

De Marinis, R. C. 1997. "L'età del bronzo nella regione benacense e nella pianura padana a nord del Po." In Bernarbò Brea, Cardarelli, and Cremaschi, *Le Terramare*, 405–422.

De Marinis, R. C. 1996. "Comprensori protourbani e articulaione sociale nella cultura di Golasecca." In Bietti Sestieri and Kruta, *The Iron Age in Europe*, 23–33.

De Marinis, R. C. 1991. "L'abitato etrusco del Forcello: Opere di difesa e di drenaggio e importanza delle vie di comunicazione fluviale." In Bergamini, *Gli Etruschi maestri di idraulica*, 75–85.

De Marinis, R. C. 1998. "I Liguri tra Etruschi e Celti." In Sena Chiesa, *Tesori della Postumia*,59–75.

De Marinis, R. C., ed. 1986–87. *Gli Etruschi a nord del Po*. 2 vols. Udine: Campanotto.

De Marinis, R. C., and G. Spadea, eds. 2004. *I Liguri: Un antico populo europeo tra Alpi e Mediterraneo*. Milan: Skira.

De Min, M. 1987. "Adria." In *Il Veneto nell'età romana*. Vol. 2, *Note di urbanistica e di archae-*

ologia del territorio, edited by G. Cavalieri Manasse, 257–268. Verona: Banca popolare di Verona.

Dench, E. 2005. *Romulus' Asylum: Roman Identities from theAge of Alexander to the Age of Hadrian*. Oxford: Oxford University Press.

Denti, M. 1991. *I Romani a nord del Po*. Milan: Longanesi.

D'Ercole, M. C. 2011. "Sharing New Worlds: Mixed Identities around the Adriatic (Sixth to Fourth Centuries B.C.E)." In *Cultural Identity in the Ancient Mediterranean*, edited by E. Gruen, 428–451. Los Angeles: Getty Research Institute.

D'Ercole, M. 2002. *Importuosa Italiae litora: Paysage et échanges dans l'Adriatique méridionale à l'époque archaïque*. Naples: Publications du Centre Jean Bérard.

De Salieu, G. 2013. "Rock Carvings and Alpine Statue-menhirs, from the Chalcolithic to the Middle Bronze Age." In *The Oxford Handbook of the European Bronze Age*, edited by H. Fokkens and A. Harding, 291–310. Oxford: Oxford University Press.

Desantis, P. 2015a. "Bologna nel III secolo a.C." In Malnati and Manzelli, *Roma e le genti del Po*, 76–77.

Devijver, H. 1988. "Les militiae equestres de P. Helvius Pertinax." *Zeitschrift für Papyrologie und Epigraphie* 75: 207–214.

Dey, H. 2015. *The Afterlife of the Roman City: Architecture and Ceremony in Late Antiquity and the Early Middle Ages*. Cambridge: Cambridge University Press.

Di Filippo Balestrazzi, E. 2013. "La romanizzazione." In Gamba, *Venetkens*, 162–171.

Dix, T. K.1996. "Pliny's library at Comum." *Libraries & Culture* 31: 85–102.

Dmitriev, S. 2005. *City Government in Hellenistic and Roman Asia Minor*. Oxford: Oxford University Press.

Donati, A. 2002. "Un imperatore ligure: Pertinace di Alba Pompeia." In *Liguria nell'impero Romano: Gli imperatori liguri. Atti del convegno, Genova, 30 novembre 2000*, edited by A. Bertinelli, 23–28. Genova: Accademia ligure di scienze e lettere.

Drews, R. 1993. *The End of the Bronze Age: Changes in Warfare and theCcatastrophe ca. 1200 B.C.* Princeton: Princeton University Press.

Duncan-Jones, R. 1992. *Structure and Scale in the Roman Economy*. Cambridge: Cambridge University Press.

Duncan-Jones, R. 1982. *The Economy of the Roman Empire: Quantitative Studies*. 2nd ed. Cambridge: Cambride University Press.

Duncan-Jones, R. 1964. "The purpose and organisation of the Alimenta." *Papers of the British School at Rome* 32: 123–146.

Duthoy, R. 1976. "Augustalis et sevir dans l'empire romain." *Epigraphische Studien* 11: 143–214.

Dyson, S. L. 1992. *Community and Society in Roman Italy*. Baltimore: Johns Hopkins University Press.

Dyson, S. L. 1985. *The Creation of the Roman Frontier*. Princeton: Princeton University Press.

Ebel, C. 1975. "Pompey's Organization of Transalpina." *Phoenix* 29: 358–373.

Eck, W. 2001. "Die grosse Pliniusinschrift aus Comum: Funktion und Monument." *Epigrafia e antichità* 17: 225–235.

Eck, W. 1997. "Rome and the Outside World: Senatorial Families and the World They

Lived In." In *The Roman Family in Italy: Status, Sentiment, Space*, edited by B. Rawson and P. Weaver, 73–99. Oxford: Oxford University Press.

Eck, W. 1979. *Die staatliche Organisation Italiens in der hohen Kaisertzeit*. Munich: Beck.

Eckstein, A. 2012. "Polybius, the Gallic crisis, and the Ebro Treaty." *Classical Philology* 107: 206–229.

Edmondson, J. 2006. "Cities and Urban Life in the Western Provinces of the Roman Empire 30 BCE–250 CE 250." *A Companion to the Roman Empire*, edited by D. Potter, 250–280.Malden: Blackwell.

Erdkamp, P. 2009. "Polybius, the Ebro Treaty, and the Gallic invasion of 225 B.C.E." *Classical Philology* 104: 495–510.

Everettt, N. 2003. *Literacy in Lombard Italy, c. 568–774*. Cambridge: Cambridge University Press.

Ewins, U. 1955, "The enfranchisement of Cisalpine Gaul." *Papers of the British School at Rome* 23: 73–98.

Ewins, U. 1952. "The early colonisation of Cisalpine Gaul." *Papers of the British School at Rome* 20: 54–71.

Facchini, G. M. 2005. "Il ruolo di Aquileia nella diffusione del vetro a mosaico nell'Italia Settentrionale." *Antichità Altoadriatiche* 61: 547–562.

Facchini, G. M. 1997. "Romanizzazione e Romanità nelle regione insubrica." In *Archeologia della Regio Insubrica: Dalla Preistoria all'Alto Medioevo. Atti del convegno, Chiasso 5–6 ottobre 1996*, edited by F. Ricci, 55–66. Como: Società Archeologica Comense.

Fagan, G. 1999. *Bathing in Public in the Roman World*. Ann Arbor: University of Michigan Press.

Farney, G. D. 2011. "Aspects of the Emergence of Italian Identity in the Early Roman Empire." In Gleba and Horsnæs, *Communicating Identity in Iron Age Communities*, 223–232.

Farney, G. D. 2007. *Ethnic Identity and Aristocratic Competition in Republican Rome*. Cambridge: Cambridge University Press.

Feeney, D. 2007. *Caesar's Calendar: Ancient Time and the Beginnings of History*. Berkeley: University of California Press.

Fishwick, D. 1987–2005. *The Imperial Cult in the Latin West*. Leiden: Brill.

Fitz, J. 1966. Der markomannisch-quadische Angriff gegen Aquileia und Opitergium." *Historia* 15: 336–367.

Fletcher, R. N. 2007. *Patterns of Imports in Iron Age Italy*. Oxford: Archaeopress.

Foglari, G., and G. Gambacurta, eds. 2001. *Materiali veneti preromani eromani del santuario diLagole di Calalzo al Musea di Pieve di Cadore*. Rome: L'Erma di Bretschneider.

Fontana, F. 2010. *I culti isiaci nell'Italia settentrionale. 1, Verona, Aquileia, Trieste*. Edizioni Università di Trieste.

Fontana, F. 1997. *I culti di Aquileia repubblicana: Aspetti della politica religiosa in Gallia Cisalpina tra il 3. e il 2. sec. a.C.* Rome: Quasar.

Forbis, E. 1996. *Municipal Virtues in the Roman Empire: The Evidence of Italian Honorary Inscriptions*. Stuttgart: Teubner.

Forni, G. 1989. "La tribù Velina degli Aquileiesi." *Antichità Altoadriatiche* 35: 51–81.

Fortunati Zuccala, M. 1993. "Alcune considerazioni sulla documentazione archeologica di età Romana." In *Carta Archeologica della Lombardia*. Vol. 4, *La Provincia di Lecco*, edited by S. Casini, 185–212. Modena: F. C. Panini.

Francovish, R., and R. Hodges. 2003. *Villa to Village: The Transformation of the Roman Countryside in Italy, c. 400–1000*. London: Duckworth.

Frasinetti P. 1972. "Sisenna e la guerra sociale." *Athenaeum* 50: 78–113.

Frayn, J. 1993. *Markets and Fairs in Roman Italy: Their Social and Economic Importance from the Second Century BC to the Third Century AD*. Oxford: Clarendon Press.

Frayn, J. 1984. *Sheep-rearing and the Wool Trade in Italy during the Roman Period*. Liverpool:Cairns.

Frederickson, M. 1964. "The Lex Rubria: Reconsiderations." *Journal of Roman Studies* 54: 129–134.

Freis, H. 1967. *Die Cohortes Urbanae*. Köln: Böhlau,

Frey, O.-H. 1995. "The Celts in Italy." In *The Celtic World*, edited by M. Green, 515–532. London: Routledge.

Frey, O.-H. 1984. "Die Bedeutung der Gallia Cisalpina für die Entstehung der Oppida-Kultur." In *Studien zu Siedlungsfragen der Latenezeit*, edited by O.-H. Frey and H. Roth, 1–38. Marburg: Vorgeschichtliches Seminar Marburg.

Frova, A. 1994. "Il teatro romano di Brescia." *Antichità Altoadriatiche* 41: 347–365.

Gabba, E. 2001. "Plinio Fraccaro e la storia antica." *Athenaeum* 89: 3–40.

Gabba, E. 2000. *Pavia: Domicilium sapientie, note storiche*. Como: Edizioni New Press.

Gabba, E. 1991. "I rapporti politici dei Galli con gli altri populi dell'Italia antica." In *Linguistici e culturali tra i popoli dell'Italia antica*, edited by E. Campanile, 149–155. Pisa: Giardini. Reprinted in E. Gabba, 1994: *Italia Romana*: 231–236. Como: Edizioni New Pres

Gabba, E. 1988. "Significato storico della conquista augustea delle Alpi." In *La Valle d'Aosta e l'arco alpino nella politica del mondo antico*, edited by M. C. Vacchina, 53–61. Reprinted in E. Gabba, 1994: *Italia Romana: 267–273*. Como: Edizioni New Pres

Gabba, E. 1987. "Le fonti storiche, la romanizzazione e l'età imperial." In *Libarna*, edited by S, Finocchi, 27–34. Turin: Quadrante Edizioni.

Gabba, E. 1979. "Caio Flaminio e la sua legge sulla colonizzazione dell'agro Gallico."*Athenaeum* 57: 159–63.

Gabba, E. 1954. *Le origini della guerra sociale e la vita politica romana dopo l'89 a.C.* Pavia: Tipografia del Libro.

Gabba, E., and G. Tibiletti, 1960. "Una signora di Treviri sepolta a Pavia." *Athenaeum* 68: 253.

Gaggero, E. 2004. "I popoli liguri testimoniati dagli autori classici." In De Marinis and Spadea, *I Liguri*, 399–401.

Galsterer, H. 1994. "Regionen and Regionalismus im römischen Italien." *Historia* 43: 306–323.

Galsterer, H. 1976. "Urbanisation und Municipalisation Italiens im 2. und 1. Jh. v. Chr." In *Hellenismus in Mittelitalien*, edited by P. Zanker, 327–333. Göttingen: Vandenhoeck and Ruprecht.

Gamba, M., ed. 2013. *Venetkens: Viaggio nella terra dei veneti antichi*. Venice: Marsilio.

Gambacurta, G., and M. Tirelli. 1996. "Le sepolture di cavallo nella necropoli 'Le Brustolade.'" In *La protostoria tra Sile e Tagliamento: Antiche genti fra Veneto e Friuli, Catalogo della Mostra*, edited by R. Salerno, G. Tasca, and A. Vigoni, 71–74. Padua: Esedra.

Gambacurta, G., D. Locatela, A. Marinetti, and A. Ruta Serafini, 2005. "Delimitazione dello spazio e rituale funerario nel Veneto preromano." In "*Terminavit sepulcrum*": *I recinti funerari nelle necropoli di Altino. Atti del Convegno Venezia 2003*, edited by G. Cresci Marrone and M. Tirelli, 9–40. Rome: Quasar.

Gambari, F. 1997. "L'Italia nord-occidentale nell'età del bronzo media e recente." In Bernarbò Brea, Cardarelli, and Cremaschi, *Le Terramare*, 441–444.

Gambari, F., and A. Bondoni. 2013. "Poco differenti per usi e costumi: Veneti e Celti." In Gamba, *Venetkens*, 156–161.

Gambaro, L. 1999. *La Liguria costiera tra 3. e 1. secolo a.C. : una lettura archeologica della romanizzazione*. Mantova: Editrice S.A.P.-Societá Archeologica Padana.

Garnsey, P. 1976. "Economy and society of Mediolanum under the Principate." *Papers of the British School at Rome* 44: 13–27.

Garnsey, P. 1968. "Trajan's alimenta: Some problems." *Historia* 17: 367–381.

George, M. 2005. *The Roman Family in the Empire: Rome, Italy, and Beyond*. Oxford: Oxford University Press.

George, M. 1997. *The Roman Domestic Architecture of Northern Italy*. Oxford:Archaeopress.

Ghedini, F. 2012. "Soluzioni e modelli abitativi tra tarda Repubblica e tardo Impero." In *Atria Longa Patescunt: Le forme dell'abitare nella cisalpina romana*, edited by F. Ghedini and M. Annibaletto, 291–332. Rome: Quasar.

Ghiacchero, M. 1974. *Edictum Diocletiani et collegarum de pretiis rerum venalium*. Genoa: Istituto di Storia Antica e Scienze Ausiliarie.

Giardina, A. 1997. *L'Italia Romana: Storie di un'identità incompiuta*. Rome: Laterza.

Giardina, A. 1994. "L'identità incompiuta dell'Italia romana." In *L'Italie d'Auguste à Dioclétien*, 1–89. Rome: École française de Rome.

Gibson, R., and R. Morello. 2012. *Reading the* Letters *of Pliny the Younger: An Introduction*. Cambridge: Cambridge University Press.

Gillett, A. 2003. *Envoys and Political Communication in the Late Antique West, 411–533*. Cambridge: Cambridge University Press.

Gillett, A. 2001. "Rome, Ravenna, and the last Western emperors." *Papers of the British School at Rome* 69: 131–167.

Giostra, C. 2011. "Goths and Lombards in Italy: The potential of archaeology with respect to ethnocultural identification." *Post-Classical Archaeologies* 1: 7–36.

Giovannini, A. 2002. "Le Ambre di Aquileia: Connotazioni generali e correlazioni cultuali." In Buora, *Roma sul Danubio*, 159–164.

Glas, T., and U. Hartmann. 2008. "Die Provinzverwaltung." In *Die Zeit der Soldatenkaiser: Krise und Transformation des Römischen Reiches im 3. Jahrhundert n. Chr. (235–284)*, edited by K.-P. Johne, 641–672. Berlin: Akademie Verlag.

Gleba, M. 2012. "Italy: Iron Age." In *Textiles and Textile Production in Europe from Prehistory to AD 400*, edited by M. Gleba and U. Mannering, 215–241. Oxford: Oxbow Books.

Gleba, M., and H. W. Horsnæs, eds. 2011. *Communicating Identity in Iron Age Communities*. Oxford: Oxbow Books.

Gleba, M. 2002. "Linen production in pre-Roman and Roman Italy." In *Purpureae vestes: Actas del I symposium internacional sobre textiles y tintes del Mediterráneo en época romana (Ibiza, 8 al 10 de noviembre, 2002)*, edited by C. Alfaro, J. P. Wild and B. Costa, 9–38. València: Consell insular d'Eivissa i Formentera.

Godechot, J. 1988. "The New Concept of the Nation and Its Diffusion in Europe." In *Na-*

tionalism in the Age of the French Revolution, edited by O. Dann and J. Dinwiddy, 13–26. London: Hambledon.

Gonzato, F. 2010. "Possibili influenze egeo-orientali negli strumenti da tessitura in osso provenieti dalla necropoli di Narde di Fratta Polesine." In Colonna and Salzani, *La fragilità dell'urna*, 101–104.

Gradel, I. 2002. *Emperor Worship and Roman Religion*. Oxford: Clarendon.

Grassi, M. T. 1998. "Gli Insubri." In Sena Chiesa, *Tesori della Postumia*, 84–87.

Grassi, M. T. 1995. *La romanizzazione degli insubri: Celti e Romani in Transpadana attraverso la documentazione storica ed archeologica*. Milan: Edizioni ET.

Grassi, M. T. 1991. *I Celti in Italia*. Milan: Longanesi.

Gregori, G. L. 2008. "Il funzionamento della amministrativi locali a Brixia e nella res publica Camunnorum." In Berrendonner, Cébeillac-Gervasoni, and Lamoine, *Le quotidien municipal dans l'occident Romain*, 53–66.

Gregori, G. L. 1999. *Brescia romana: Ricerche di prosopografia e storia sociale*. Rome: Quasar.

Grazia Maioli, M. 2000. "Cesena." In Marini Calvani, *Aemilia*, 495–499.

Gruen, E. 1974. *The Last Generation of the Roman Republic*. Berkeley: University of California Press.

Guarnieri, C. 2000. "Faenza." In Marini Calvani, *Aemilia*, 471–475. Hall, J. 2002. *Hellenicity: Between Ethnicity and Culture*. Chicago: University of Chicago Press.

Hall, J. 1997. *Ethnic Identity in Greek Antiquity*. Cambridge: Cambridge University Press.

Handley, M. 2011. *Dying on Foreign Shores: Travel and Mobility in the Late-Antique West*. Portsmouth, RI: Journal of Roman Archaeology.

Harari, M. 2000. *Gli Etruschi del Po*. Pavia: Edizioni Libreria Cardano.

Harl, K. 1996. *Coinage in the Roman Economy, 300 B.C. to A.D. 700*. Baltimore: Johns Hopkins University Press.

Harris, W. V. 1985. *War and Imperialism in Republican Rome, 327–70 B.C.* Oxford: Clarendon Press.

Harris W. V. 1971. *Rome in Etruria and Umbria*. Oxford: Clarendon Press.

Häussler, R. 2013. *Becoming Roman?: Diverging Identities and Experiences in Ancient Northwest Italy*. New York: Routledge.

Häussler, R. 2007. "At the Margins of Italy: Celts and Ligurians in North-West Italy." In *Ancient Italy: Regions without Boundaries*, edited by G. J. Bradley, E. Isayev, and C. Riva, 45–78. Exeter: University of Exeter Press.

Häussler, R. 2002. "Writing Latin—from Resistance to Assimilation: Language, Culture, and Society in N. Italy and S. Gaul." In *Becoming Roman, Writing Latin? Literacy and Epigraphy in the Roman West*, edited by A. Cooley, 61–76. Portsmouth, RI: Journal of Roman Archaeology.

Häussler, R. 2000. "The Dynamics of State Societies in Northwest Italy." In Lomas and Herring, *The Emergence of State Identities*, 131–156.

Häussler, R., and J. Pearce. 2007. "Towards an Archaeology of Literacy." In *Literacy and the State in the Ancient Mediterranean*, edited by Kathryn Lomas, Ruth Whitehouse, and John Wilkins, 219–236. London: Accordia.

Hempl, G. 1932. "Venetic." *Language and Literature* 5: 343–354.

Henderson, J. 2002. *Pliny's Statue: The Letters, Self-Portraiture, and Classical Art*. Exeter: University of Exeter Press.

Herring, E. 2000. "'To see oursels as others see us!': The Construction of Native Identities in Southern Italy." In Lomas and Herring, *The Emergence of State Identities*, 45–77.

Hoffer, S. 1999. *The Anxieties of Pliny the Younger*. Oxford: Oxford University Press.

Højte, J. 2005. *Roman Imperial Statue Bases: From Augustus to Commodus*. Aarhus: Aarhus University Press.

Holloway, R. R. 1981. *Italy and the Aegean: 3000–700 B.C.* Louvain-la-Neue: Institut supérieur d'archéologie et d'histoire de l'art.

Hölscher, T. 2011. "Myths, Images, and the Typology of Identities in Early Greek Art." In *Cultural Identity in the Ancient Mediterranean*, edited by E. Gruen, 47–65. Los Angeles: Getty Research Institute.

Hope, V. 2001. *Constructing Identity: The Roman Funerary Monuments of Aquileia, Mainz, and Nîmes*. Oxford: Archaeopress.

Horden, P., and N. Purcell. 2000. *The Corrupting Sea: A Study of Mediterranean History*. Malden: Blackwell.

Horster, M. 2001. *Bauinschriften römischer Kaiser: Untersuchungen zu Inschriftenpraxis und Bautätigkeit in Städten des westlichen Imperium Romanum in der Zeit des Prinzipats*. Stuttgart: Franz Steiner Verlag.

Humphries, M. 1999. *Communities of the Blessed: Social Environment and Religious Change in Northern Italy, AD 200–400*. Oxford: Oxford University Press.

Isayev, E. 2011. "Corfinium and Rome: Changing Place in the Social War." In Gleba and Horsnæs, *Communicating Identity in Iron Age Communities*, 210–222.

Jacques, F. 1984. *Le privilège de liberté: Politique impériale et autonomie municipale dans les cités de l'Occident romain (161–244)*. Rome: École française de Rome.

Jacques, F. 1983. *Les curateurs des cités dans l'Occident romain de Trajan à Gallien*. Paris: Nouvelles Éditions Latines.

Jennings, B. 2014. *Breaking with Tradition: Cultural Influences for the Decline of the Circum-Alpine Region Lake-dwellings*. Leiden: Brill.

Jongman, W. 2000. "Wool and the Textile Industry of Roman Italy: A Working Hypothesis." In Lo Cascio, *Mercati Permanenti e Mercati Periodici nel Mondo Romano: Atti degli Incontri capresi di storia dell'economia antica (Capri 13–15 ottobre 1997)*, 189–197. Bari: Edipuglia.

Jorio, S. 2004. "Como, piazza Cacciatori delle Alpi-via Gallio, Scavo di un'area extraurbana." *Notiziario della Soprintendenza Archeologica della Lombardia* 2001–2002, 71–76.

Keppie, L. 2000. "Colonisation and veteran settlement in Italy, 47–14 BC: New evidence and further thoughts." *Legions and Veterans: Roman Army Papers, 1971–2000*: 249–262.

Keppie, L. 1983. *Colonisation and Veteran Settlement in Italy, 47–14 B.C.* London: British School at Rome.

König, J., K. Oikonomopoulou, and G. Woolf, eds. 2013. *Ancient Libraries*. Cambridge: Cambridge University Press.

Kouroumali, M. 2013. "The Justinianic Reconquest of Italy: Imperial Campaigns and Local Responses." In *War and Warfare in Late Antiquity*, edited by A. Sarantis and N. Christie, 969–999. Leiden: Brill.

Krautheimer, R. 1983. *Three Christian Capitals: Topography and Politics*. Berkeley: University of California Press.

Kristiansen, K. 2000. *Europe before History*. Cambridge: Cambridge University Press.

Kristiansen, K., and T. Larsson. 2005. *The Rise of Bronze Age Society: Travels, Transmissions and Transformations*. Cambridge: Cambridge University Press.

Kron, G. Forthcoming. "The Population of Northern Italy and the Debate over the Augustan Census Figures: Weighing the Documentary, Literary and Archaeological Evidence." In *Popolazione e risorse nell'Italia settentrionale dall'età preromana ai Longobardi*, edited by E. Lo Cascio and M. Balbo. Bari: Edipuglia.

Kruta, V. 1999. "The First Celtic Expansion: Prehistory to History." In Moscti et al., *The Celts*, 206–224.

Laffi, U. 2007. *Colonie e municipi nello Stato romano*. Rome: Edizioni di Storia e Letteratura.

Laffi, U. 1997. "Osservazioni sul contenuto e sul testo del Fragmentum Atestinum." *Athenaeum* 1: 119–138.

Laffi, U. 1966. *Adtributio e Contributio: Problemi del sistema politicoamministrativo dello stato romano*. Pisa: Scuola Normale Superiore di Pisa.

Lanzani, V. 1984. "Ticinum: le origini della citta Cristiana." In *Storia di Pavia*, 1:349–368. Milan: Banca del Monte di Lombardia.

Latte, Kurt. 1940. "Livy's Patavinitas." *Classical Philology* 35: 56–60.

Laurence, R., A. S. Esmonde Cleary, and G. Sears, eds. 2011. *The City in the Roman West, c. 250 BC–c. AD 250*. Cambridge: Cambridge University Press.

Laurence, R. 1999. *The Roads of Roman Italy: Mobility and Cultural Change*. London: Routledge.

Legrottaglie, G. 2005. "L'autorappresentazione del cittadino aquileiese fra tarda repubblica e prima età imperiale." *Antichità Altoadriatiche* 61: 125–150.

Lejeune, M. 1988. *Recueil des inscriptions gauloises (R.I.G.)*. Vol. 2, fasc. 1, *Textes gallo-étrusques, textes gallo-latins sur pierre*. Paris: Éditions du Centre National de la Recherche Scientifique.

Lejeune, M. 1974. *Manuel de la langue vénète*. Heidelberg: C. Winter.

Lejeune, M. 1971. *Lepontica*. Paris: Société d'Édition "Les Belles Lettres."

Lendon, J. E. 2006. "The Legitimacy of the Roman Emperor: Against Weberian Legitimacy and Imperial "strategies of legitimation." In *Herrschaftsstrukturen und Herrschaftspraxis: Konzepte, Prinzipien und Startegien der Administration im römischen Kaiserreich: Akten der Tagung an der Universität Zürich, 18.-20.10.2004*, edited by A. Kolb, 53–63. Berlin: De Gruyter.

Lendon, J. E. 1997. *Empire of Honour: The Art of Government in the Roman World*. Oxford: Clarendon Press.

Leonardi, G., ed. 2004. *La tomba bisoma di uomo e di cavallo nella necropoli del Piovego-Padova*. Venice: Marsiglio.

Letta, C. 1976. "La dinastia del Cozii e la romanizazzione delle Alpi occidentali." *Athenaeum* 54: 37–76.

Lettich, G. 2003. *Itinerari epigrafici aquileiesi: Guida alle epigrafi esposte nel Museo Archeologico Nazionale di Aquileia*. Trieste: Editreg.

Lettich, G. 1982. "Concordia e Aquileia: Note sullurganizzazione difensiva del confine orientale d'Italia nel IV secolo." *Antichità Altoadriatiche* 22: 67–87.

Levene, D. S. 2010. "Roman Historiography in the Late Republic." In *A Companion to Greek and Roman Historiography*, edited by J. Marincola, 275–289. Malden: Blackwell.

Levick, B.1999. *Vespasian*. London: Routledge.

Liebeschuetz, J. H. W. G. 2005. *Ambrose of Milan: Political Letters and Speeches*. Liverpool: Liverpool University Press.

Lipkin, S. 2012. *Textile Making in Central Tyrrhenian Italy from the Final Bronze Age to the Republican Period*. Oxford: Archaeopress.

Liu, J. 2013. "Trade, Traders, and Guilds(?) in Textiles: The Case of Southern Gaul and Northern Italy (1st–3rd centuries AD)." In *Making Textiles in Pre-Roman and Roman Times: People, Places, Identities*, edited by M. Gleba and J. Pásztókai-Szeőke, 126–141. Oxford: Oxbow Books.

Liu, J. 2009. *Collegia centonariorum: The Guilds of Textile Dealers in the Roman West*. Leiden: Brill.

Livy. *The Early History of Rome: Books I-V of The History of Rome from Its Foundation*. Translated by A. de Selincourt. Harmondsworth: Penguin, 1960.

Lizzi Testa, R. 1989. "Vescovi e strutture ecclesiastiche nella città tardoantica." In *L'Italia Annonaria nel IV–Vsecolo d.C.* Como: Edizioni New Press.

Lo Cascio, E. 2005. "The Emperor and His Adminstration." In *Cambridge Ancient History*. Vol. 12, edited by A. Bowman, P. Garnsey, and A. Cameron, 131–168. Cambridge: Cambridge University Press.

Lo Cascio, E. 2000. *Il princeps e il suo impero*. Bari: Edipuglia.

Lo Cascio, E. 1978. "Gli alimenta, l'agricoltura italica e l'approvigionamento di Roma." *Rendiconti della Accademia Nazionale dei Lincei* 33: 311–351.

Locatelli, D., L. Malnati, and D. Maras, eds. 2013. *Le origini della città alla luce delle nuove scoperte archeologiche*. Rome: Newton Compton.

Lomas, K. 2011. "Communicating Identities in Funerary Iconography: The Inscribed Stelae of Northern Italy." In Gleba and Horsnæs, *Communicating Identity in Iron Age Communities*, 7–25.

Lomas, K. 2009. "Gender Identities in the Veneto in the First Millennium BC." In *Gender Identities in Italy in the First Millennium BC*, edited by E. Herring and K. Lomas, 13–26. Oxford: Archaeopress.

Lomas, K. 2008. "Script Obsolescence in Ancient Italy: From Pre-Roman to Roman Writing." In *The Disappearance of Writing Systems: Perspectives on Literacy and Communication*, edited by J. Baines, J.Bennet, and S. D. Huston, 109–138. London: Equinox.

Lomas, K. 2007. "The Ancient Veneti: Community and State in Northern Italy." In *Ancient Italy: Regions without Boundaries*, edited by G. J. Bradley, E. Isayev, and C. Riva, 21–41. Exeter: University of Exeter Press.

Lomas, K. 2003. "Public Building, Urban Renewal and Euergetism in Early Imperial Italy." In Lomas and Cornell, *Bread and Circuses*, 28–45.

Lomas, K., and T. Cornell, eds. 2003. *"Bread and Circuses": Euergetism and Municipal Patronage in Roman Italy*. London: Routledge.

Lomas, K., and T. Cornell, 2003. "Introduction: Patronage and Benefaction in Ancient Italy." In Lomas and Cornell, *Bread and Circuses*, 1–11.

Lønstrup Dal Santo, G. 2015. "Rites of Passage: On Ceremonial Movements and Vicarious Memories." In *The Moving City: Processions, Passages, and Promenades in Ancient Rome*, edited by I. Ostenberg, S. Malmberg, and J. Bjørnebye, 145–154. London: Bloomsbury.

Lott, J. B. 2004. *The Neighborhoods of Augustan Rome*. Cambridge: Cambridge University Press.

Luraschi, G. 2013. "Storia di Como romana: vicende, istituzioni, società." in Rumi, *Storia di Como*, 7–57.

Luraschi, G. 1984. "Aspetti di vita pubblica nella Como dei Plinii." In *Plinio, i suoi luoghi e il suo tempo*, 71–105. Como: Società archeologica comense.

MacKinnon, M. 2001. "High on the hog: Linking zooarchaeological, literary, and artistic data for pig breeds in Roman Italy." *American Journal of Archaeology* 105: 649–673.

Maggi, S. 2013. "L'urbanistica di Como Romana." In Rumi, *Storia di Como*, 131–147.

Maggi, S. 2006. "Modelli e tipologie forensi in Cisalpina: alcune puntualizzazioni." In Brecciaroli Taborelli, *Forme etempi dell'urbanizzazione nella Cisalpina*, 283–286.

Maggi, S. 1999. *Le sistemazioni forensi nelle città della Cisalpina romana dalla tarda repubblica al principato augusteo (e oltre)*. Brussells: Latomus.

Maggiani, A. 2004. "The Etruscans in Liguria." In Camporeale, *The Etruscans outside Etruria*, 158–167.

Magnani, S. 2001. "La Ravenna preromana: Fonti e documenti." In *Ravenna Romana*, edited by M. Mauro, 25–45. Ravenna: Adriapress.

Magny, M. 2004. "The Contributions of Paleoclimatology to the Lake-dwelling." In Menotti, *Living on the Lake in Prehistoric Europe*, 132–143.

Mainardis, F. 2008. *Iulium Carnicum: Storia ed Epigrafia*. Trieste: Editreg.

Malkin, I. 2011. *A Small Greek World: Networks in the Ancient Mediterranean*. New York: Oxford University Press.

Malnati, L. 2013. "Gallica Parma." In Locatelli, Malnati, and Maras, *Storia della prima Parma*, 59–61.

Malnati, L. 2004. "Galli, Liguri Veleiati e Friniati nell'Emilia occidentale." In De Marinis and Spadea, *I Liguri*, 361–365.

Malnati, L. 2003a. "Le fonti greche e latine sull'antico populo dei Veneti." In *I Veneti dai bei cavalla*, edited by L. Malnati and M. Gama, 11–22. Treviso: Canova.

Malnati, L. 2003b. "Verona da capaluogo dei Cenomani a città romana." In *I Veneti dai bei cavalla*, edited by L. Malnati and M. Gama, 98–99. Treviso: Canova.

Malnati, L. 1996. "Il fenomeno urbano nell'Italia settentrionale in Età preromana." In Bietii Sestieri and Kruta, *The Iron Age in Europe*, 181–190.

Malnati, L., and V. Manzelli, eds. 2015. *Roma e le genti del Po: Un incontro di culture, III–I secolo a.C.* Florence: Giunti.

Malnati, L., and M. Catarsi. 2013. "Parma in età repubblicana." In Locatelli, Malnati, and Maras, *Storia della prima Parma*, 62–64.

Malnati, L., M. Catarsi, and C. Pedrelli. 2013. "Il santuario al guado del fiume: Prime risultanze dello scavo archeologico in Piazza Ghiaia." In Locatelli, Malnati, and Maras, *Storia della prima Parma*, 71–72.

Malnati, L., and V. Manfredi. 1991. *Gli Etruschi in Val Padana*. Milan: Mondadori.

Mancassola, M., and F. Saggioro. 2001. "Insediamento rurale e campagne tra antichità e alto-medioevo. Territori tra Verona, Brescia, e Mantova." *Antiquite tardive* 9: 307–330.

Mandolesi, A. 2009. *Etruschi in Piemonte: L'Etruria e l'area subalpina occidentale attraverso i contatti del primo Millennio a. C. e i documenti archeologici e artistici conservati in Piemonte*. Turin: Fondazione per l'Arte della Compagnia di San Paolo.

Mansuelli, G. A. 1941. *Ariminum (Rimini)*. Rimini: Istituto di Studi Romani.

Manzelli, V. 2015. "Ravenna nel III a.C." In Malnati and Manzelli, *Roma e le genti del Po*, 104–105.

Manzelli, V. 2001. "La *forma urbis* di Ravenna in età romana." In *Ravenna Romana*, edited by M. Mauro, 45–61. Ravenna: Adriapress.

Maraldi, L.. 2006. *Il popolamento di età romana nel territorio della centuriazione cesenate: Rinvenimenti archeologici fra via del Confine, via Emilia, via Dismano e fiume Rubicone*. Cesena: Società di studi romagnoli.

Marchesini, M. 2013. "Paesaggio e ambiente durante la colonizazzione romana." In Locatelli, Malnati, and Maras, *Storia della prima Parma*, 66–67.

Marini Calvani, M., ed. 2000. *Aemilia: La cultura romana in Emilia Romagna dal III secolo a.C. all'età constantiniana*. Venice: Marsilio.

Marzano, A. 2007. *Roman Villas in Central Italy: A Social and Economic History*. Leiden: Brill.

Marzatico, F. 2014. "Il mondo Retico fra Etruschi e Celti." In Barral et al., *Les Celtes*, 189–210.

Marzatico, F. 2004. "150 Years of Lake-dwelling Research in Northern Italy." In Menotti, *Living on the Lake in Prehistoric Europe*, 83–97.

Marzatico, F. 1997. "L'architettura del legno negli abitati palafitticoli del Trentino." In Bernarbò Brea, Cardarelli, and Cremaschi, *LeTerramare*, 263–271.

Maselli Scotti, F., L. Mandruzzato, and C. Tiussi. 2006. "Primo impianto coloniario di Aquileia: L'area tra foro e macellum." In Brecciaroli Taborelli, *Forme e tempi dell'urbanizzazione nella Cisalpina*, 35–40.

Masselli Scotti, F., and P. Ventura. 2001. "Strutture portuali di *Tergeste* Romana." In *Strutture Portuali e Rotte Marittime nell'Adriatico di Età Romana*, edited by C. Zaccaria, 201–209. Trieste: Centro di antichita altoadriatiche.

Maselli Scotti, F. 2002a. "Riflessioni sull'urbanistica di Aquileia." In Buora, *Roma sul Danubio*, 57–68.

Maselli Scotti, F. 2002b. "I culti oritentali ad Aquileia." In Buora, *Roma sul Danubio*, 139–144.

Mattingly, D. J. 2011. *Imperialism, Power, and Identity: Experiencing the Roman Empire*. Princeton: Princeton University Press.

McLynn, N. 1994. *Ambrose of Milan: Church and Court in a Christian Capital*. Berkeley: University of California Press.

Mench, F. 1968. *The Cohortes Urbanae of Imperial Rome: An Epigraphic Study*. PhD diss., Yale University.

Menotti, F., ed. 2004. *Living on the Lake in Prehistoric Europe: 150 years of Lake-dwelling Research*. London: Routledge.

Menotti, F. 2004. "Introduction: The Lake-dwelling Phenomenon and Wetland Archaeology." In Menotti, *Living on the Lake in Prehistoric Europe*, 1–16.

Mercando, L. 2003. "Variazioni urbane in Piemonte." In *Abitare in Citta: La Cisalpina tra Impero e Medioevo*, edited by J. Ortalli and M. Heinzelman, 9–25. Wiesbaden: Ludwig Reichert Verlag.

Metlich, M. 2004. *The Coinage of Ostrogothic Italy*. London: Spink.

Mian, G., and L. Villa. 2013. "La residenza imperial tardoantica e il circo." In *Costantino e Teodoro: Aquileia nel IV secolo*, edited by C. Tiussi, L. Villa, and M. Novello, 75–81. Milan: Electa.

Michels, A. 1967. Calendar of the Roman Republic. Princeton: Princeton University Press.

Michelucci, M. 1985. "Armi e attrezzi agricoli: I ripostagli di Talamone." In *Laromanizzazione dell'Etruria: Il territorio di Vulci*, edited by A. Carandini, 44–47. Milan: Electa.

Mihovilić, K. 2012. "Bronzo finale in Istria." In *Le origini degli Etruschi: Storia, archeologia, antropologia*, edited by V. Bellelli, 411–453. Rome: L'Erma di Bretschneider.

Milano, H., and V. Pistarino. 2008. "Le iscrizioni sepolcrali con una forumula *LDDD* in Italia." In Berrendonner, Cébeillac-Gervasoni, and Lamoine, *Le quotidien municipal dans l'occident Romain*, 687–713.

Millar, F. 1995. "The last century of the Republic: Whose history?" *Journal of Roman Studies*, 236–243.

Millar, F. 1977. *The Emperor in the Roman World, 31 BC–AD 337*. Ithaca: Cornell University Press.

Millo, F. 2013. "Quattro Cavalli dalle teste superbe gettò sulla pira." In Gamba, *Venetkens*, 364–366.

Mirabella Roberti, M. 1974. "L'urbanistica romana di Como e alcune recenti scoperte." In *Atti del Convegno celebrativo del Centenario della Rivista archeologica Comense*, 31–35. Como: Noseda.

Mirabella Roberti, M. 1963. "Archeologia ed arte di Brescia romana." In *Storia di Brescia*. Vol. 1, *Dalle origini alla caduta della signoria viscontea*, edited by G. Treccani degli Alfieri, 233–320. Brescia: Banco San Paolo.

Mlinar, M., ed. 2011. *Keltskih konj topot: Najdišče Bizjakova hiša v Kobaridu. Katalog Razstave* [Hear the Horses of Celts: The Bizjakova hiša Site in Kobarid. Exhibition Catalogue.] Tolmin: Tolminski Muzej.

Mócsy, A. 1974. *Pannonia and Upper Moesia: A History of the Middle Danube Provinces of the Roman Empire*. London: Routledge.

Molà, L., R. C. Mueller, and C. Zanier, eds. 2000. *La seta in Italia dal Medioevo al Seicento*. Venice: Marsilio.

Mollo. S. 1997. *L'augustalità a Brescia*. Rome: Accademia nazionale dei Lincei.

Monnas, L. 2008. *Merchants, Princes, and Painters: Silk Fabrics in Italian and Northern Paintings, 1300–1550*. New Haven, CT: Yale University Press.

Montagnari Kokelj, E. 1989. "Periodo protostorico." In *Il Carso Goriziano tra protostoria e Storia: Da Castellazzo a San Polo*, edited by E. Montagnari Kokelj, 22–25. Gorizia: Museo provinciale di Borgo Castello.

Moore, T. 2011. "Detribalizing the later prehistoric past: Concepts of tribes in Iron Age and Roman studies." *Journal of Social Archaeology* 11: 334–359.

Moorhead, J. 1992. *Theoderic in Italy*. Oxford: Clarendon Press.

Morandi, A. 2004. Vol. 2 of Agostinetti and Morandi 2004, *Celti d'Italia*. Rome: Spazio Tre.

Moreschini, C. 2013a. "Plinio il Vecchio." In Rumi, *Storia di Como*, 247–257.

Moreschini, C. 2013b. "Plinio il Giovane." In Rumi, *Storia di Como*, 259–268.

Morigi Govi, C., and G. Sassatelli. 1996. "Felsina Etrusca." In *Atlante storico delle citta italiane, Emilia-Romagna*. Vol. 2, *Bologna*, edited by F. Bocchi, 11–27. Bologna: Grafis.

Morselli, C., ed. 2007. *Trieste antica: Lo scavo di Crosada*. Trieste: Editreg.

Morselli, C. 2007. "La formazione del paesaggio costruito." In Moselli, *Trieste antica*, 137–145.

Moscati, S., O.-H. Frey, V. Kruta, B. Raftery, M. Szabó, E. Arslan, and D. Vitali, eds. 2005. *The Celts*. New York: Rizzoli.

Mouritsen, H. 2005. "Freedmen and decurions: Epitaphs and social history in Imperial Italy." *Journal of Roman Studies* 95: 38–63.

Mouritsen, H. 1998. *Italian Unification*. London: Institute of Classical Studies, University of London.

Mouritsen, H. 1997. "Mobility and Social Change in Italian Towns during the Principate." In *Roman Urbanism: Beyond the Consumer City*, edited by H. Parkins, 59–82. London: Routledge.

Negroni Catacchio, N., A. Massari, and B. Raposso. 2006. "L'ambra come indicatore di scambi nell'Italia pre- e protostorica." In *Atti della XXXIX Riunione Scientifica IIPP materie prime e scambi nella preistoria italiana: Nel cinquantenario della fondazione dell'Istituto italiano di preistoria e protostoria, Firenze 25–27 novembre 2004*, 1439–1475. Florence: Istituto italiano di preistoria e protostoria.

Nicolet, C. 1991. *Space, Geography, and Politics in the Roman Empire*. Ann Arbor: University of Michigan Press.

Nicolet, C. 1988. *The World of the Citizen in Republican Rome*. Berkeley: University of California Press.

Nicolis, N. 2013. "Northern Italy." In *The Oxford Handbook of the European Bronze Age*, edited by H. Fokkens and A. Harding, 692–705. Oxford: Oxford University Press.

Nicols, J. 2013. *Civic Patronage in the Roman Empire*. Leiden: Brill.

Noreña, C. 2011a. *Imperial Ideals in the Roman West: Representation, Circulation, Power*. Cambridge: Cambridge University Press.

Noreña, C. 2011b. "Self-Fashioning in the Panegyricus." In *Pliny's Praise: The Panegyricus in the Roman World*, edited by P. Roche, 29–44. Cambridge: Cambridge University Press.

Noreña, C. 2009. "The Ethics of Autocracy in the Roman World." In *A Companion to Greek and Roman Political Thought*, edited by in R. Balot, 266–279. Malden: Wiley-Blackwell.

Noreña, C. 2007. "The social economy of Pliny's correspondence with Trajan." *American Journal of Philology* 128.2: 239–277.

Ortalli, J., ed. 2003. *Abitare in città: La Cisalpina tra impero e medioevo*. Wiesbaden: Ludwig Reichert Verlag.

Ortalli, J. 2003. "L'insediatmento residenziale urbano nella Cispadana." In Ortalli, *Abitare in città*, 92–119.

Ortalli, J. 2000. "Bologna." In Marini Calvani, *Aemilia, la cultura romana in Emilia Romagna dal 3. secolo a.C. all'età costantiniana*, 439–449. Venice: Marsilio.

Ortalli, J. 1992. "Edilizia residenziale e crisi urbana nella tarda antichità: fonti archeologiche per la Cispadana." *Corsi di cultura sull'arte ravennate e bizantina* 39: 584–599.

Osgood, J. 2011. *Claudius Caesar: Image and Power in the Early Roman Empire*. Cambridge: Cambridge University Press.

Panciera, S. 1987. "I patroni di Aquileia fra la città e Roma." *Antichità Altoadriatiche* 30: 77–95.

Panciera, S. 1981. "Aquileiesi in Occidente ed occidentali in Aquileia." *Antichità Altoadriatiche* 19: 105–138.

Panciera, S. 1977. "Aquileia, Ravenna e la flotta militare." *Antichità Altoadriatiche* 13: 107–134.

Panciera, S. 1976. "Strade e commerci tra Aquileia e le regioni Alpine." *Antichità Altoadriatiche* 9: 153–172.

Panciera, S. 1972. "Porti e commerci nell'Alto Adriatico." *Antichità Altoadriatiche* 2: 79–112.

Pare, C. 2000. "Bronze and the Bronze Age." In Pare, *Metals Make the World Go Round*, 1–38.

Pare, C., ed. 2000. *Metals Make the World Go Round: The Supply and Circulation of Metals in Bronze Age Europe. Proceedings of a Conference Held at the University of Birmingham in June 1997*. Oxford: Oxbow Books.

Parker, G. 2008. *The Making of Roman India*. Cambridge: Cambridge University Press.

Passerini, A. 1939. *Le coorti pretorie*. Rome: Centro editoriale internazionale.

Passi Pitcher, L., ed. 1996. *Bedriacum: Ricerche archeologiche a Calvatone*. Milan: Edizioni ET.

Patterson, J. R. 2006a. "The Relationship of the Italian Ruling Classes with Rome: Friendship, Family Relations, and Their Consequences." In *Herrschaftsstrukturen und Herrschaftspraxis: Konzepte, Prinzipien und Startegien der Administration im römischen Kaiserreich. Akten der Tagung an der Universität Zürich, 18–20.10.2004*, edited by A. Kolb, 139–154. Berlin: De Gruyter.

Patterson, J. R. 2006b. *Landscapes and Cities: Rural Settlement and Civic Transformation in Early Imperial Italy*. Oxford: Oxford University Press.

Patterson, J. R. 2003. "The Emperor and the Cities of Italy." In Lomas and Cornell, *Bread and Circuses*, 89–104.

Patterson, J. R. 1994. "The Collegia and the Transformation of the Towns in Italy in the Second Century AD." In *L'Italie d'Auguste à Dioclétien: Actes du colloque international organisé par l' École française de Rome (Rome, 1992)*, 227–238. Rome: École française de Rome.

Patterson, J. R. 1990. "Food, poverty and patronage: The significance of the epigraphy of the Roman alimentary schemes in early imperial Italy." *Papers of the British School at Rome* 58: 197–228.

Patterson, J. R. 1987. "Crisis: What crisis? Rural change and urban development in Imperial Apennine Italy." *Papers of the British School at Rome* 55: 115–146.

Pauli, L. 1999. "The Alps at the Time of the First Celtic Migrations." In Moscati et al., *The Celts*, 225–229.

Pautasso, A. 1994. *Monetazione celtica dell'Arco Alpino*. Aosta: Keltia.

Pautasso, A. 1966. *Le monete preromane dell'Italia settentrionale*. Varese: Centro di Studi Preistorici ed Archeologici.

Pearce, M. 2007. *Bright Blades and Red Metal: Essays on North Italian Prehistoric Metalwork*. London: Accordia Research Institute.

Pearce, M. 2000. "Metals Make the World Go Round: The Copper Supply for Frattesina." In Pare, *Metals Make the World Go Round*, 108–115.

Pearce, M.1998. "New research on the *terramare* of northern Italy." *Antiquity* 72: 743–746.

Pearce, M. 1994. *Il territorio di Milano e Pavia tra Mesolitico e Prima età del Ferro: Dalla carta archeologica alla ricostruzione del paesaggio*. Florence: Nuova Italia editrice.

Pearce, M., and A. De Guio. 1999. "Between the Mountains and the Plain: An Integrated Metals Production and Circulation System in Later Bronze Age North-eastern Italy." In *Prehistoric Alpine Environment, Society, and Economy. Papers of the International Colloquium Paese '97 in Zurich*, edited by P. Della Casa, 289–293. Bonn: Rudolf Habelt.

Pellegrini, G. B., and A. Prosdocimi. 1967. *La lingua venetica*. Padua: Istituto di glottologia dell'Università di Padova.

Péré-Noguès, S. 2014. "L'arivée des Celtes en Italie du Nord à travers les lectures historiographiques grecques et romaines." In Barral et al., *Les Celtes*, 145–150.

Peretto, R. 2007. "Modelli insediativi protostorici in ambito perifluviale nell'area veneta del Delta del Po." In Berti, *Genti nel delta di Spina a Comacchio*, 33–47.

Peretto, R. 2010. "Villaggi e vie d'acqua." In Colonna and Salzani, *La fragilità dell'urna*, 13–19.

Peroni, R. 1997. "Le terramare nel quadro dell'età del bronzo europea." In Bernarbò Brea, Cardarelli, and Cremaschi, *Le Terramare*, 30–36.

Perry, J. S. 2006, *The Roman Collegia: The Modern Evolution of an Ancient Concept*. Leiden: Brill.

Peyre, C. 1979. *La Cisalpine Gauloise du III au I siècle avant J.-C.* Paris: Presses de l'École normale supérieure.

Piccoli, F. 2004. *Il vino nel Nord Italia in epoca romana: storia della coltivazione della vite, della produzione e del commercio del vino in Cisalpina*. Verona: Della Scala.

Piccottini, G. 1976. "L'influenza di Aquileia sull'arte sepolcrale del Norico Mediterraneo." *Antichità altoadriatiche* 9: 141–151.

Pina Polo, F. 2006. "Deportation, Kolonisation, Migration: Bevölkerungsverschiebungen im republikanischen Italien und Formen der Identitätsbildung." In *Herrschaftsstrukturen und Herrschaftspraxis: Konzepte, Prinzipien und Startegien der Administration im römischen Kaiserreich: Akten der Tagung an der Universität Zürich, 18.-20.10.2004*, edited by A. Kolb, 171–206. Berlin: De Gruyter.

Pizzirani, C. 2009. "Il sepolcreto etrusco della Galassina di Castelvetro (MO)." In *Archeologia Preromana in Emilia Occidentale: La ricerca oggi tra monti e pianura*, edited by C. Chiaramonte Treré, 65–179. Milan: Cisalpino.

Pobjoy, M. 2000. "The first *Italia*." In Lomas and Herring, *The Emergence of State Identities*, 187–211.

Polybius. *The Rise of the Roman Empire*. Translated by I. Scott-Kilvert. Harmondsworth: Penguin, 1979.

Potter, T. W. 1987. *Roman Italy*. Berkeley: University of California Press.

Prag, J. 2008. "Sicilia and Britiannia: Epigraphic Evidence for Civic Administration." In Berrendonner, Cébeillac-Gervasoni, and Lamoine, *Le quotidien municipal dans l'occident Romain*, 67–81.

Prenc, F. 2002. *Le pianificazioni agrarie di età romana nella pianura aquileiese*. Trieste: Editreg.

Price, S. R. F. 1985. *Rituals and Power: The Roman Imperial Cult in Asia Minor*. Cambridge: Cambridge University Press.

Primas, M.1997. "Rapporti tra le arée a nord e a sud delle Alpi durante l'età del bronzo media e Recente." In Bernarbò Brea, Cardarelli, and Cremaschi, *Le Terramare*, 37–44.

Prosdocimi, A. 2003. "Il sacrificio del cavallo in alcune fonti di tradizione indeuropea." In *Produzioni, merci e commerci in Altino preromana e romana*, edited by G. Cresci Marrone and M. Tirelli, 61–88 Rome: Quasar.

Purcell, N. 2005. "Romans in the Roman World." In The *Cambridge Companion to the Age of Augustus*, edited by K. Galinsky, 85–105. Cambridge: Cambridge University Press.

Purcell, N. 1996. "Rome and the Management of Water: Environment, Culture and Power."

In *Human Landscapes in Classical Antiquity*, edited by G. Shipley and J. B. Salmon, 180–212. London: Routledge.
Purcell, N. 1990. "The Creation of Provincial Landscape: The Roman Impact on Cisalpine Gaul." In Blagg and Millett, *The Early Roman Empire in the West*, 7–29. Oxford: Oxbow Books.
Purcell, N. 1985. "Wine and wealth in ancient Italy." *Journal of Roman Studies* 75: 1–19.
Ramsl, P. 2014. "The Relationship between Austrian and North-Italian Sites in the Iron Age." In Barral et al., *Les Celtes*, 179–188.
Rask, K. A. 2014. "Etruscan animal bones and their implications for sacrificial studies." *History of Religions* 53: 269–312.
Rebecchi, F. 1993. "La città dell'Italia annonaria." In *Storia di Roma*. Vol. 3, pt. 2, *L'età tardoantica*, 199–227. Turin: G. Einaudi.
Rebecchi, F. 1980. "Sull'origine dell'insediamento in Grado e sul suo porto tardoantico." *Antichità Altoadriatiche* 17: 41–56.
Rees, R. 2004. *Diocletian and the Tetrarchy*. Edinburgh: Edinburgh University Press.
Reidel, A. 1984. "The Paleovenetian horse of Le Brustolade (Altino)." *Studi Etruschi* 50: 227–256.
Reynolds, J. 1981. "Diocletian's edict on maximum prices: The chapter on wool." *Zeitschrift für Papyrologie und Epigraphie* 42: 283–284.
Richardson, J. S. 1983. "The Tabula Contrebiensis: Roman Law in Spain in the Early First Century B.C." *Journal of Roman Studies* 73, 1983: 33–41.
Richmond, I. A., and W. G. Holford. 1935. "Roman Verona: The archaeology of its town-plan." *Papers of the British School at Rome* 13: 69–76
Roffia, E. 1994. "Sirmione in età romana." In *Catullo e Sirmione: Società e cultura della Cisalpina alle soglie dell'impero*, edited by N. Criniti, 111–131. Brescia: Grafo.
Roncaglia, C. 2015. "'Pliny Country' Revisited: Connectivity and Regionalism in Roman Italy." In *Ancient Documents and Their Contexts*, edited by J. Bodel and N. Nimotrova, 199–211. Leiden: Brill.
Roncaglia, C. 2013. "Client prefects? Rome and the Cottians in the western Alps." *Phoenix* 67: 353–372.
Rossi, C. 2014. *Le necropoli urbane di Padova romana*. Padua: Padova University Press.
Rossi, F., ed. 2002. *Nuove ricerche sul Capitolium di Brescia: Scavi, studi, e restauri*. Milan: Edizioni ET.
Rossignani, M. P. 2006. "Processi di transformazione negli insediamenti indigeni della Cisalpina tra II e I secolo a.C." In Brecciaroli Taborelli, *Forme e tempi dell'urbanizzazione nella Cisalpina*, 29–34.
Rossini, F. 1975 "Verona Scaligera." *Verona e il suo territorio* 3:3 343. Verona: Istituto per gli studi storici Veronesi.
Rottoli, M., and M. Marchesini. 2015. "L'impatto sul territorio: La trasformazione del Paesaggio." In Malnati and Manzelli, *Roma e le genti del Po*, 286–287.
Rowe, G. 2002. *Princes and Political Cultures*. Ann Arbor: University of Michigan Press.
Rubinich, M. 2013. "Le *Thermae Felices Constantinianiae*." In Tiussi, Villa, and Novello, *Costantino e Teodoro*, 85–90.
Rumi, G., ed. 2013. *Storia di Como. Dalla romanizzazione alla caduta dell'Impero (196 a.C.–476 d.C.)*. Como: Storia di Como srl.

Rüpke, J. 1995. *Kalender und Öffentlichkeit: Die Geschichte der Repräsentation und religiösen Qualifikation von Zeit in Rom*. Berlin: de Gruyter.

Ruta Serafini, A. 2001. "Il celtismo in area veneta: nuovi dati." In Vitri and Oriolo, *I Celti in Carnia e nell'arco alpino centro orientale*, 197–210.

Ruta Serafini, A., C. Balista, L. De Vanna, and G. Gambacurta. 1992. "La scavo della necropoli romana e preromana tra via Tiepolo e via S.Massimo: nota prliminare." *Quaderni di Archeologia del Veneto* 8: 15–25.

Rutter, N. K. 2001. *Historia Numorum: Italy*. London: British Museum Press.

Sacchi, F. 2013. "Como romana: Gli aspestti monumentali della città e del suburbia." In Rumi, *Storia di Como*, 149–182.

Sacchi, F. 2012. *Mediolanum e i suoi monumenti dalla fine del II secolo a. C. all'età severiana*. Milan: Società editrice Vita e Pensiero.

Sacchi, F. 2006. "Elementi architettonici di un ignoto edificio dell'età di Plinio il Giovane?." In *Extra Moenia*, Vol. 1, *Ricerche Archeologiche nell'area suburbana occidentale di Como Romana*, edited by D. Caporusso, 245–252. Como: New Press.

Sailor, D. 2008. *Writing and Empire in Tacitus*. Cambridge: Cambridge University Press.

Salmon, E. T. 1982. *The Making of Roman Italy*. Ithaca: Cornell University Press.

Sandrone, Silvia. 2004. "La produzione artigianale d'età romana nella Cispadana occidentale." In *Artigianato e produzione nella Cisalpina*, edited by S. Santoro and A. Besozzi, 115–146. Florence: All'Insegna del Giglio.

Santoro, S., and A. Besozzi, eds. 2004. *Artigianato e produzione nella Cisalpina*. Florence: All'Insegna del Giglio.

Sartori, A. 2013. "Le pietre e la storia." In Rumi, *Storia di Como*, 219–244.

Sartori, A. 1994a. *Guida alla sezione epigrafica delle raccolte archeologiche di Milano*. Milan: Comune di Milano.

Sartori, A. 1994b. *Le iscrizioni romane*. Como: Comune di Como.

Sartori, A. 1965. *Pollentia ed Augusta Bagiennorum: Studi sulla romanizzazione in Piemonte*. Turin: Deputazione Subalpina di Storia Patria.

Sartori A., L. Passi Pitcher, and E. Natta. 1996. "I materiali dei vecchi rinvenimenti." In Pitcher, *Bedriacum*, 119–128. Milan: Edizioni ET.

Sartori, F. 1964. "Colonia Augusta Verona Nova Gallieniana," *Athenaeum* 42: 39–44.

Sartori, F. 1960. "Verona Romana: Storia politica, economica, amministrativa." In *Verona e il suo Territorio*, Vol. 3, 159–259. Verona: Istituto per gli studi storici Veronesi.

Sartori, M. 1989. "Osservazioni sul ruolo del curator rei publicae." *Athenaeum* 67: 5–20.

Šašel, J., and P. Petru. 1971. *Claustra Alpium Iuliarum*. Ljubljana: Narodni muzej.

Šašel, J. 1972. "Zur Rekrutierung der Prätorianer." *Historia* 21.3: 474–480.

Šašel, J. 1966. "Barbii." *Eirene* 5: 117–137.

Šašel Kos, M. 2001. "The Roman inscriptions of Celeia commemorating emperors." In *Varia Epigraphica: Atti del Colloquio Internazionale di Epigrafia Bertinoro, 8–10 giugno 2000*, edited by G. A. Bertinelli and A. Donati, 383–402. Faenza: Fratelli Lega.

Šašel Kos, M. S. 1998. "Caesarian Inscriptions in the Emona Basin?" In *Epigrafia romana in area Adriatica. Actes de la IXe Rencontre franco-italienne sur l'epigraphie du monde romain*, edited by E. Marín, 101–112. Macerata: Università degli Studi di Macerata.

Sassatelli, G. 2013. "Etruschi, Veneti e Celti: Relazioni culturali e mobilità individuale." In

Mobilità Geografica e Mercenariato nell'Italia Preromana: Atti del XX convegno internazionale di Studi sulla Storia e l'archeologia dell'etruria, 397–427. Rome: Quasar.

Sassatelli, G. 2008. "Gli Etruschi nella Valle del Po: Riflessioni, problemi e prospettive di Ricerca." *Annali Faina* 15: 71–114.

Sassatelli, G. 2005. "L'arrivo dei Galli." In *Storia di Bologna: Bologna nell'antichità*, edited by G. Sassatelli and A. Donati, 339–385. Bologna: Bologna University Press.

Sassatelli, G. 2004. "The Etruscans on the Po Plain." In Camporeale, *The Etruscans outside Etruria*, 168–191.

Sassatelli, G. 1994a. *Iscrizioni e graffiti della città etrusca di Marzabotto*. Bologna: Bologna University Press.

Sassatelli, G. 1994b. "Problemi del populamento: Etruria Padana con particolare riguardo a Bologna." In *La presenza etrusca nella Campania meridionale: Atti delle giornate di studio (Salerno-Pontecagnano 1990)*, 497–508. Florence: Olschki.

Sassatelli, G. 1993. "Spina nelle immagini etrusche." In *Spina, storia di una città tra Greci ed Eruschi*, edited by F. Berti and P. G. Guzzo, 115–127. Ferrara: Ferrara arte.

Sassatelli, G. 1991. "Opere idrauliche nella città etrusca di Marzabotto." In Bergamini, *Gli Etruschi maestri di idraulica*, 179–208.

Sassatelli, G. 1990. "La situazione in Etruria padana." In *Crise et transformation des sociétés archaiques de l'Italie antique au Ve siécle av. J. C. Actes de la table ronde, Rome, 19–21 novembre 1987*, 51–100. Rome: École française de Rome.

Sassatelli, G., and E. Govi. 2013. "Etruria on the Po and the Adriatic Sea" In *The Etruscan World*, edited by J. Turfa, 281–300. London: Routledge.

Schäfer, T. 1989. *Imperii insignia: Sella curulis und fasces. Zur Repräsentation römischer Magistrate*. Mainz: Von Zabern

Sebesta, J. L. 1994. Sebesta, "Tunica Ralla, Tunica Spissa: The Colors and Textiles of Roman Costume." In *The World of Roman Costume*, edited by J. L. Sebasta and L. Bonfante, 65–76. Madison: University of Wisconsin Press.

Sena Chiesa, G. 2015. "Cultura e arte: Assenze e presenze fra integrazione e innovazione." In Malnati and Manzelli, *Roma e le genti del Po*, 30–37.

Sena Chiesa, G. 2014. "Gli asparagi di Cesare: Reiflessioni su cinquant'anni di archeologia cisalpina." In *Gli asparagi di Cesare: Studi sulla Cisalpina Romana*, 9–22. Florence: All'Insegna del Giglio.

Sena Chiesa, G. 2003. "Agglomerati insediativi minori." In Ortalli, *Abitare in città*, 205–221. Sena Chiesa, G., ed. 1998. *Tesori della Postumia: Archeologia e storia intorno a una grande strada romana alle radici dell-Europa*. Milan: Skira.

Sena Chiesa, G. 1993. "Il territorio di Comum: insediamenti, necropoli, popolamento." In *Novum Comum 2050: Atti del convegno celebrativo della fondazione di Como romana, Como 1993*, 185–220. Como: Società archeologica Comense.

Seston, W. 1978. "La lex Julia de 90 av. J.-C. et l'intégration des Italiens dans le citoyenneté Romaine." *Comptes Rendus des Academie des inscriptions et Belles-Lettres*, 529–542.

Sfameni, C. 2008. *Ville residenziali nell'Italia tardoantica*. Bari: Edipuglia.

Sheeres, M., C. Knipper, M. Hauschild, M. Schönfelder, M. Siebel, D. Vitali, C. Pare, and K. Alt 2013. "Evidence for 'Celtic migrations'? Strontium isotope analysis at the early La Tène (LT B) cemeteries of Nebringen (Germany) and Monte Bibele (Italy)." *Journal of Archaeological Science* 40.10: 3614–3625.

Sherratt, S. 2000. "Circulation of Metals and the End of the Bronze Age in the Eastern Mediterranean." In Pare, *Metals Make the World Go Round*, 82–95.

Sherwin-White, A. N. 1973. *The Roman Citizenship*. 2nd ed. Oxford: Clarendon Press.

Sherwin-White, A. N. 1966. *The Letters of Pliny: A Historical and Social Commentary*. Oxford: Oxford University Press.

Simshäuser, W. 1973. *Iuridici und Munizipalgerichtsbarkeit in Italien*. Munich: Beck.

Skegro, A. 2006. "The economy of Roman Dalmatia." In *Dalmatia, Research in the Roman Province 1970–2001: Papers in Honour of J. J. Wilkes*, edited by D. Davison, V. Gaffney, and E. Marin, 149–174. Oxford: British Archaeological Reports.

Smith, R. 2007. "The Imperial Court of the Late Roman Empire." In *The Court and Court Society in Ancient Monarchies*, edited by A. Spawforth, 82–120. Cambridge: Cambridge University Press.

Solano, S. 2015. "Brixia: l'abitato dei Cenomani." In Malnati and Manzelli, *Roma e le genti del Po*, 86–88.

Spadoni, M. 2004. *I prefetti nell'amministrazione municipale dell'Italia romana*. Bari: Edipuglia.

Stella Busana, M. 1995. *Oderzo: Forma urbia: Saggio di topografia antica*. Rome: L'Erma di Bretschneider.

Susini, G. 1976. "I profughi della Sabatina." In *L'Italia settentrionale nell'età antica: Convegno in memoria di Plinio Fraccaro nel 1150. Anniversario della fondazione dello Studio Pavese (Pavia, 8–10 settembre 1975)*, 172–176. Pavia: Tipografia del Libro.

Susini, G. 1958. "Supplemento epigrafico faventino." *Studi Romagnoli* 9: 167–198.

Syme, R. 1999. *The Provincial at Rome, and Rome and the Balkans, 80 BC–AD 14*. Exeter: University of Exeter Press.

Syme, R. 1985. "Correspondents of Pliny." *Historia* 34: 324–359.

Syme, R. 1968. "People in Pliny." *Journal of Roman Studies* 58: 135–151.

Syme, R. 1939. *The Roman Revolution*. Oxford: Clarendon Press.

Tagliaferri, A. 1978. *Relazioni dei rettori veneti in Terraferma*. Vol. 1, *Podestaria e capitanato di Brescia*. Milan: Giuffrè.

Tamassi, K. 2002. "Necropoli Ca' Cima, tomba 9." In *AKEO: I tempi della scrittura: Veneti antichi, alfabeti e documenti*, edited by A. Marinetti, 175–181. Montebelluna: Museo di Storia Naturale e Archeologia.

Tchernia, A. 2016. *The Romans and Trade*. Oxford: Oxford University Press.

Tchernia, A. 1986. *Le vin de l'Italie romaine: Essai d'histoire économique d'après les amphores*. Rome: École Française de Rome.

Thomas, E. 2007. *Monumentality and the Roman Empire: Architecture in the Antonine Age*. Oxford: Oxford University Press.

Tiussi, C., M. Verzár, and L. Villa. 2013. "Aquileia *splendida Civitas:* La città tardoantica." In *Costantino e Teodoro: Aquileia nel IV secolo*, edited by C. Tiussi, L. Villa, and M. Novello, 54–67. Milan: Electa.

Todisco, E. 1999. *I veterani in Italia in età imperiale*. Bari: Edipuglia.

Tonni, A. 2012. "The Renaissance Studs of the Gonzagas of Mantua." In *The Horse as Cultural Icon: The Real and Symbolic Horse in the Early Modern World*, edited by P. Edwards, K. A. E. Enenkel, and E. Graham, 261–277. Leiden: Brill.

Torelli, M. 2004. "I Liguri nel Sannio" In De Marinis and Spadea, *I Liguri*, 452–454.

Torelli, M. 1999. *Tota Italia: Essays in the Cultural Formation of Roman Italy*. Oxford: Clarendon Press.

Torelli, M. 1998. "La Gallia transpadana, laboratorio della romanizzazione." In Sena Chiesa, *Tesori della Postumia*, 27–36.

Torelli, M. 1991. "L'acqua degli Etrusci dalle forme ideologiche alle pratiche sociale." In Bergamini, *Gli Etruschi maestri di idraulica*, 19–28.

Tosi, G. 1994. "Gli edifici per spettacolo di Verona." *Antichità Altoadriatiche* 41: 241–257.

Tozzi, P. 1984a. "Il territorio di Ticinum romana." In *Storia di Pavia*, 1:151–182. Milan: Banca del Monte di Lombardia.

Tozzi, P. 1984b. "L'impianto urbano di Ticinum romana." In *Storia di Pavia*, 1:183–203. Milan: Banca del Monte di Lombardia.

Towle, A., J. Henderson, P. Bellintani, and G. Gambacurta. 2001. "Frattesina and Adria: Report of scientific analyses of early glass from the Veneto." *Padusa* 37: 7–68.

Tran, N. 2006. *Les membres des associations romaines: Le rang social des collegiati en Italie et en Gaules, sous le haut-empire*. Rome: École française de Rome.

Traviglia, A., and C. Morselli. 2007. "La destinazione agricola dell'area il definitivo Abbandono." In Morselli, *Trieste antica*, 151–157.

Uggeri, G. 1991. "Interventi idraulici nell'Etruria padana." In Bergamini, *Gli Etruschi maestri di idraulica*, 69–72.

Urbano, A. 2005. "Donation, dedication, and *damnatio memoriae*: The Catholic reconciliation of Ravenna and the Church of Sant'Apollinare Nuovo." *Journal of Early Christian Studies* 31: 71–110.

Vannacci Lunazzi, G. 2001. "L'insediamento di Colle Mazéit a Verzegnis." In Vitri and Oriolo, *I Celti in Carnia e Nell'arco alpino centro orientale*, 149–171.

Vavazzori, M. 1993. "Considerazioni sulle epigrafi romane del territorio lecchese." In *Carta Archeologica della Lombardia*. Vol. 4, *La Provincia di Lecco*, edited by S. Casini, 261–283. Modena: F. C. Panini.

Vedaldi Iasbez, V. 1994. *La Venetia orientale e l'Histria: Le fonti letterarie greche e latine fino alla caduta dell'Impero romano d'Occidente*. Rome: Quasar.

Vedaldi Iasbez, V. 1989. "Magistrati romani ad Aquileia in età repubblicana." *Antichità Altoadriatiche* 35: 99–103.

Verboven, K. 2011. "Professional collegia: Guilds or social clubs?." *Ancient Society* 41: 187–195.

Verzár-Bass, M. 2003. "L'assetto urbano di Aquileia." In Ortalli, *Abitare in città*, 73–83.

Verzár-Bass, M. 1996. "Arte funeraria lungo la via dell'ambra." In Buora, *Lungo la via dell'ambra*, 245–265.

Veyne, P. 1976. *Le pain et le cirque*. Paris: Éditions du Seuil. Translated and abridged by B. Pearce as *Bread and Circuses: Historical Sociology and Political Pluralism*. London: Penguin, 1990.

Vicari, F. 1994. "Economia della Cispadana Romana: la produzione tessile." *Rivista di Storia Antica* 24: 239–260.

Vitali, D. 2008. "Torquis e Boi cisalpini." In *Taurini sul confine Il Bric San Vito di Pecetto Nell'età del Ferro*, edited by F. Gambari, 13–19. Turin: Celid.

Vitali, D. 2006. "Cavalli in tombe—tombe di cavalli in necropoli lateniane d'Italia." In *Animali tra uomini e dei: Archeozoologia del mondo preromano: Atti del convegno inter-*

nazionale, 8–9 novembre 2002, edited by A. Curci, D. Vitali, and A. Penzo, 127–137. Bologna: Ante Quem.

Vitali, D. 2004. "I Celti in Italia." In *Guerrieri, Principi ed Eroi fra il Danubio e il Po dalla preistoria all'Alto Medioevo. Exposition, Trento, Castello del Buonconsiglio, 2004*, edited by F. Marzatico and P. Gleirscher, 315–330. Trento: Castello del Buonconsiglio.

Vitali, D. 2003. "Introduzione." In *La necropoli di Monte Tamburino a Monte Bibele*, edited by D. Vitali, 15–38. Bologna: Gedit.

Vitali, D. 1999. "The Celts in Italy." In Moscati et al., *The Celts*, 230–247.

Vitali, D. 1998. "I Celti e Spina." In *Spina e il delta Padano*, edited by F. Rebecchi, 253–273. Rome: L' Erma di Bretschneider.

Vitri, S., and F. Oriolo, eds. 2001. *I Celti in Carnia e nell'arco alpino centro orientale: Atti della giornata di studio, Tolmezzo, 30 aprile 1999*. Trieste: Editreg.

Vitri, S. 2001. "Lo stato della ricerca protostorica in Carnia." In Vitri and Oriolo, *I Celti in Carnia e nell'arco alpino centro orientale*, 19–50.

Voisin, J. 1984. "Les Romans, chasseurs de *têtes*." *Du châtiment dans la cité: Supplices corporels et peine de mort dans le monde antique. Table ronde (Rome 9–11 novembre 1982)*, 241–293. Rome: École française de Rome.

Von Vacano, O. W. 1975. "Der Tempelgiebel von Telamon." *Mitteilungen des Deutschen Archäologischen Instituts: Römische Abteilung* 82: 127–150.

Wallace, R. 2004. "Venetic." In *The Cambridge Encyclopedia of the World's Ancient Languages*, edited by R. Woodard, 840–856. Cambridge: Cambridge University Press.

Ward-Perkins, B. 2005. *The Fall of Rome and the End of Civilization*. Oxford: Oxford University Press.

Ward-Perkins, B. 1997. "Continuists, catastrophists, and the towns of post-Roman northern Italy." *Papers of the British School at Rome* 65: 157–76.

Ward-Perkins, B. 1984. *From Classical Antiquity to the Middle Ages: Urban Public Building in Northern and Central Italy, AD 300–850*. Oxford: Oxford University Press.

Watson, A. 2004. *Aurelian and the Third Century*. London: Routledge.

Wells, P. 2014. "Material Culture and Identity: The Problem of Identifying Celts, Germans, and Romans in Late Iron Age Europe." In *Fingerprinting the Iron Age: Approaches to Identity in the European Iron* Age, edited by C. N. Popa and S. Stoddart, 306–322. Oxford: Oxbow Books.

Wells, P. 1999. *The Barbarians Speak: How the Conquered Peoples Shaped Roman Europe*. Princeton: Princeton University Press.

Wells, P. 1984. *Farms, Villages, and Cities: Commerce and Urban Origins in Late Prehistoric Europe*. Ithaca: Cornell University Press.

Wells, P. 1980. *Culture Contact and Culture Change: Early Iron Age Central Europe and the Mediterranean World*. Cambridge: Cambridge University Press.

Whatmough, J. 1943. "A Last Word on *patavinitas*." *Classical Philology* 38: 205.

Whatmough, J. 1933. *The Prae-Italic Dialects of Italy*. Cambridge, MA: Harvard University Press.

Whittaker, C. 2004. *Rome and Its Frontiers: The Dynamics of Empire*. London: Routldge.

Wielowiejski, J. 1996. "Il significato della via dell'ambra per i contatti tra l'Italia e le popolazioni alla luce delle ultime ricerche." In Buora, *Lungo la via dell'ambra*, 295–312.

Wild, J. P. 1976. "The *Gynacea*." In *Aspects of the Notitia Dignitatum: Papers Presented to the*

Conference in Oxford, 1974, edited by R. Goodburn and P. Bartholomew, 51–58. Oxford: British Archaeological Reports.

Wilkes, J. J. 1992. *The Illyrians*. Oxford: Blackwell.

Williams, D. 1995. *Ambrose of Milan and the End of the Nicene-Arian Conflicts*. Oxford: Clarendon Press.

Williams, J. H. C. 2001a. *Beyond the Rubicon: Romans and Gauls in Republican Italy*. Oxford: Oxford University Press.

Williams, J. H.C. 2001b. "Roman Intentions and Romanization: Republican Northern Italy, c. 200–100 BC." In *Italy and the West: Comparative Issues in Romanization*, edited by S. Keay and N. Terrenato, 91–101. Oxford: Oxbow Books.

Williams, J. H. C. 1997. "Celtic Ethnicity in Northern Italy: Problems Ancient and Modern." In *Gender and Ethnicity in Ancient Italy*, edited by T. Cornell and K. Lomas, 69–81. London: Accordia Research Institute.

Wiseman, T. P. 1993. "Sirmio, Sir Ronald, and the Gens Valeria." *Classical Journal* 88: 223–229.

Wiseman, T. P. 1990. *Le grotte di Catullo: Una villa romana e i suoi proprietari*. Brescia: Ecoedizioni.

Wiseman, T. P. 1987. *Catullus and His World: A Reappraisal*. Cambridge: Cambridge University Press.

Witcher, R. 2000. "Globalisation and Roman Imperialism: Perspectives on Identities in Roman Italy." In Lomas and Herring, *The Emergence of State Identities*, 213–225.

Witschel, C. 2004. "Re-evaluating the Roman West in the 3rd c. A.D." *Journal of Roman Archaeology* 17: 251–281.

Woolf, G. 2015. "Pliny/Trajan and the Poetics of Empire." *Classical Philology* 110: 132–151.

Woolf, G. 1998. *Becoming Roman: The Origins of Provincial Civilization in Gaul*. Cambridge: Cambridge University Press.

Woolf, G. 1993. "Rethinking the *oppida*." *Oxford Journal of Archaeology* 12: 223–234.

Woolf, G. 1992. "The unity and diversity of Romanisation." *Journal of Roman Archaeology* 5: 349–352.

Woolf, G. 1990. "Food, poverty, and patronage: The significance of the epigraphy of the Roman alimentary schemes in early imperial Italy." *Papers of the British School at Rome* 58: 197–228.

Zaccaria, C. 2002. "Marco Aurelio ad Aquileia e provvedimenti dopo la calata dei Marcomanni in Italia." In Buora, *Roma sul Danubio*, 75–79.

Zaccaria, C. 1996. "Aspetti degli *emporia* del *Caput Adriae* in età romana." In Buora, *Lungo la via dell'ambra*, 139–149.

Zaccaria, C. 1989. "Forme di promozione sociale ad Aquileia nei primi secoli." *Antichità Altoadriatiche* 35: 133–149.

Zaccaria, C. 1985. "Testimonianze epirafiche dei rapporti tra Aquileia e l'Illyrico in età imperiale Romana." *Antichità Altoadriatiche* 26: 85–129.

Zahrnt, M. 1988. "Antinoopolis in Agypten: die hadrianische Gründung und ihre Privilegien in der neueren Forschung." *Aufstieg und Niedergang der römischen Welt*, vol. 2, 10.1: 669–706

Zanda, E. 1998. "Centuriazione e città." In *Archeologia in Piemonte*. Vol. 2, *L'età romana*, edited by L. Mercando, 49–66. Turin: U. Allemandi.

Zanker, P. 1990. *The Power of Images in the Age of Augustus*. Ann Arbor: University of Michgan Press.

Zuiderhoek, A. 2011. "Oligarchs and Benefactors: Elite demography and euergetism in the Greek East of the Roman Empire." In *Political Culture in the Greek City after the Classical Age*, edited by O. van Nijf, R. Alston, and C. Williamson, 185–195. Leuven: Peeters.

Zuiderhoek, A. 2007. "The ambiguity of munificence." *Historia* 56: 196–213.

Index

Page numbers in *italics* refer to illustrations.